# A Commentary on Demosthenes'
# *Philippic* I

AMERICAN PHILOLOGICAL ASSOCIATION

TEXTS AND COMMENTARIES SERIES

Series Editor
Justina Gregory

*Sallust's* Bellum Catilinae, Second Edition
J. T. Ramsey

*A Commentary on Demosthenes'* Philippic I: With Rhetorical
*Analyses of* Philippics II *and* III
Cecil Wooten

# A Commentary on Demosthenes' *Philippic* I

## With Rhetorical Analyses of *Philippics* II and III

Cecil Wooten

OXFORD
UNIVERSITY PRESS

2008

# OXFORD
## UNIVERSITY PRESS

Oxford University Press, Inc., publishes works that further
Oxford University's objective of excellence
in research, scholarship, and education.

Oxford   New York
Auckland   Cape Town   Dar es Salaam   Hong Kong   Karachi
Kuala Lumpur   Madrid   Melbourne   Mexico City   Nairobi
New Delhi   Shanghai   Taipei   Toronto

With offices in
Argentina   Austria   Brazil   Chile   Czech Republic   France   Greece
Guatemala   Hungary   Italy   Japan   Poland   Portugal   Singapore
South Korea   Switzerland   Thailand   Turkey   Ukraine   Vietnam

Copyright © 2008 by the American Philological Association

Published by Oxford University Press, Inc.
198 Madison Avenue, New York, New York 10016

www.oup.com

Library of Congress Cataloging-in-Publication Data
Wooten, Cecil W., 1945–
A commentary on Demosthenes' Philippic I:
with rhetorical analyses of Philippics II and III /
Cecil Wooten.
p. cm.
ISBN 978–0–19–533326–8; 978–0–19–533327–5 (pbk.)
1. Demosthenes. Philippicae.   I. Title.
PA3950.P6.W66 2008
885'.01—dc22   2007011352

Printed in the United States of America
on acid-free paper

George Alexander Kennedy

magistro atque amico optimo

# Preface

The most recent commentary in English on Demosthenes' *Philippics* appeared in 1907; it has been out of print since the 1960s. In part because of the lack of a modern commentary, what are arguably the finest deliberative speeches from antiquity are not often read these days in American colleges and universities. I hope that the present volume will correct that lack and will encourage more study of Demosthenes. The commentary is aimed at advanced undergraduates and first-year graduate students, and it addresses rhetorical and stylistic matters, historical background, and grammatical issues. In the rhetorical analysis I rely primarily on the theories of ancient rhetoricians, especially Hermogenes, who was particularly interested in Demosthenes. I have prepared a commentary for the *First Philippic* only; for each of the other two speeches I have provided a brief historical introduction, an outline, and an essay emphasizing its differences from *Philippic* I. I have organized the book in this way because it seemed to me that in some courses only one of the speeches, most likely the first, would be read. If students, having already been introduced to Demosthenic language and rhetorical technique and the historical background, then wanted to read the second and third *Philippics*, they could, I felt, manage on their own if provided with some general guidance about structure, argument, and style.

I have chosen not to treat *Philippic* IV. There has always been some controversy about its authenticity, and, in any case, a very thorough commentary appeared in 2002: István Hajdu, *Kommentar zur 4. Philippischen Rede des Demosthenes* (Berlin).

I would like to thank many friends who have unfailingly given me support, encouragement, and sustenance of various sorts during the last few years as I worked on this project: Francis and Helen Barlow, Niko Endres, Allan Gurganus, Jane Holding, Sharon James, Sara Mack, Harriet Horwitz and Rick Meyer, and Daisy Thorp. I would also like to thank Galen Rowe, now deceased, who read my first analysis of *Philippic* I, and in particular Bill Race, who encouraged me from beginning to end, meticulously read many versions of the manuscript, and gave me many invaluable suggestions. Everyone should be so lucky to have such a good colleague and friend. Finally, I want to express my gratitude to Victor Bers and Harvey Yunis, who, like the mythical heroes who made two trips to the underworld, read the manuscript not once but twice and gave me many useful suggestions, to the members of the Publications Committee of the American Philological Association, in particular to the chairman of that committee, Justina

Gregory, who has been encouraging, helpful, and extremely professional throughout the process of submission, to the staff at Oxford University Press, who have been wonderful to work with, and to Mary Bellino, who did a superb job of copyediting the manuscript. I also want to thank the University Research Council at the University of North Carolina at Chapel Hill for their financial assistance in the publication of this book.

George Kennedy has been kind and generous to me since the beginning of my career almost forty years ago. He has been a good mentor and a good friend, and it is to him that I gratefully dedicate this book.

# Contents

# Abbreviations and Bibliography

A complete annotated bibliography of work on Demosthenes, arranged topic-
ally and by speech, can be found in Donald Jackson and Galen Rowe, "Demosthenes 1915–1965," *Lustrum* 14 (1969): 7–109, and for the period after
1965 in Felipe G. Hernández Muñoz, "Demostenes 1965–1997: Repertorio
Bibliográfico," *Tempus* 21 (1999): 37–71. The line numbers in the analysis refer
to the Oxford Classical Text by M. R. Dilts (Oxford, 2002).

| | |
|---|---|
| Aristides | *Aristidis Qui Feruntur Libri Rhetorici II*, ed. W. Schmid (Leipzig, 1926). |
| Aristotle | *Ars Rhetorica*. ed. W. D. Ross (Oxford, 1959). All translations from this work come from George Kennedy, *Aristotle: On Rhetoric* (Oxford, 1991). |
| Bers | Victor Bers, *Speech in Speech: Studies in Incorporated "Oratio Recta" in Attic Drama and Oratory* (London, 1997). |
| Black | E. Black, "The Second Persona," *Quarterly Journal of Speech* 56 (1970): 109–19. |
| Blass | Friedrich Blass, *Die Attische Beredsamkeit*, 2nd ed., vol. 3.1 (Leipzig, 1893). |
| Borza | Eugene N. Borza, *In the Shadow of Olympus: The Emergence of Macedon* (Princeton, 1990). |
| Carlier | Pierre Carlier, *Démosthène* (Paris, 1990). |
| Cawkwell | G. L. Cawkwell, "Eubulus," *Journal of Hellenic Studies* 83 (1963): 47–67. |
| CIA | *Corpus Inscriptionum Atticarum* (Berlin, 1873–95) |
| [Cicero] | *Rhetoric to Herennius*. All quotations from this work come from the translation by H. Caplan in the Loeb Classical Library (Cambridge, Mass., 1954). |
| Davies | Gilbert A. Davies, ed., *Demosthenes: Philippics I, II, and III* (Cambridge, 1907). |
| Denniston GP | J. D. Denniston, *The Greek Particles* (Oxford, 1954). |
| Denniston GPS | J. D. Denniston, *Greek Prose Style* (Oxford, 1952). |
| Demetrius | *On Style*. All quotations from this work come from the translation by Doreen Innes, based on that of W. Rhys Roberts, in the Loeb Classical Library (Cambridge, Mass., 1995). |
| Devine and Stephens | A. M. Devine and Laurence Stephens, *Discontinuous Syntax: Hyperbaton in Greek* (Oxford, 2000). |

Dik          Helma Dik, *Word Order in Ancient Greek: A Pragmatic Account of Word Order Variation in Herodotus* (Amsterdam, 1995).

Dilts        M. R. Dilts, ed., *Scholia Demosthenica*, vol. 1 (Leipzig, 1983).

Dionysius    *Critical Essays.* All quotations from these works come from the translation by S. Usher in the Loeb Classical Library (Cambridge, Mass., 1974).

Donnet       D. Donnet, "Aspects du rhythme dans la première Philippique de Démosthène," *Les Études Classiques* 43 (1975): 407–17.

Dover        K. J. Dover, *The Evolution of Greek Prose Style* (Oxford, 1997).

Gotoff       Harold C. Gotoff, *Cicero's Caesarian Speeches: A Stylistic Commentary* (Chapel Hill, N.C., 1993).

Griffith     G. W. Griffith, "The Reign of Philip the Second," in *A History of Macedonia*, ed. N. G. L. Hammond and G. W. Griffith, vol. 2 (Oxford, 1979): 203–315.

Hammond      N. G. L. Hammond, *A History of Greece to 322 B.C.* (Oxford, 1967).

Hansen       Mogens Hansen, *The Athenian Democracy in the Age of Demosthenes: Structure, Principles, and Ideology,* trans. J. A. Crook (Oxford, 1991).

Hermogenes   *Opera,* ed. Hugo Rabe (Leipzig, 1913). All references to Hermogenes are to page numbers in this edition. All translations from Hermogenes, unless otherwise noted, come from Cecil Wooten, *Hermogenes' On Types of Style* (Chapel Hill, N.C., 1987).

Jaeger       Werner Jaeger, *Demosthenes: The Origin and Growth of his Policy,* trans. Edward Robinson (Berkeley, 1938).

Kennedy      George Kennedy, "The Focusing of Arguments in Greek Deliberative Oratory," *Transactions of the American Philological Association* 90 (1959): 131–38.

Lausberg     H. Lausberg, *Handbook of Literary Rhetoric,* trans. M. Bliss, A. Jansen, and D. Orton (Leiden, 1998).

Longinus     *On the Sublime.* All quotations from this work come from the translation by W. H. Fyfe, revised by Donald Russell, in the Loeb Classical Library (Cambridge, Mass., 1995).

LSJ          H. G. Liddell, R. Scott, H. Stuart Jones, *A Greek-English Lexicon,* 9th edn. (Oxford, 1940), with revised supplement (1996).

McCabe       D. F. McCabe, *The Prose-Rhythm of Demosthenes* (New York, 1981).

Ober         Josiah Ober, *Mass and Elite in Democratic Athens: Rhetoric, Ideology, and the Power of the People* (Princeton, 1989).

Pearson AD   Lionel Pearson, *The Art of Demosthenes* (Chico, Calif., 1981).

Pearson DD   Lionel Pearson, "The Development of Demosthenes as a Political Orator," *Phoenix* 18 (1964): 95–109.

Pearson H    Lionel Pearson, "Hiatus and Its Purposes in Attic Oratory," *American Journal of Philology* 96 (1975): 138–59.

Pearson HA    Lionel Pearson, "Historical Allusions in the Attic Orators," *Classical Philology* 36 (1941): 209–29.

Pearson VP    Lionel Pearson, "The Virtuoso Passages in Demosthenes' Speeches," *Phoenix* 29 (1975): 214–30.

Quintilian    *The Orator's Education*. All quotations from this work come from the translation by Donald Russell in the Loeb Classical Library (Cambridge, Mass., 2001).

Ronnet    Gilberte Ronnet, *Étude sur le style de Démosthène dans les discours politiques* (Paris, 1951).

Rowe SM    Galen Rowe, "Demosthenes' *First Philippic*: The Satiric Mode," *Transactions of the American Philological Association* 99 (1968): 361–74.

Rowe UL    Galen Rowe, "Demosthenes' Use of Language," in *Demosthenes' On the Crown*, ed. James Murphy (New York, 1967), 175–99.

Sandys    John Edwin Sandys, ed., *The First Philippic and Olynthiacs of Demosthenes* (London, 1897).

Sandys 2    John Edwin Sandys, ed., *On the Peace, Second Philippic, On the Chersonesus, and Third Philippic* (London, 1900).

Sealey    Raphael Sealey, *Demosthenes and His Time* (Oxford, 1993).

Smyth    H. W. Smyth, *Greek Grammar* (Cambridge, Mass., 1963).

Tarbell    Frank Bigelow Tarbell, ed., *The Philippics of Demosthenes* (Boston, 1880).

Usher    Stephen Usher, *Greek Oratory: Tradition and Originality* (Oxford, 1999).

Vince    J. H. Vince, trans., *Demosthenes*, vol. 1, Loeb Classical Library (Cambridge, Mass., 1930).

Wooten A    Cecil Wooten, "Abruptness in Demetrius, Longinus, and Demosthenes," *American Journal of Philology* 112 (1991): 493–505.

Wooten CP    Cecil Wooten, *Cicero's Philippics and their Demosthenic Model: The Rhetoric of Crisis* (Chapel Hill, N.C., 1983).

Wooten DH    Cecil Wooten, "Dionysius of Halicarnassus and Hermogenes on the Style of Demosthenes," *American Journal of Philology* 110 (1989): 576–88.

Wooten FO    Cecil Wooten, "A Few Observations on Form and Content in Demosthenes," *Phoenix* 31 (1977): 258–61.

Wooten TD    Cecil Wooten, "A Triple Division in Demosthenes," *Classical Philology* 94 (1999): 450–54.

Wooten UM    Cecil Wooten, "Unnoticed Medical Language in Demosthenes," *Hermes* 107 (1979): 157–60.

Worthington    Ian Worthington, ed., *Demosthenes: Statesman and Orator* (London, 2000).

Yunis    Harvey Yunis, *Taming Democracy: Models of Political Rhetoric in Classical Athens* (Ithaca, N.Y., 1996).

# A Commentary on Demosthenes'
## *Philippic* I

# Introduction: *Philippic* I

## HISTORICAL BACKGROUND

### Philip and Athens Until 351

In 359, Philip succeeded his brother Perdiccas, who had been killed fighting the Illyrians, as king of Macedon. Two years later, when the Athenians were preoccupied with the outbreak of the Social War, Philip attacked Amphipolis and captured it.[1] Athens had established Amphipolis as a colony in 436. In the winter of 424/23, Brasidas had come to the aid of the pro-Spartan faction in the city, freed it of Athenian control, and established a Spartan garrison there. Three years later, according to the terms of the Peace of Nicias, the Spartan garrison was removed and Amphipolis was given back to the Athenians, who, nevertheless, failed to reassert their control over the city, although they never gave up their claim to it (Griffith, 231–33).

The kings of Macedon had been interested in Amphipolis for two reasons. First of all, it enjoyed a very strategic location; it sat on the route from east to west across the Strymon River and gave access to the passage along the river into the interior of Macedon. The city, therefore, could act as a fortress protecting the eastern parts of the kingdom. Second, it was near the gold and silver mines of Mount Pangaeum and thus an important source of income. Perdiccas had put a Macedonian garrison there in 360. Philip had withdrawn it in 359, when he was trying to assert his control over Macedon, in an effort to appease the Athenians and to keep them from interfering in the north. Two years later, when his position was stronger, Athens still had not taken advantage of the opportunity to occupy the city, and Philip took it back. When Amphipolis felt threatened by Philip, the city had appealed to Athens for help; Philip forestalled Athenian intervention, however, by sending Athens a note claiming that he intended to take the city only to return it to its rightful owner, that is, Athens. He never did (Griffith, 233–40).

Soon after the fall of Amphipolis, Philip took Pydna, which, like Methone (see below), had been secured for Athens by Timotheus in 364. It seems that

---

[1] All dates are B.C. I intend for this historical background to be only a bare outline, giving just enough information to place this speech in its broad historical context. I will explain some of the facts presented here in more detail in the commentary itself when they become relevant to the argument of the speech. To the reader who wants more continuous historical background, I highly recommend Sealey, 3–136, particularly 88–136.

Philip wanted to eliminate any possible base of operations that Athens might use in its attempt to regain Amphipolis (Griffith, 242). The Athenians declared war (Diodorus 16.8.3). Philip realized that an alliance between Athens and the towns of the Chalcidian League, which were beginning to look on Philip as a threat, could be formidable. Therefore, in order to keep the Chalcidians from allying with Athens, Philip offered to give them Potidaea, knowing that as long as this bone of contention existed between them they would never join together against him (Griffith, 244–47). Potidaea, originally a Corinthian colony, had joined the Delian League but revolted in 432. It was destroyed by the Athenians after a long siege of two years, and the area settled by Athenian colonists. At the end of the Peloponnesian War, in 404, it had come under the control of the Chalcidian League but was retaken for Athens by Timotheus in 363 and repopulated with Athenian colonists.

In 356 Philip laid siege to Potidaea. The Athenians voted to send an expedition to relieve the town, but Philip took it before the expedition could be sent out. He let the Athenian settlers there go free, which indicates that he was trying to be conciliatory toward Athens (Diodorus 16.8.3–5).[2] Philip needed to protect himself, but he clearly did not want to provoke Athens unnecessarily. Late in 355, he attacked Methone, Athens' last base on the Macedonian coast, which surrendered the following year. Athens made no attempt to relieve the town (Diodorus 16.31.6, 16.34.4–5).

Preoccupation with the Social War might have dampened the Athenian response to these attacks on their possessions or former possessions in the north. Or they might not have perceived these areas to be vital to their interests. Amphipolis gave access to timber in the Strymon valley, which the Athenians needed for their ships. But although they had not controlled Amphipolis in over fifty years, they still had the largest fleet in the Aegean. It is clear that they had worked out some means of obtaining timber in the north, probably through trade. The loss of Pydna, Potidaea, and Methone seems to have done no harm— except to Athenian prestige (Sealey, 110–12; Griffith, 231).

The factors of undoubted importance to Athenian security and well-being were the defense of Thermopylae, which gave access to central Greece, and the protection of the grain routes from the Black Sea. Philip's actions in the north from 357 to 355 had threatened neither (Sealey, 111). Once Methone had been taken back, however, Macedonia was free from the threat of an attack by a foreign foe from within its own territories. Moreover, Philip's enemies in the north and northwest had been soundly defeated. Philip soon, therefore, began to look south

---

[2] Philip had acted similarly two years earlier. When he was trying to establish his power, Athens had supported a pretender to the throne named Argaeus and had sent him to Macedonia accompanied by three thousand mercenaries and an Athenian general. Philip handily defeated the force near Methone but returned the prisoners to Athens without ransom (Griffith, 211–12). We do not know exactly who this Argaeus was (cf. Borza, 296–97); however, as Borza notes, "it surely must have stuck in the new king's mind that the first Greeks to oppose him at the moment of his accession were Athenian" (201).

and east. In 353 he moved an army into Thessaly in support of his allies, the cities of the Thessalian League, against Lycophron of Pherae (Diodorus 16.35.1). The kings of Macedon had traditionally been interested in Thessaly for three reasons. First, a strong and united Thessaly could have been a threat to Macedon. Second, Thessaly had the best cavalry in the Greek world. And, third, it could act as a buffer against Thebes, which had occasionally threatened Macedon in the first half of the fourth century. Philip himself, in fact, had been taken to Thebes as a hostage after one of these incursions (Griffith, 205, 219, 226).[3]

When Philip moved into Thessaly, the Pheraeans sought help from Onomarchus and the Phocians, who were engaged in the Sacred War, primarily against Thebes. In the late summer or early fall of 353, Onomarchus and his Thessalian allies defeated Philip, who withdrew from Thessaly (Diodorus 16.35.2). He returned the following year, however, and in 352, at the battle of the Crocus Field, Philip and his Thessalian allies defeated Onomarchus and the Pheraeans (Diodorus 16.35.5–6). It was probably after this battle that Philip was made archon of the Thessalian League (Sealey, 122). He had thus extended his power to the south and was approaching central Greece. After settling affairs in Thessaly, he did, in fact, move toward Thermopylae in pursuit of the Phocians. Athens sent out a force to block the pass, and Philip withdrew to Macedon (Diodorus 16.37.3, 16.38.1–2).

Philip was still at war with the Athenians, although they had inflicted no damage on him. In Thessaly he had found allies against them. Athens supported Phocis in the Sacred War; therefore, Thebes and the cities of the Thessalian League were enemies of Athens. And the search for allies against the Athenians may have been one of the reasons that had taken Philip south in the first place (Griffith, 263).

Meanwhile, in the east, Cersobleptes, an ally of Athens who ruled the eastern part of Thrace, was trying to unify the eastern Thracians; in the process, he sometimes threatened Greek cities (Borza, 215). Late in 352, Byzantium and Perinthus called in Philip to protect them against Cersobleptes. During this campaign Philip laid siege to Heraion Teichos on or near the Propontis. The Athenians voted to send a relief force; however, before the ships could be dispatched, news reached Athens that Philip had fallen ill. This was probably true, for he abandoned the siege and returned to Macedon at the end of the winter (D 3.4–5).

This is the general situation in which D delivered the *First Philippic*, probably in the late spring or summer of 351 (Griffith, 297). Although Philip had begun to show interest in areas that were vital to Athenian security, he had been blocked at Thermopylae in the summer of 352 and had withdrawn from the Propontis in the winter of 351. Most Athenians probably did not perceive a crisis (Sealey, 125–26).

---

[3] R. M. Errington argues that most of Philip's military activity in the 350s was aimed at the establishment of security for Macedonia; "Review Discussion: Four Interpretations of Philip II," *American Journal of Ancient History* 6 (1981): 82.

## D and Athens Until 351

D is one of the few ancient Greeks about whose private life we know a good deal.[4] He was born about 384, the son of Demosthenes of the deme of Paeonia, who, according to Plutarch (*Dem.* 4.1), was a wealthy gentleman nicknamed "Cutler" (μαχαιροποιός) because he owned a large factory where slaves produced knives. Pseudo-Plutarch, in the *Lives of the Ten Orators* (844A), tells us that his mother's name was Cleobule. His political rival Aeschines says (3.172) that his grandmother was a Scythian, but since this is the type of slander often found in Greek oratory little credence should be given to the statement. His father died when D was seven and left him, his five-year-old sister, and his mother in the charge of three guardians, Aphobus, Demophon, and Therippides. The will stipulated that the estate, which amounted to thirteen talents, forty-three minai, was to be divided in the following way: Aphobus was to marry D's mother and receive eighty minai as dowry, Demophon was to marry D's sister when she came of age and receive two talents, and Therippides was to receive the interest on seventy minai until D came of age. The remainder of the estate was to be invested, the interest going to D. If we are to believe D, who is our only source, the guardians appropriated their legacies without fulfilling the conditions attached to them, and rather than investing the rest of the estate they slowly diverted it for their own use and squandered it.

When D came of age at eighteen, probably in 366, less than one-tenth of the original estate remained. D decided to recover what he had lost and spent two years studying oratory, probably with Isaeus, an expert in the inheritance laws, in preparation for the case. D may have known and actually studied with Plato during this period. It is also quite probable that he learned something about delivery from the actor Satyrus, although pseudo-Plutarch says (845B) that the actor in question was Andronicus.

Two years later, probably in 364, D instituted three separate suits against his guardians. The suit against Aphobus was tried first; the other two were postponed and may have never been tried. When the case came before the archon, he referred it to an arbiter. The decision went against Aphobus, but he had the right to appeal it to a jury, and he did. The trial was decided in D's favor, and Aphobus was fined ten talents, only a small part of which, in all probability, D actually received. It is also likely that this decision against Aphobus persuaded the other two guardians to submit to arbitration and compromise.

As D himself tells us (21.78–80, 205–7, 28.17), not long before the case against Aphobus was to be heard, Thrasylochus, one of Aphobus's friends, challenged D either to exchange property with him or to assume a financial responsibility that had been imposed on him by the state (see discussion in the commentary on 36.27). If D had agreed to exchange property, Thrasylochus would have then

---

[4] The most important sources are his own speeches and letters and the biography of Plutarch. For a modern account of D's life until 351, see also Carlier, 35–55, 75–87, 102–17.

been in a position to drop the suit against Aphobus, since the suit was related to D's property. D refused the exchange and accepted the financial obligation. This episode foreshadowed conflicts later in D's life: Thrasylochus was the brother of Meidias, who was a friend of Eubulus.

At the conclusion of the suits against his guardians, which seem to have dragged on for several years, D had developed a good deal of oratorical skill and legal knowledge, and he put it to use as a "logographer," a writer of speeches for others to deliver in court, some of which are still extant. D continued in this profession for years, possibly until the middle of the 340s, and seems to have been so successful that he became a fairly wealthy man. In his later life, D, like Isocrates, was not particularly proud of the fact that he had made his living in this way.

D's true calling, however, was as a political orator. When he was nineteen, D had witnessed the trial of Callistratus. Although we are not sure exactly what his role was, Callistratus was evidently accused of having lost for Athens the important town of Oropus by his opposition to Thebes and his cool treatment of the Thebans at a council in 371. It has been argued that this experience inspired D to become a political orator (Plut., *Dem.* 5.1–3). During his youth, Athens had begun to recover some of the power and prestige lost at the end of the Peloponnesian War—a process that began with the formation of the Second Athenian League in 378. The rise of Athens to a new position of strength in Greek politics must have greatly impressed and excited the young man.

Plutarch, who wrote hundreds of years after the death of D, is our only source for the story that Callistratus inspired the young man to become an orator. The anecdote rings true, however, since D seems to have learned from Callistratus the importance of pragmatism in politics. Callistratus had been instrumental in bringing into existence the Second Athenian League and in effecting a rapprochement between Athens and Sparta in the 370s: "Both undertakings were inspired by a judicious realism, such as characterizes statesmanship of a high order" (Sealey, 95).

D's first real interest in politics is seen in three judicial speeches of an avowedly political nature that he wrote between 355 and 353 attacking the members of the political faction of Aristophon, a pro-Theban, who had succeeded Callistratus as the leader of Athens. The speech *Against Androtion* was written for a man named Diodorus who prosecuted Androtion, one of the supporters of Aristophon, for having proposed an illegal motion in the Assembly. The speech is much broader than that, however; it is an attack on Androtion's whole career. The speech *Against Timocrates*, another supporter of Aristophon, was also written for Diodorus, who prosecuted Timocrates on charges of owing money to the state. A large section of this speech, devoted to a discussion of the tax-collecting policies of Androtion, is very similar to an attack in the earlier speech written for Diodorus against him. The third of this series, *Against Leptines*, was delivered by D himself, who appeared as an advocate for Ctesippus, a son of the general Chabrias, in a case questioning the legality of a law proposed by Leptines (probably also a supporter of

Aristophon) to do away with the privilege of tax-exemption for the descendants of very deserving Athenian citizens. Chabrias and his descendants had been awarded such an exemption. One scholar argues that in these speeches, at least in the speeches *Against Androtion* and *Against Leptines*, D was attacking politicians who had favored the imperialistic policies that had led to the Social War and thus supporting the conservative position of those politicians who were opposed to an aggressive foreign policy abroad (Carlier, 76, 78).

In particular, in these speeches D seems to be supporting the conservative political faction of Eubulus,[5] who was in favor of abandoning Athens' maritime confederacy and turning the city into a peaceful state with a sound economic policy (Cawkwell, 61), even though D was probably not a close associate of Eubulus or a member of his inner circle (Carlier, 81).[6] Aristophon's harsh treatment of the allies had provoked the Social War, which lasted from 357 to 355 and had greatly weakened the state. Both his foreign policy and his economic practices had proved disastrous. In 354, Eubulus became the most prominent figure in Athenian politics. Although later, in 349, D would argue that Eubulus's conservative financial policies had impeded Athenian military enterprises abroad (1.19–20, 3.10–13), when Eubulus was in the ascendancy the Athenians did send, or propose to send, armed expeditions abroad, for example to Thermopylae in 352, to the Propontis in 351, and to Olynthus in 349. It seems, therefore, that Eubulus was not opposed to armed intervention abroad on principle but felt that the Athenians should intervene only to defend what were clearly their vital interests when those interests were obviously being threatened (Sealey, 124–25; Cawkwell, 53, 67). In his first purely political speech D advocates this same kind of cautious, restrained policy.

Relations between Persia and Athens had been strained since 359, when Artaxerxes III came to the throne, because Athenian mercenaries had participated in revolts against the king. There were rumors that Artaxerxes was preparing for war with Athens, and the adherents of Aristophon felt that Athens should take the initiative and declare war on Persia. At an assembly held to debate this situation in 354, D, then thirty, delivered his first public oration, the speech *On the Symmories*, in which he proposed a reorganization of the naval boards, which were responsible for outfitting the fleet, in an attempt to spread the tax burden over a larger number of citizens and to lower the tax rate on the rich, who tended to be supporters of Eubulus. By his exalted demands and his descriptions of the sacrifices that a war with Persia would require, D was instrumental in averting one. The naval boards were in fact reorganized in 340, but along different lines from those envisioned in this speech.

---

[5] Political parties as such did not exist in Athens, although there were groups of political leaders who cooperated with one another (Hansen, 277–87).

[6] Carlier even speculates that the ambitious young politician may have eventually abandoned Eubulus's policies precisely because he was not in his inner circle.

It is in the speech *For the Megalopolitans*, delivered in 353/52, that D first breaks away from the policies of Eubulus and strikes out on his own, advocating a more aggressive, more interventionist foreign policy whose goal was to expand Athenian influence abroad. Megalopolis had been supported by Thebes against Sparta; however, when the Thebans became involved in the Sacred War, the Megalopolitans began to fear that Sparta would renew its aggressions and appealed to Athens for an alliance. Eubulus advocated a policy of nonintervention, but D, arguing on the basis of the balance of power in Greek politics, a principle that he had probably learned from Callistratus, supported the Megalopolitan request and tried to persuade the Athenians to build up a base of power by supporting smaller states against both Sparta and Thebes. Athens turned down the Megalopolitan request, and Megalopolis applied to Philip, thus giving him, for the first time, the opportunity to interfere in the affairs of central Greece.

D's growing interest in foreign policy is seen in a judicial speech, *Against Aristocrates*, written by D but delivered in 352 by his friend Euthycles of Thria. Euthycles was attacking as illegal a law proposed by Aristocrates to give special privileges to Charidemus, an Athenian mercenary, then in the service of King Cersobleptes of Thrace, whose kingdom bordered the Hellespont. D realized that it was essential for Athens to keep control of the grain routes through the Hellespont, and was afraid that if Cersobleptes were too strong he might threaten Athenian control in this area. D, therefore, supported a policy that would favor Cersobleptes' brother Amodocus, whose kingdom lay between that of Cersobleptes and Macedon, in an effort to keep Cersobleptes as weak as possible. He was here again adhering to the theory of balance of power that he had sketched out in *For the Megalopolitans*. D failed to see, however, that the real threat to Athenian interests in the Hellespont would come, not from Thrace, but from Macedon. Although he did see in Amodocus a bulwark against possible intrusions by Macedon as well as a means of keeping Cersobleptes weak, he did not realize that when Philip's attack came only a strong, united Thrace would be of any help to Athens.

The Athenians decided to support Cersobleptes, who was promising that he would return to Athens the town of Amphipolis, taken by Philip in 357. Amodocus allied with Philip, and in the winter of 352 Philip laid siege to Heraion Teichos, an important town held by Cersobleptes that could be used as a threat to the grain routes from the Hellespont. D now realized who was Athens' most dangerous enemy, and, probably in the spring of 351, he delivered the *First Philippic*. This is the first speech in which he deals fully with the relationship between Athens and Philip. D had been trying, with no success, to forge a position for himself in Athenian foreign policy since 354. Now he seized upon the aggressions of Philip as an "opportunity to give renewed impetus and focus to a political career which had seemingly stalled in the face of the rejection or disregard of his earlier proposals" (Usher, 218).

Opposition to Macedonia was to become the hallmark of D's political career. The motivation behind the development of that policy has been a topic of controversy.[7] Many scholars have seen in D a great patriot, struggling against tremendous odds to preserve a participatory form of government, and a way of life, against the encroachments of monarchy: "From 351 right through to the Macedonian king's death in 336 Demosthenes used his oratorical and diplomatic skills in support of his unrelenting belief that Philip was a dire threat to the freedom of the Greek world in general and of the Athenians in particular and should be resisted."[8] It has also been argued that this policy was self-interested, that D was trying to preserve the only political form in which he himself could be influential: "Having created for himself a major role, both as a courtroom advocate and as a politician, in the democratic city-state that he so admired, Demosthenes was determined to defend at all costs the system in which he could best function, that is, in which he could use oratory to his greatest advantage."[9] Other scholars have maintained that D was simply an ambitious politician looking for a cause he could use to advance his political career. Badian writes of the early political speeches: "They were all patently devoid of real conviction. He wanted to become a leader in glorious action, but had no policy of his own, no assessment of political and strategic priorities."[10] Of the *First Philippic* he says:

> It belongs in a context of a young and ambitious orator's seeking a cause in which he can advocate Athenian activism: against Sparta, against Philip, against Caria or even the King. The advocacy of moderation in the *Symmories* had proved ineffective in terms of his career, and so (it seems) had the wooing of important Athenians in *Leptines*. Demosthenes had cut his losses and decided that the advocacy of activism in foreign policy had the greatest promise. (33)

It is quite possible that all of these factors played some role in the development of his policy. What is not in dispute, however, is the quality of D's speeches, the instruments that he forged to wage his political battles, and it is to the speech itself that I now turn.

### GENERAL APPROACH OF THE SPEECH

D faced a challenging rhetorical situation when he delivered the *First Philippic*. Bitzer defines rhetorical situation as "a complex of persons, events, objects, and relations presenting an actual or potential exigence which can be completely or partially removed if discourse, introduced into the situation, can so constrain human decision or action as to bring about the significant modification of the

---

[7] And since the 1960s, as scholars have come better to understand the history of the fourth century, the wisdom of D's policy has been brought into serious question; see, for example, G. L. Cawkwell, "The Crowning of Demosthenes," *Classical Quarterly* 19 (1969): 163–80.

[8] T. T. B. Ryder, "Demosthenes and Philip II," in Worthington, 45.

[9] Wooten CP, 20.

[10] "The Road to Prominence," in Worthington, 36.

exigence."[11] The exigence, which Bitzer defines as a "thing that is other than it should be" (6), was an aggressive and apparently determined foreign king who had threatened Athenian possessions abroad but was not yet a direct threat to Athens itself, "a distant enemy... not a threat impinging directly on the needs or the security of the Athenians" (Sealey, 125). The audience, which Bitzer describes as consisting of "those persons who are capable of being influenced by discourse and of being mediators of change" (8), was complacent: "The situation was simply not so clear as Demosthenes portrayed it" (Yunis, 258). D, therefore, still fairly young and inexperienced, with no particular reputation for skill in foreign policy, had to devise a speech that could prod an audience disinclined to act to face a problem that still seemed far away, a discourse, as Bitzer puts it, "of such a character that the audience, in thought and action, is so engaged that it becomes mediator of change" (4).

The *First Philippic*, therefore, was an experiment with various types of what Bitzer calls "constraints" (8). It differs in style and structure from the two deliberative speeches closest to it in date, *For the Megalopolitans*, delivered in the preceding year, and *On the Freedom of the Rhodians*, delivered in 351/50.[12] Having been unsuccessful in *For the Megalopolitans*, D seems to have decided to experiment with a new form of oratory in which he used a more emotional style and transferred to deliberative speaking many of the techniques, particularly the use of narration and characterization, that he had developed in his judicial oratory (Pearson AD, 122–27). Probably he was somewhat dissatisfied with the results, for he returned, in *On the Freedom of the Rhodians*, to many of the techniques seen in *For the Megalopolitans*. In the deliberative speeches of the next decade, however, he would return to many of the techniques seen in the *First Philippic*, although in a more restrained and moderate fashion. This speech, consequently, can be regarded as one of the springs from which would flow D's greatest deliberative oratory, and therein lies its major importance, at least from a rhetorical point of view. The speech seems to have had little impact on Athenian policy at the end of the decade of the 350s, but it was to have a decided influence on the great oratory of the 340s. I would like to examine here how this speech differs from *For the Megalopolitans* and *On the Freedom of the Rhodians*.

The first difference is the clear, sharp focus. Kennedy has demonstrated that in the fifth century there was a tendency, seen most clearly in the speeches in Thucydides, to rely on a single argument, particularly the argument from

---

[11] L. F. Bitzer, "The Rhetorical Situation," *Philosophy and Rhetoric* 1 (1968): 6.

[12] For this chronology, see Sealey, 129, 132–33. The *First Philippic* is hard to date precisely because it does not deal with a specific crisis. The traditional date is spring of 351, although it has been dated as late as January of 350; cf. J. R. Ellis, "The Date of Demosthenes' First Philippic," *Revue des Études Grecques* 79 (1966): 636–39. Carlier argues (87) that the speech *On the Freedom of the Rhodians* was delivered before the *First Philippic*, in 353 or the spring of 352; however, he demands of a young politician working out his policies a sort of consistency that is unreasonable. I see no reason not to accept the traditional dating, which goes back to Dionysius of Halicarnassus.

expediency. In the fourth century, however, Kennedy argues, there is a tendency to synthesize arguments, to appeal to expediency but also to possibility, justice, and honor. This is seen most clearly in the speeches of Isocrates. It is the fourth-century approach that is generally found in D's early political speeches. Kennedy notes that

> The earliest speeches show an attempt to combine arguments in the manner of Isocrates. For example, the speech *On the Symmories* aims at pointing out what is expedient *and* honorable *and* just (28 and 35), and the speech *On the Liberty of the Rhodians* shows the same characteristics: practicality, expediency, and honor all point in one direction (2, 8, 28). (136)[13]

We see the same tendency in *For the Megalopolitans*. There D argues that expediency is the principle that dictates how states should conduct their foreign policy and that Athens should make decisions based on this principle (§29); yet, he is hesitant to abandon the moral and ethical appeal of a synthesis of arguments. There is, consequently, much stress laid on the justice of the policy that he proposes (§§14–15, 23–26) and on the argument that it is honorable (§§6–10).

In the *First Philippic*, however, as Kennedy notes, "a new vigor appears which is unlike anything in Greek oratory since the fifth century and which involves a return to focus on a single form of argument" (136). And this argument is expediency, as is usually the case in the fifth century: "It is assumed that Philip acts in his own interests and Athens must act in hers" (137). Kennedy also points out that the focus of the speech is very sharp: "Demosthenes so focuses Athenian interests that the question seems not one of advantage but of necessity, not the choice of a course of action but the adoption of the only possibility" (137).

Second, in keeping with this sharp focus, D concentrates in the *First Philippic* on a few crucial arguments that recur in various forms throughout the speech (Rowe SM, 362). This approach not only makes these arguments emphatic; it also makes the speech easier for the audience to follow. In addition, in order to give these arguments weight, D also provides a good deal of information, often in the form of historical narrative, to back up his points (Pearson AD, 119). In *For the Megalopolitans*, by contrast, and to a lesser extent in *On the Freedom of the Rhodians*, D presents many arguments. They are developed one by one, in a linear fashion, and little information is given to back them up. Vince, in his introduction to *For the Megalopolitans*, observes that "the appeal of Demosthenes on behalf of the Arcadians contains more argument than passion, and some of the arguments are more ingenious than sound" (438). He also notes that because of the large number of arguments this speech is "not an easy one to follow." The tone of these speeches, moreover, is calm and logical. Usher says of

---

[13] In the latter speech D attempts to prove that what he is proposing is just (§§8, 25–27), honorable (§§2–4, 22–24), possible (§§9–13, 30), and expedient (§§14–16, 28–29).

*For the Megalopolitans* that "the mood of the speech is cerebral, calculating and unsentimental, even when justice and fairness enter the argument" (212). Blass remarks about *On the Freedom of the Rhodians* that "on the whole the tone remains calm and measured" ("im allgemeinen der Ton ruhig und gemessen bleibt," 308). The tone of the *First Philippic*, however, is very different. It is primarily "an emotional appeal, an appeal to the Athenians' confidence in themselves and their pride as free men" (Pearson AD, 126).

This emotional tone is created to a great extent by the third factor that distinguishes the *First Philippic* from the other two speeches: language that is much more highly patterned, relying particularly on those figures of speech and thought that create emphasis and that convey and evoke emotion. In *For the Megalopolitans*, for example, there are, on average, .70 rhetorical questions and .35 direct addresses to the audience per page (a sum total of 6 and 3, respectively, out of approximately 8.5 pages of text). In *On the Freedom of the Rhodians* there are .60 rhetorical questions and one direct address to the audience (6 and 10, respectively, in about 10 pages of text). In the *First Philippic* there is an average of 1.6 rhetorical questions per page of text and 1.8 direct addresses to the audience (26 and 29, respectively, in 16 pages of text).

There are similar incidences of hyperbaton (the separation of elements that naturally go together, which gives emphasis to one or both of them) and the figure that involves negation and affirmation (κατὰ ἄρσιν καὶ θέσιν), which allows the orator to emphasize an idea by stating it twice, once positively and once negatively (e.g., "We are always defeated and never win a single war"). In *For the Megalopolitans* there is an average of 3.3 examples of hyperbaton per page of text (28 examples). Similarly, in *On the Freedom of the Rhodians* the average is about 3 (30 examples). Moreover, most of these examples are of the "mild" type, found commonly in all the orators, which normally involves the separation of an adjective from its noun, usually by a verb (e.g., τὴν αὐτὴν ἔχειν διάνοιαν, *On the Freedom of the Rhodians*, §32.3).[14] In the *First Philippic*, however, the incidence of hyperbaton is almost twice as high as in the other two speeches, about 5 examples per page (78 instances). Moreover, there are many examples of the more "violent" type of hyperbaton, which involves the interpolation of several words between the elements that naturally go together (e.g., τὴν ἱερὰν ἀπὸ τῆς χώρας ᾤχετ᾽ ἔχων τριήρη, §34.15–16).[15] Likewise, there is a much higher proportion of examples of the figure that involves negation and affirmation in the *First Philippic* as opposed to the other two speeches, an average of 1.6 per page (25 examples) as compared with .5 in the speech *On the Freedom of the Rhodians* (5 examples) and .8 in the speech *For the Megalopolitans* (5 examples).

---

[14] For a discussion of different degrees of hyperbaton, see Denniston GPS, 47–59.
[15] Devine and Stephens use (133) the terms "short" and "long" rather than mild and violent. They note, moreover, that "there is a high degree of hyperbaton with a more emotive style" (59).

Epanadiplosis (the emphatic repetition of a word at the beginning of a sentence), which Ronnet describes as being "unknown to orators before Demosthenes, but familiar to the tragic poets" ("inconnue des orateurs avant Démosthène, mais familière aux poètes tragiques," 69), is used once in *For the Megalopolitans* (§23) and not at all in *On the Freedom of the Rhodians*. It is used three times in the *First Philippic* (§§10, 18, 46). Anaphora and antistrophe (the repetition of a word at the beginning or end of successive clauses) are used in the *First Philippic* four times (§§7, 27, 36, 43), not at all in *For the Megalopolitans* and only twice (§§18, 34) in *On the Freedom of the Rhodians*: "New again here, the *First Philippic* offers us at the same time vivid and expressive examples of antistrophe and the first attempts at anaphora" ("Novatrice encore ici, la 1<sup>re</sup> *Philippique* nous offre à la fois des exemples vivants et expressifs d'antistrophe et les premières tentatives d'anaphore"; Ronnet, 66). Similarly, in the *First Philippic* D uses one instance of a paradoxical statement followed by a rhetorical question that demands an answer to the riddle, a good technique for arousing the audience's attention (§2), three instances of dramatic dialogue to give an aura of spontaneity, immediacy, and urgency to the speech (§§10–11, 25–26, 44), and three instances of bold and striking images that provoke an emotional response from the audience (§§9, 26, 40). None of these techniques is used in the other two speeches, and that is one reason why they have a cool, expository tone as compared with the lively, dramatic, emotionally compelling quality of the *First Philippic*.[16]

One of the aspects of judicial oratory that D transferred to his deliberative speeches is taking the stance of a plaintiff (Pearson AD, 123). In his view there were two major problems facing Athens in the middle of the fourth century, the aggressions of Philip and the unwillingness of the Athenians to take vigorous action abroad. The former problem, he felt, was simply a symptom of the latter: the most fundamental difficulty facing the Athenians was their own attitude (Wooten UM, 157–60). In the *First Philippic*, therefore, D had to prosecute, as it were, first the Athenians for their unwillingness to defend their own interests, and second Philip for taking advantage of Athenian indifference. Reflecting what he saw as the relative importance of these two problems, the vast majority of this speech, approximately 80 percent (41 sections out of 51), is devoted to a discussion of internal problems in Athens. Much of this discussion is critical of the audience, and some of that criticism is written in a style that Hermogenes, the late second-century A.D. author of *On Types of Style*, calls Asperity (τραχύτης). Blass, in fact, says that the speech could be described as "against the people" ("gegen das Volk," 189).

Asperity involves open and strong criticism of more important people, here the Athenian populace, by someone who is less important, here an individual orator (Hermogenes, 255). This style uses figurative language, commands, impatient rhetorical questions, and short, choppy clauses, which are often little more than phrases, all elements of language usually employed by people who are

---

[16] I do not understand Sealey's description of *Philippic* I as "not imbued with the earnestness of the later *Philippics*" or of the speech *On the Freedom of the Rhodians* as being "filled with passion" (133).

angry (258–59). In fact, Hermogenes cites (259) two passages from this speech as examples of Asperity, although he also notes (256) that there are few instances of such a style in D, since they run the risk of offending the audience:[17]

πότ᾽ οὖν, ὦ ἄνδρες Ἀθηναῖοι, πότε ἃ χρὴ πράξετε; ἐπειδὰν τί γένηται; ἐπειδὰν νὴ Δία ἀνάγκη τις ᾖ. νῦν δὲ τί χρὴ τὰ γιγνόμενα ἡγεῖσθαι; (§10)

εἶτα τοῦτο ἀναμενοῦμεν; καὶ τριήρεις κενὰς καὶ τὰς παρὰ τοῦ δεῖνος ἐλπίδας ἂν ἀποστείλητε, πάντ᾽ ἔχειν οἴεσθε καλῶς; οὐκ ἐμβησόμεθα; οὐκ ἔξιμεν αὐτοὶ μέρει γέ τινι στρατιωτῶν οἰκείων νῦν, εἰ καὶ μὴ πρότερον; οὐκ ἐπὶ τὴν ἐκείνου πλευσόμεθα; (§§43–44)

There are other examples of this sort of prosecutorial style. In section 25, for example, D uses a sarcastic imaginary dialogue similar to the one cited by Hermogenes, employing the same sort of choppy phrases:

εἰ γὰρ ἔροιτό τις ὑμᾶς, "εἰρήνην ἄγετε, ὦ ἄνδρες Ἀθηναῖοι;" "μὰ Δί᾽ οὐχ ἡμεῖς γε," εἴποιτ᾽ ἄν, "ἀλλὰ Φιλίππῳ πολεμοῦμεν."

This is followed in section 26 by an example of the kind of figurative language that Hermogenes sees as being typical of Asperity: ὥσπερ γὰρ οἱ πλάττοντες τοὺς πηλίνους, εἰς τὴν ἀγορὰν χειροτονεῖτε τοὺς ταξιάρχους καὶ τοὺς φυλάρχους, οὐκ ἐπὶ τὸν πόλεμον. Another example follows in section 40: οὐδὲν δ᾽ ἀπολείπετε, ὥσπερ οἱ βάρβαροι πυκτεύουσιν, οὕτω πολεμεῖν Φιλίππῳ. Hermogenes notes that images can make a passage either harsher or less severe, depending on the nature of the image and the general tone of the passage in which it appears (246, 248, 258, 333–34).

Only a small percentage of the speech is devoted to a discussion of Philip. In fact, he is not mentioned until the end of section 3. The criticism of Philip, moreover, is less harsh and more indirect than that of the Athenians. In sections 5 and 6, D even holds Philip up as an example for the Athenians to imitate, a man who was not discouraged by Athens' former power, who acts and realizes that the prizes of war belong to those who are willing to take risks.

Some of the passages that discuss Philip are written in a style that Hermogenes calls Florescence (ἀκμή). Florescence, the mildest form of criticism in the Hermogenic system, involves reproach, like Asperity, but it tones down this reproach by using stylistic characteristics associated with Brilliance (λαμπρότης), which deals with remarkable and praiseworthy human actions (265), mainly long clauses, parallelism, figures of speech that tend to make language pleasing to the ear, and rhythm, such as the dactylic, associated with Solemnity (σεμνότης): "By using longer clauses and those figures of speech, such as anaphora, that are often associated with poetry and that consequently give a pleasing effect, the orator can soften his reproach and make the criticism

---

[17] Syrianus, in his commentary on Hermogenes, makes this point (Rabe, 59–60), adding that too much criticism can also undermine the ethical appeal of the orator.

in a less harsh way."[18] For example, at the end of his first discussion of Philip's aggressions against Athenian possessions in the north, D says:

ἀλλ᾽ εἶδεν, ὦ ἄνδρες Ἀθηναῖοι, τοῦτο καλῶς ἐκεῖνος, ὅτι ταῦτα μέν ἐστιν
ἅπαντα τὰ χωρία ἆθλα τοῦ πολέμου κείμενα ἐν μέσῳ, φύσει δ᾽ ὑπάρχει
τοῖς παροῦσι τὰ τῶν ἀπόντων, καὶ τοῖς ἐθέλουσι πονεῖν καὶ κινδυνεύειν τὰ
τῶν ἀμελούντων. (§5)

The sentence takes the form of an analytical period, with the main clause put first and the ramifications of it spun out in subordinate clauses that follow. There is much parallelism and antithesis (τοῖς παροῦσι τὰ τῶν ἀπόντων, καὶ τοῖς ἐθέλουσι πονεῖν καὶ κινδυνεύειν τὰ τῶν ἀμελούντων), and rhyming in the homoioteleuton seen at the end of ἀπόντων and ἀμελούντων. In the next section, in describing the reaction of potential allies to people like Philip, D uses a dactylic hexameter: καὶ προσέχειν τὸν νοῦν τούτοις ἐθέλουσιν ἅπαντες (˘˘ ˘ | ¯ ¯ | ¯ ¯ | ˘ ˘ ˘ | ¯ ˘ ˘ | ¯ ¯).

Even toward the end of the speech, when the criticism of Philip becomes harsher and that of the audience milder (see commentary), reproaches of Philip are still cast in the form of long periodic sentences rather than the choppy clauses associated with Asperity:

ἐγὼ δὲ οἶμαι μέν, ὦ ἄνδρες Ἀθηναῖοι, νὴ τοὺς θεοὺς ἐκεῖνον μεθύειν τῷ
μεγέθει τῶν πεπραγμένων καὶ πολλὰ τοιαῦτα ὀνειροπολεῖν ἐν τῇ γνώμῃ,
τήν τ᾽ ἐρημίαν τῶν κωλυσόντων ὁρῶντα καὶ τοῖς πεπραγμένοις ἐπηρμένον,
οὐ μέντοι γε μὰ Δί᾽ οὕτω προαιρεῖσθαι πράττειν ὥστε τοὺς ἀνοητοτάτους
τῶν παρ᾽ ἡμῖν εἰδέναι τί μέλλει ποιεῖν ἐκεῖνος (§49).

In these passages, the longer sentences, combined with the parallelism and rhythm, distend and dilute the criticism. This is not because D does not feel hostile toward Philip, whom he clearly despises; however, he wants to make it clear to his audience, by the tone that he uses when he discusses him, that Philip is not the real problem.

Through the techniques described above D created a very different kind of oratory from what he had practiced earlier. In *For the Megalopolitans* he had used a calm, orderly, cerebral approach and had been unsuccessful. In *Philippic I* he devised an approach that was much more energetic and emotional and also failed. In *Philippic III* he would learn to blend these two extremes to create what is probably the finest deliberative speech from the ancient world.

---

[18] Cecil Wooten, trans., *Hermogenes' On Types of Style* (Chapel Hill, N.C., 1987), xiv.

# Structure of the Speech

I. Proemium: D explains why he has risen to speak before the older orators and asks for the audience's indulgence (§1).

II. Preliminary Arguments (§§2–12).

   A. First Topic: The Athenians should not be discouraged by the difficult situation, since they have done nothing to make it better, but should be encouraged by the examples of their ancestors and of Philip himself, who overcame formidable foes by taking vigorous action (§§2–7).

   B. Second Topic: Philip's position is not as sure as it seems, since his allies and subjects resent his arrogance; the Athenians should take advantage of their animosity toward him (§§8–9).

   C. Third Topic: Philip has grown great only because of Athenian negligence and carelessness; they will never be able to defeat him if they are unorganized and unprepared (§§10–12).

III. Specific Proposals (§§13–30).

   A. Partition: D outlines the subjects that he will discuss and requests a fair hearing (§§13–15).

   B. First Proposal: The Athenians must equip fifty triremes and enough ships to transport half the cavalry, so that Philip will know that they are prepared to act (§§16–18).

   C. Second Proposal: They need to station a standing force in the north to harass Philip; D discusses the nature of this force (§§19–22).

   D. D explains the reasons for the size and composition of the force that he has proposed (§§23–27).

   E. D gives an estimate of expenses and discusses the source of funds (§§28–29).

   F. D concludes the part of the speech about specific proposals (§30).

IV. Resumption of General Argument (§§31–50).

   A. First Topic: Geographical and climatic considerations make a standing force in the north attractive (§§31–32).

   B. Second Topic: The general in charge will decide how exactly the force is to be deployed, but this force will deprive Philip of his ability to harass Athenian shipping and possessions and thus of a major source of revenue (§§33–34).

C. Third Topic: There is a tremendous contrast between the careful way in which festivals are organized and the haphazard manner in which military objectives are carried out (§§35–37).

D. Fourth Topic: Statesmen must tell the truth, even if it is unpleasant to hear; otherwise the city will never be prepared to act (§§38–39).

E. Fifth Topic: Athenian policy has been reactive rather than proactive, but this is no longer possible (§§40–41).

F. Sixth Topic: Some god seems to be goading Philip on in the hope that his aggressions might arouse the Athenians from their torpor (§42).

G. Seventh Topic: D draws a contrast between the beginning of the war and how it has ended up and makes a call to action (§§43–44).

H. Eighth Topic: If citizens will participate in the war, the gods will be on Athens' side, but unpaid mercenaries will never be successful (§§45–46).

I. Ninth Topic: Citizens in the army must monitor the actions of the general (§47).

J. Tenth Topic: Rumor-mongers deceive the people and only make the situation worse; the Athenians must face facts (§§48–50).

V. Epilogue: D has spoken bluntly in the best interests of the city; he hopes that it will not be to his own detriment (§51).

# ΔΗΜΟΣΘΕΝΟΥΣ ΚΑΤΑ ΦΙΛΙΠΠΟΥ Α΄

1. Εἰ μὲν περὶ καινοῦ τινος πράγματος προὐτίθετο, ὦ ἄνδρες Ἀθηναῖοι, λέγειν, ἐπισχὼν ἂν ἕως οἱ πλεῖστοι τῶν εἰωθότων γνώμην ἀπεφήναντο, εἰ μὲν ἤρεσκέ τί μοι τῶν ὑπὸ τούτων ῥηθέντων, ἡσυχίαν ἂν ἦγον, εἰ δὲ μή, τότ᾽ ἂν αὐτὸς
5 ἐπειρώμην ἃ γιγνώσκω λέγειν· ἐπειδὴ δ᾽ ὑπὲρ ὧν πολλάκις εἰρήκασιν οὗτοι πρότερον συμβαίνει καὶ νυνὶ σκοπεῖν, ἡγοῦμαι καὶ πρῶτος ἀναστὰς εἰκότως ἂν συγγνώμης τυγχάνειν. εἰ γὰρ ἐκ τοῦ παρεληλυθότος χρόνου τὰ δέοντα οὗτοι συνεβούλευσαν, οὐδὲν ἂν ὑμᾶς νῦν ἔδει βουλεύεσθαι.
10 2. Πρῶτον μὲν οὖν οὐκ ἀθυμητέον, ὦ ἄνδρες Ἀθηναῖοι, τοῖς παροῦσι πράγμασιν, οὐδ᾽ εἰ πάνυ φαύλως ἔχειν δοκεῖ. ὃ γάρ ἐστι χείριστον αὐτῶν ἐκ τοῦ παρεληλυθότος χρόνου, τοῦτο πρὸς τὰ μέλλοντα βέλτιστον ὑπάρχει. τί οὖν ἐστι τοῦτο; ὅτι οὐδέν, ὦ ἄνδρες Ἀθηναῖοι, τῶν δεόντων ποιούντων
15 ὑμῶν κακῶς τὰ πράγματα ἔχει· ἐπεί τοι, εἰ πάνθ᾽ ἃ προσῆκε πραττόντων οὕτως εἶχεν, οὐδ᾽ ἂν ἐλπὶς ἦν αὐτὰ βελτίω γενέσθαι. (3) ἔπειτα ἐνθυμητέον καὶ παρ᾽ ἄλλων ἀκούουσι καὶ τοῖς εἰδόσιν αὐτοῖς ἀναμιμνησκομένοις, ἡλίκην ποτ᾽ ἐχόντων δύναμιν Λακεδαιμονίων, ἐξ οὗ χρόνος οὐ πολύς, ὡς

καλῶς καὶ προσηκόντως οὐδὲν ἀνάξιον ὑμεῖς ἐπράξατε τῆς
πόλεως, ἀλλ᾽ ὑπεμείνατε ὑπὲρ τῶν δικαίων τὸν πρὸς ἐκείνους
πόλεμον. τίνος οὖν εἵνεκα ταῦτα λέγω; ἵν᾽ ἴδητε, ὦ ἄνδρες
Ἀθηναῖοι, καὶ θεάσησθε, ὅτι οὐδὲν οὔτε φυλαττομένοις ὑμῖν
ἐστιν φοβερόν, οὔτ᾽, ἂν ὀλιγωρῆτε, τοιοῦτον οἷον ἂν ὑμεῖς    5
βούλοισθε, παραδείγμασι χρώμενοι τῇ τότε ῥώμῃ τῶν
Λακεδαιμονίων, ἧς ἐκρατεῖτε ἐκ τοῦ προσέχειν τοῖς πράγμασι τὸν νοῦν, καὶ τῇ νῦν ὕβρει τούτου, δι᾽ ἣν ταραττόμεθα
ἐκ τοῦ μηδὲν φροντίζειν ὧν ἐχρῆν. (4) εἰ δέ τις ὑμῶν, ὦ
ἄνδρες Ἀθηναῖοι, δυσπολέμητον οἴεται τὸν Φίλιππον εἶναι,   10
σκοπῶν τό τε πλῆθος τῆς ὑπαρχούσης αὐτῷ δυνάμεως καὶ
τὸ τὰ χωρία πάντ᾽ ἀπολωλέναι τῇ πόλει, ὀρθῶς μὲν οἴεται,
λογισάσθω μέντοι τοῦτο, ὅτι εἴχομέν ποτε ἡμεῖς, ὦ ἄνδρες
Ἀθηναῖοι, Πύδναν καὶ Ποτείδαιαν καὶ Μεθώνην καὶ πάντα
τὸν τόπον τοῦτον οἰκεῖον κύκλῳ, καὶ πολλὰ τῶν μετ᾽ ἐκείνου   15
νῦν ὄντων ἐθνῶν αὐτονομούμενα καὶ ἐλεύθερ᾽ ὑπῆρχε, καὶ
μᾶλλον ἡμῖν ἐβούλετ᾽ ἔχειν οἰκείως ἢ ᾽κείνῳ. (5) εἰ τοίνυν
ὁ Φίλιππος τότε ταύτην ἔσχε τὴν γνώμην, ὡς χαλεπὸν
πολεμεῖν ἐστιν Ἀθηναίοις ἔχουσι τοσαῦτα ἐπιτειχίσματα τῆς
αὐτοῦ χώρας ἔρημον ὄντα συμμάχων, οὐδὲν ἂν ὧν νυνὶ   20
πεποίηκεν ἔπραξεν οὐδὲ τοσαύτην ἐκτήσατο δύναμιν. ἀλλ᾽
εἶδεν, ὦ ἄνδρες Ἀθηναῖοι, τοῦτο καλῶς ἐκεῖνος, ὅτι ταῦτα
μέν ἐστιν ἅπαντα τὰ χωρία, ἆθλα τοῦ πολέμου κείμενα ἐν

μέσῳ, φύσει δ' ὑπάρχει τοῖς παροῦσι τὰ τῶν ἀπόντων, καὶ
τοῖς ἐθέλουσι πονεῖν καὶ κινδυνεύειν τὰ τῶν ἀμελούντων.
(6) καὶ γάρ τοι ταύτῃ χρησάμενος τῇ γνώμῃ πάντα κατέστραπται καὶ ἔχει, τὰ μὲν ὡς ἂν ἑλών τις ἔχοι πολέμῳ, τὰ
5 δὲ σύμμαχα καὶ φίλα ποιησάμενος· καὶ γὰρ συμμαχεῖν καὶ
προσέχειν τὸν νοῦν τούτοις ἐθέλουσιν ἅπαντες, οὓς ἂν ὁρῶσι
παρεσκευασμένους καὶ πράττειν ἐθέλοντας ἃ χρή. (7) ἂν
τοίνυν, ὦ ἄνδρες Ἀθηναῖοι, καὶ ὑμεῖς ἐπὶ τῆς τοιαύτης
ἐθελήσητε γενέσθαι γνώμης νῦν, ἐπειδήπερ οὐ πρότερον, καὶ
10 ἕκαστος ὑμῶν, οὗ δεῖ καὶ δύναιτ' ἂν παρασχεῖν αὑτὸν
χρήσιμον τῇ πόλει, πᾶσαν ἀφεὶς τὴν εἰρωνείαν ἕτοιμος
πράττειν ὑπάρξῃ, ὁ μὲν χρήματα ἔχων εἰσφέρειν, ὁ δ' ἐν
ἡλικίᾳ στρατεύεσθαι, συνελόντι δ' ἁπλῶς ἂν ὑμῶν αὐτῶν
ἐθελήσητε γενέσθαι, καὶ παύσησθε αὐτὸς μὲν οὐδὲν ἕκαστος
15 ποιήσειν ἐλπίζων, τὸν δὲ πλησίον πάνθ' ὑπὲρ αὑτοῦ πράξειν,
καὶ τὰ ὑμέτερα αὐτῶν κομιεῖσθε, ἂν θεὸς θέλῃ, καὶ τὰ
κατερρᾳθυμημένα πάλιν ἀναλήψεσθε, κἀκεῖνον τιμωρήσεσθε.
(8) μὴ γὰρ ὡς θεῷ νομίζετ' ἐκείνῳ τὰ παρόντα πεπηγέναι
πράγματα ἀθάνατα, ἀλλὰ καὶ μισεῖ τις ἐκεῖνον καὶ δέδιεν, ὦ
20 ἄνδρες Ἀθηναῖοι, καὶ φθονεῖ, καὶ τῶν πάνυ νῦν δοκούντων
οἰκείως ἔχειν· καὶ ἅπανθ' ὅσα περ καὶ ἐν ἄλλοις τισὶν
ἀνθρώποις ἔνι, ταῦτα καὶ ἐν τοῖς μετ' ἐκείνου χρὴ νομίζειν
ἐνεῖναι. κατέπτηχε μέντοι πάντα ταῦτα νῦν, οὐκ ἔχοντα
ἀποστροφὴν διὰ τὴν ὑμετέραν βραδυτῆτα καὶ ῥαθυμίαν· ἣν
25 ἀποθέσθαι φημὶ δεῖν ἤδη. (9) ὁρᾶτε γάρ, ὦ ἄνδρες Ἀθηναῖοι,

21

τὸ πρᾶγμα, οἷ προελήλυθεν ἀσελγείας ἄνθρωπος, ὃς οὐδ᾽
αἵρεσιν ὑμῖν δίδωσι τοῦ πράττειν ἢ ἄγειν ἡσυχίαν, ἀλλ᾽
ἀπειλεῖ καὶ λόγους ὑπερηφάνους, ὥς φασι, λέγει, καὶ οὐχ
οἷός ἐστιν ἔχων ἃ κατέστραπται μένειν ἐπὶ τούτων, ἀλλ᾽ ἀεί
τι προσπεριβάλλεται καὶ κύκλῳ πανταχῇ μέλλοντας ἡμᾶς    5
καὶ καθημένους περιστοιχίζεται. (10) πότ᾽ οὖν, ὦ ἄνδρες
Ἀθηναῖοι, πότε ἃ χρὴ πράξετε; ἐπειδὰν τί γένηται; ἐπειδὰν
νὴ Δία ἀνάγκη τις ᾖ. νῦν δὲ τί χρὴ τὰ γιγνόμενα ἡγεῖσθαι;
ἐγὼ μὲν γὰρ οἶμαι τοῖς ἐλευθέροις μεγίστην ἀνάγκην τὴν
ὑπὲρ τῶν πραγμάτων αἰσχύνην εἶναι. ἢ βούλεσθε, εἰπέ μοι,    10
περιόντες αὐτῶν πυνθάνεσθαι, "λέγεταί τι καινόν;" γένοιτο
γὰρ ἄν τι καινότερον ἢ Μακεδὼν ἀνὴρ Ἀθηναίους καταπολεμῶν καὶ τὰ τῶν Ἑλλήνων διοικῶν; (11) "τέθνηκε
Φίλιππος;" "οὐ μὰ Δία, ἀλλ᾽ ἀσθενεῖ." τί δ᾽ ὑμῖν διαφέρει;
καὶ γὰρ ἂν οὗτός τι πάθῃ, ταχέως ὑμεῖς ἕτερον Φίλιππον    15
ποιήσετε, ἄνπερ οὕτω προσέχητε τοῖς πράγμασι τὸν νοῦν·
οὐδὲ γὰρ οὗτος παρὰ τὴν αὑτοῦ ῥώμην τοσοῦτον ἐπηύξηται
ὅσον παρὰ τὴν ἡμετέραν ἀμέλειαν. (12) καίτοι καὶ τοῦτο· εἴ
τι πάθοι καὶ τὰ τῆς τύχης ἡμῖν, ἥπερ ἀεὶ βέλτιον ἢ ἡμεῖς
ἡμῶν αὐτῶν ἐπιμελούμεθα, καὶ τοῦτο ἐξεργάσαιτο, ἴσθ᾽ ὅτι    20

πλησίον μὲν ὄντες, ἅπασιν ἂν τοῖς πράγμασι τεταραγμένοις
ἐπιστάντες ὅπως βούλεσθε διοικήσαισθε, ὡς δὲ νῦν ἔχετε,
οὐδὲ διδόντων τῶν καιρῶν Ἀμφίπολιν δέξασθαι δύναισθ᾽ ἄν,
ἀπηρτημένοι καὶ ταῖς παρασκευαῖς καὶ ταῖς γνώμαις.

5  ⌈13. Ὡς μὲν οὖν δεῖ τὰ προσήκοντα ποιεῖν ἐθέλοντας
ὑπάρχειν ἅπαντας ἑτοίμως, ὡς ἐγνωκότων ὑμῶν καὶ πεπεισμένων, παύομαι λέγων· τὸν δὲ τρόπον τῆς παρασκευῆς ἣν
ἀπαλλάξαι ἂν τῶν τοιούτων πραγμάτων ἡμᾶς οἴομαι, καὶ τὸ
πλῆθος ὅσον, καὶ πόρους οὕστινας χρημάτων, καὶ τἆλλα ὡς
10  ἄν μοι βέλτιστα καὶ τάχιστα δοκεῖ παρασκευασθῆναι, καὶ δὴ
πειράσομαι λέγειν, δεηθεὶς ὑμῶν, ὦ ἄνδρες Ἀθηναῖοι, τοσοῦτον. (14) ἐπειδὰν ἅπαντα ἀκούσητε κρίνατε, μὴ πρότερον
προλαμβάνετε· μηδ᾽ ἂν ἐξ ἀρχῆς δοκῶ τινι καινὴν παρα-
σκευὴν λέγειν, ἀναβάλλειν με τὰ πράγματα ἡγείσθω. οὐ γὰρ
15  οἱ "ταχὺ" καὶ "τήμερον" εἰπόντες μάλιστα εἰς δέον λέγουσιν
(οὐ γὰρ ἂν τά γ᾽ ἤδη γεγενημένα τῇ νυνὶ βοηθείᾳ κωλῦσαι
δυνηθείημεν), (15) ἀλλ᾽ ὃς ἂν δείξῃ τίς πορισθεῖσα παρασκευὴ καὶ πόση καὶ πόθεν διαμεῖναι δυνήσεται, ἕως ἂν ἢ
διαλυσώμεθα πεισθέντες τὸν πόλεμον ἢ περιγενώμεθα τῶν
20  ἐχθρῶν· οὕτω γὰρ οὐκέτι τοῦ λοιποῦ πάσχοιμεν ἂν κακῶς.
οἶμαι τοίνυν ἐγὼ ταῦτα λέγειν ἔχειν, μὴ κωλύων εἴ τις ἄλλος
ἐπαγγέλλεταί τι. ἡ μὲν οὖν ὑπόσχεσις οὕτω μεγάλη, τὸ δὲ
πρᾶγμα ἤδη τὸν ἔλεγχον δώσει· κριταὶ δ᾽ ὑμεῖς ἔσεσθε.

16. Πρῶτον μὲν τοίνυν, ὦ ἄνδρες Ἀθηναῖοι, ⌈τριήρεις
25  πεντήκοντα⌉ παρασκευάσασθαί φημι δεῖν, εἶτ᾽ αὐτοὺς οὕτω

τὰς γνώμας ἔχειν ὡς, ἐάν τι δέῃ, πλευστέον εἰς ταύτας
αὐτοῖς ἐμβᾶσιν. πρὸς δὲ τούτοις τοῖς ἡμίσεσιν τῶν ἱππέων
ἱππαγωγοὺς τριήρεις καὶ πλοῖα ἱκανὰ εὐτρεπίσαι κελεύω.
(17) ταῦτα μὲν οἶμαι δεῖν ὑπάρχειν ἐπὶ τὰς ἐξαίφνης ταύτας
ἀπὸ τῆς οἰκείας χώρας] αὐτοῦ στρατείας εἰς Πύλας καὶ   5
Χερρόνησον καὶ Ὄλυνθον καὶ ὅποι βούλεται (δεῖ γὰρ ἐκείνῳ
τοῦτο ἐν τῇ γνώμῃ παραστῆσαι, ὡς ὑμεῖς ἐκ τῆς ἀμελείας
ταύτης τῆς ἄγαν, ὥσπερ εἰς Εὔβοιαν καὶ πρότερόν ποτε
φασιν εἰς Ἁλίαρτον καὶ τὰ τελευταῖα πρώην εἰς Πύλας, ἴσως
ἂν ὁρμήσαιτε· (18) οὗτοι παντελῶς, οὐδ᾽ εἰ μὴ ποιήσαιτ᾽ ἂν   10
τοῦτο, ὡς ἔγωγέ φημι δεῖν, εὐκαταφρόνητόν ἐστιν) ἵν᾽ ἢ διὰ
τὸν φόβον εἰδὼς εὐτρεπεῖς ὑμᾶς (εἴσεται γὰρ ἀκριβῶς· εἰσὶ
γάρ, εἰσὶν οἱ πάντ᾽ ἐξαγγέλλοντες ἐκείνῳ παρ᾽ ἡμῶν αὐτῶν
πλείους τοῦ δέοντος) ἡσυχίαν ἔχῃ, ἢ παριδὼν ταῦτα ἀφύλα-
κτος ληφθῇ, μηδενὸς ὄντος ἐμποδὼν πλεῖν ἐπὶ τὴν ἐκείνου   15
χώραν ὑμῖν, ἂν ἐνδῷ καιρόν. (19) ταῦτα μέν ἐστιν ἃ πᾶσι
δεδόχθαι φημὶ δεῖν καὶ παρεσκευάσθαι προσήκειν οἴομαι·
πρὸ δὲ τούτων δύναμίν τινα, ὦ ἄνδρες Ἀθηναῖοι, φημὶ
προχειρίσασθαι δεῖν ὑμᾶς, ἣ συνεχῶς πολεμήσει καὶ κακῶς
ἐκεῖνον ποιήσει. μή μοι μυρίους μηδὲ δισμυρίους ξένους,   20
μηδὲ τὰς ἐπιστολιμαίους ταύτας δυνάμεις, ἀλλ᾽ ἣ τῆς
πόλεως ἔσται, κἂν ὑμεῖς ἕνα κἂν πλείους κἂν τὸν δεῖνα κἂν
ὁντινοῦν χειροτονήσητε στρατηγόν, τούτῳ πείσεται καὶ
ἀκολουθήσει. καὶ τροφὴν ταύτῃ πορίσαι κελεύω. (20) ἔσται
δ᾽ αὕτη τίς ἡ δύναμις καὶ πόση, καὶ πόθεν τὴν τροφὴν ἕξει,   25

καὶ πῶς ταῦτ' ἐθελήσει ποιεῖν; ἐγὼ φράσω, καθ' ἕκαστον
τούτων διεξιὼν χωρίς. ξένους μὲν λέγω—καὶ ὅπως μὴ
ποιήσεθ' ὃ πολλάκις ὑμᾶς ἔβλαψεν· πάντ' ἐλάττω νομίζον-
τες εἶναι τοῦ δέοντος, καὶ τὰ μέγιστ' ἐν τοῖς ψηφίσμασιν
5 αἱρούμενοι, ἐπὶ τῷ πράττειν οὐδὲ τὰ μικρὰ ποιεῖτε· ἀλλὰ
τὰ μικρὰ ποιήσαντες καὶ πορίσαντες τούτοις προστίθετε, ἂν
ἐλάττω φαίνηται. (21) λέγω δὴ τοὺς πάντας στρατιώτας
δισχιλίους, τούτων δὲ Ἀθηναίους φημὶ δεῖν εἶναι πεντα-
κοσίους, ἐξ ἧς ἄν τινος ὑμῖν ἡλικίας καλῶς ἔχειν δοκῇ,
10 χρόνον τακτὸν στρατευομένους, μὴ μακρὸν τοῦτον, ἀλλ' ὅσον
ἂν δοκῇ καλῶς ἔχειν, ἐκ διαδοχῆς ἀλλήλοις· τοὺς δ' ἄλλους
ξένους εἶναι κελεύω. καὶ μετὰ τούτων ἱππέας διακοσίους,
καὶ τούτων πεντήκοντα Ἀθηναίους τοὐλάχιστον, ὥσπερ τοὺς
πεζούς, τὸν αὐτὸν τρόπον στρατευομένους· καὶ ἱππαγωγοὺς
15 τούτοις. (22) εἶεν· τί πρὸς τούτοις ἔτι; ταχείας τριήρεις
δέκα· δεῖ γάρ, ἔχοντος ἐκείνου ναυτικόν, καὶ ταχειῶν
τριήρων ἡμῖν, ὅπως ἀσφαλῶς ἡ δύναμις πλέῃ. πόθεν δὴ
τούτοις ἡ τροφὴ γενήσεται; ἐγὼ καὶ τοῦτο φράσω καὶ
δείξω, ἐπειδάν, διότι τηλικαύτην ἀποχρῆν οἶμαι τὴν δύναμιν
20 καὶ πολίτας τοὺς στρατευομένους εἶναι κελεύω, διδάξω.
23. Τοσαύτην μέν, ὦ ἄνδρες Ἀθηναῖοι, διὰ ταῦτα, ὅτι οὐκ
ἔνι νῦν ἡμῖν πορίσασθαι δύναμιν τὴν ἐκείνῳ παραταξομένην,
ἀλλὰ ληστεύειν ἀνάγκη καὶ τούτῳ τῷ τρόπῳ τοῦ πολέμου
χρῆσθαι τὴν πρώτην· οὐ τοίνυν ὑπέρογκον αὐτήν (οὐ γὰρ
25 ἔστι μισθὸς οὐδὲ τροφή), οὐδὲ παντελῶς ταπεινὴν εἶναι δεῖ.
(24) πολίτας δὲ παρεῖναι καὶ συμπλεῖν διὰ ταῦτα κελεύω,
ὅτι καὶ πρότερόν ποτ' ἀκούω ξενικὸν τρέφειν ἐν Κορίνθῳ

τὴν πόλιν, οὗ Πολύστρατος ἡγεῖτο καὶ Ἰφικράτης καὶ
Χαβρίας καὶ ἄλλοι τινές, καὶ αὐτοὺς ὑμᾶς συστρατεύεσθαι·
καὶ οἶδα ἀκούων ὅτι Λακεδαιμονίους παραταττόμενοι μεθ᾽
ὑμῶν ἐνίκων οὗτοι οἱ ξένοι καὶ ὑμεῖς μετ᾽ ἐκείνων. ἐξ οὗ
δ᾽ αὐτὰ καθ᾽ αὑτὰ τὰ ξενικὰ ὑμῖν στρατεύεται, τοὺς φίλους 5
νικᾷ καὶ τοὺς συμμάχους, οἱ δ᾽ ἐχθροὶ μείζους τοῦ δέοντος
γεγόνασιν. καὶ παρακύψαντα ἐπὶ τὸν τῆς πόλεως πόλεμον,
πρὸς Ἀρτάβαζον καὶ πανταχοῖ μᾶλλον οἴχεται πλέοντα, ὁ δὲ
στρατηγὸς ἀκολουθεῖ, εἰκότως· οὐ γὰρ ἔστιν ἄρχειν μὴ
διδόντα μισθόν. (25) τί οὖν κελεύω; τὰς προφάσεις ἀφελεῖν 10
καὶ τοῦ στρατηγοῦ καὶ τῶν στρατιωτῶν, μισθὸν πορίσαντας
καὶ στρατιώτας οἰκείους ὥσπερ ἐπόπτας τῶν στρατηγουμένων παρακαταστήσαντας· ἐπεὶ νῦν γε γέλως ἔσθ᾽ ὡς
χρώμεθα τοῖς πράγμασιν. εἰ γὰρ ἔροιτό τις ὑμᾶς, "εἰρήνην
ἄγετε, ὦ ἄνδρες Ἀθηναῖοι;" "μὰ Δί᾽ οὐχ ἡμεῖς γε," εἴποιτ᾽ 15
ἄν, "ἀλλὰ Φιλίππῳ πολεμοῦμεν." (26) οὐκ ἐχειροτονεῖτε
δ᾽ ἐξ ὑμῶν αὐτῶν δέκα ταξιάρχους καὶ στρατηγοὺς καὶ
φυλάρχους καὶ ἱππάρχους δύο; τί οὖν οὗτοι ποιοῦσιν; πλὴν
ἑνὸς ἀνδρός, ὃν ἂν ἐκπέμψητε ἐπὶ τὸν πόλεμον, οἱ λοιποὶ
τὰς πομπὰς πέμπουσιν ὑμῖν μετὰ τῶν ἱεροποιῶν· ὥσπερ γὰρ 20
οἱ πλάττοντες τοὺς πηλίνους, εἰς τὴν ἀγορὰν χειροτονεῖτε
τοὺς ταξιάρχους καὶ τοὺς φυλάρχους, οὐκ ἐπὶ τὸν πόλεμον.
(27) οὐ γὰρ ἐχρῆν, ὦ ἄνδρες Ἀθηναῖοι, ταξιάρχους παρ᾽
ὑμῶν, ἵππαρχον παρ᾽ ὑμῶν, ἄρχοντας οἰκείους εἶναι, ἵν᾽ ἦν

ὡς ἀληθῶς τῆς πόλεως ἡ δύναμις; ἀλλ' εἰς μὲν Λῆμνον τὸν
παρ' ὑμῶν ἵππαρχον δεῖ πλεῖν, τῶν δ' ὑπὲρ τῶν τῆς πόλεως
κτημάτων ἀγωνιζομένων Μενέλαον ἱππαρχεῖν. καὶ οὐ τὸν
ἄνδρα μεμφόμενος ταῦτα λέγω, ἀλλ' ὑφ' ὑμῶν ἔδει κεχειρο-
5 τονημένον εἶναι τοῦτον, ὅστις ἂν ᾖ. 28. Ἴσως δὲ ταῦτα μὲν ὀρθῶς ἡγεῖσθε λέγεσθαι, τὸ δὲ
τῶν χρημάτων, πόσα καὶ πόθεν ἔσται, μάλιστα ποθεῖτε
ἀκοῦσαι. τοῦτο δὴ καὶ περαίνω. χρήματα τοίνυν· ἔστι μὲν ἡ
τροφή, σιτηρέσιον μόνον, τῇ δυνάμει ταύτῃ τάλαντα ἐνενή-
10 κοντα καὶ μικρόν τι πρός, δέκα μὲν ναυσὶ ταχείαις τετταρά-
κοντα τάλαντα, εἴκοσιν εἰς τὴν ναῦν μναῖ τοῦ μηνὸς ἑκάστου,
στρατιώταις δὲ δισχιλίοις τοσαῦθ' ἕτερα, ἵνα δέκα τοῦ μηνὸς
ὁ στρατιώτης δραχμὰς σιτηρέσιον λαμβάνῃ, τοῖς δ' ἱππεῦσι
διακοσίοις οὖσιν, ἐὰν τριάκοντα δραχμὰς ἕκαστος λαμβάνῃ
15 τοῦ μηνός, δώδεκα τάλαντα. (29) εἰ δέ τις οἴεται μικρὰν
ἀφορμὴν εἶναι, σιτηρέσιον τοῖς στρατευομένοις ὑπάρχειν,
οὐκ ὀρθῶς ἔγνωκεν· ἐγὼ γὰρ οἶδα σαφῶς ὅτι, τοῦτ' ἂν
γένηται, προσποριεῖ τὰ λοιπὰ αὐτὸ τὸ στράτευμα ἀπὸ τοῦ
πολέμου, οὐδένα τῶν Ἑλλήνων ἀδικοῦν οὐδὲ τῶν συμμάχων,
20 ὥστ' ἔχειν μισθὸν ἐντελῆ. ἐγὼ συμπλέων ἐθελοντὴς πάσχειν
ὁτιοῦν ἕτοιμος, ἐὰν μὴ ταῦθ' οὕτως ἔχῃ. πόθεν οὖν ὁ πόρος
τῶν χρημάτων, ἃ παρ' ὑμῶν κελεύω γενέσθαι; τοῦτ' ἤδη
λέξω.

## ΠΟΡΟΥ ΑΠΟΔΕΙΞΙΣ

**30.** Ἃ μὲν ἡμεῖς, ὦ ἄνδρες Ἀθηναῖοι, δεδυνήμεθ' εὑρεῖν
ταῦτ' ἐστίν· ἐπειδὰν δ' ἐπιχειροτονῆτε τὰς γνώμας, {ἃ} ἂν
ὑμῖν ἀρέσκῃ, χειροτονήσετε, ἵνα μὴ μόνον ἐν τοῖς ψηφίσμασι
καὶ ταῖς ἐπιστολαῖς πολεμῆτε Φιλίππῳ, ἀλλὰ καὶ ἐν τοῖς 5
ἔργοις.

**31.** Δοκεῖτε δέ μοι πολὺ βέλτιον ἂν περὶ τοῦ πολέμου καὶ
ὅλης τῆς παρασκευῆς βουλεύσασθαι, εἰ τὸν τόπον, ὦ ἄνδρες
Ἀθηναῖοι, τῆς χώρας, πρὸς ἣν πολεμεῖτε, ἐνθυμηθείητε, καὶ
λογίσαισθε ὅτι τοῖς πνεύμασιν καὶ ταῖς ὥραις τοῦ ἔτους τὰ 10
πολλὰ προλαμβάνων διαπράττεται Φίλιππος, καὶ φυλάξας
τοὺς ἐτησίας ἢ τὸν χειμῶνα ἐπιχειρεῖ, ἡνίκ' ἂν ἡμεῖς μὴ
δυναίμεθα ἐκεῖσ' ἀφικέσθαι. **(32)** δεῖ τοίνυν ταῦτ' ἐνθυμουμένους μὴ βοηθείαις πολεμεῖν (ὑστεριοῦμεν γὰρ ἁπάντων),
ἀλλὰ παρασκευῇ συνεχεῖ καὶ δυνάμει. ὑπάρχει δ' ὑμῖν 15
χειμαδίῳ μὲν χρῆσθαι τῇ δυνάμει Λήμνῳ καὶ Θάσῳ καὶ
Σκιάθῳ καὶ ταῖς ἐν τούτῳ τῷ τόπῳ νήσοις, ἐν αἷς καὶ
λιμένες καὶ σῖτος καὶ ἃ χρὴ στρατεύματι πάνθ' ὑπάρχει· τὴν
δ' ὥραν τοῦ ἔτους, ὅτε καὶ πρὸς τῇ γῇ γενέσθαι ῥᾴδιον καὶ
τὸ τῶν πνευμάτων ἀσφαλές, πρὸς αὐτῇ τῇ χώρᾳ καὶ πρὸς 20
τοῖς τῶν ἐμπορίων στόμασι ῥᾳδίως ἔσται.

**33.** Ἃ μὲν οὖν χρήσεται καὶ πότε τῇ δυνάμει, παρὰ τὸν
καιρὸν ὁ τούτων κύριος καταστὰς ὑφ' ὑμῶν βουλεύσεται· ἃ
δ' ὑπάρξαι δεῖ παρ' ὑμῶν, ταῦτ' ἐστὶν ἁγὼ γέγραφα. ἂν
ταῦτ', ὦ ἄνδρες Ἀθηναῖοι, πορίσητε, τὰ χρήματα πρῶτον ἃ 25

λέγω, εἶτα καὶ τἆλλα παρασκευάσαντες, τοὺς στρατιώτας,
τὰς τριήρεις, τοὺς ἱππέας, ἐντελῆ πᾶσαν τὴν δύναμιν νόμῳ
κατακλείσητε ἐπὶ τῷ πολέμῳ μένειν, τῶν μὲν χρημάτων
αὐτοὶ ταμίαι καὶ πορισταὶ γιγνόμενοι, τῶν δὲ πράξεων παρὰ
5 τοῦ στρατηγοῦ τὸν λόγον ζητοῦντες, παύσεσθε ἀεὶ περὶ τῶν
αὐτῶν βουλευόμενοι καὶ πλέον οὐδὲν ποιοῦντες, (34) καὶ ἔτι
πρὸς τούτῳ πρῶτον μέν, ὦ ἄνδρες Ἀθηναῖοι, τὸν μέγιστον
τῶν ἐκείνου πόρων ἀφαιρήσεσθε. ἔστι δ᾽ οὗτος τίς; ἀπὸ τῶν
ὑμετέρων ὑμῖν πολεμεῖ συμμάχων, ἄγων καὶ φέρων τοὺς
10 πλέοντας τὴν θάλατταν. ἔπειτα τί πρὸς τούτῳ; τοῦ πάσχειν
αὐτοὶ κακῶς ἔξω γενήσεσθε, οὐχ ὥσπερ τὸν παρελθόντα
χρόνον εἰς Λῆμνον καὶ Ἴμβρον ἐμβαλὼν αἰχμαλώτους
πολίτας ὑμετέρους ᾤχετ᾽ ἔχων, πρὸς τῷ Γεραιστῷ τὰ
πλοῖα συλλαβὼν ἀμύθητα χρήματ᾽ ἐξέλεξε, τὰ τελευταῖα εἰς
15 Μαραθῶνα ἀπέβη καὶ τὴν ἱερὰν ἀπὸ τῆς χώρας ᾤχετ᾽ ἔχων
τριήρη, ὑμεῖς δ᾽ οὔτε ταῦτα δύνασθε κωλύειν οὔτ᾽ εἰς τοὺς
χρόνους, οὓς ἂν προθῆσθε, βοηθεῖν. (35) καίτοι τί δήποτε,
ὦ ἄνδρες Ἀθηναῖοι, νομίζετε τὴν μὲν τῶν Παναθηναίων
ἑορτὴν καὶ τὴν τῶν Διονυσίων ἀεὶ [τοῦ καθήκοντος χρόνου]
20 γίγνεσθαι, ἄν τε δεινοὶ λάχωσιν ἄν τε ἰδιῶται οἱ τούτων
ἑκατέρων ἐπιμελούμενοι, εἰς ἃ τοσαῦτα ἀναλίσκεται χρήματα, ὅσα οὐδ᾽ εἰς ἕνα τῶν ἀποστόλων, καὶ [τοσοῦτον ὄχλον]
καὶ [παρασκευὴν ὅσην] οὐκ οἶδ᾽ εἴ τι τῶν ἁπάντων ἔχει, τοὺς
δ᾽ ἀποστόλους πάντας ὑμῖν ὑστερίζειν τῶν καιρῶν, τὸν εἰς
25 Μεθώνην, τὸν εἰς Παγασάς, τὸν εἰς Ποτείδαιαν; (36) ὅτι
ἐκεῖνα μὲν ἅπαντα νόμῳ τέτακται, καὶ πρόοιδεν ἕκαστος
ὑμῶν ἐκ πολλοῦ τίς χορηγὸς ἢ γυμνασίαρχος τῆς φυλῆς,

πότε καὶ παρὰ τοῦ καὶ τί λαβόντα τί δεῖ ποιεῖν, οὐδὲν ἀν-
εξέταστον οὐδ' ἀόριστον ἐν τούτοις ἡμέληται· ἐν δὲ τοῖς περὶ
τοῦ πολέμου καὶ τῇ τούτου παρασκευῇ ἄτακτα, ἀδιόρθωτα,
ἀόριστα ἅπαντα. τοιγαροῦν ἅμα ἀκηκόαμέν τι καὶ τριηρ-
άρχους καθίσταμεν καὶ τούτοις ἀντιδόσεις ποιούμεθα καὶ   5
περὶ χρημάτων πόρου σκοποῦμεν, καὶ μετὰ ταῦτα ἐμβαίνειν
τοὺς μετοίκους ἔδοξε καὶ τοὺς χωρὶς οἰκοῦντας, εἶτ' αὐτοὺς
πάλιν, εἶτ' ἀντεμβιβάζειν, (37) εἶτ' ἐν ὅσῳ ταῦτα μέλλεται,
προαπόλωλεν τὸ ἐφ' ὃ ἂν ἐκπλέωμεν· τὸν γὰρ τοῦ πράττειν
χρόνον εἰς τὸ παρασκευάζεσθαι ἀναλίσκομεν, οἱ δὲ τῶν   10
πραγμάτων οὐ μένουσι καιροὶ τὴν ἡμετέραν βραδυτῆτα καὶ
εἰρωνείαν. ἃς δὲ τὸν μεταξὺ χρόνον δυνάμεις οἰόμεθ' ἡμῖν
ὑπάρχειν, οὐδὲν οἷαί τ' οὖσαι ποιεῖν ἐπ' αὐτῶν τῶν καιρῶν
ἐξελέγχονται. ὁ δ' εἰς τοῦθ' ὕβρεως ἐλήλυθεν ὥστ' ἐπι-
στέλλειν Εὐβοεῦσιν ἤδη τοιαύτας ἐπιστολάς.   15

## ΕΠΙΣΤΟΛΗΣ ΑΝΑΓΝΩΣΙΣ

**38.** Τούτων, ὦ ἄνδρες Ἀθηναῖοι, τῶν ἀνεγνωσμένων
ἀληθῆ μέν ἐστι τὰ πολλά, ὡς οὐκ ἔδει, οὐ μὴν ἀλλ' ἴσως οὐχ
ἡδέα ἀκούειν. ἀλλ' εἰ μέν, ὅσα ἄν τις ὑπερβῇ τῷ λόγῳ, ἵνα
μὴ λυπήσῃ, καὶ τὰ πράγματα ὑπερβήσεται, δεῖ πρὸς ἡδονὴν   20
δημηγορεῖν· εἰ δ' ἡ τῶν λόγων χάρις, ἂν ᾖ μὴ προσήκουσα,
ἔργῳ ζημία γίγνεται, αἰσχρόν ἐστι φενακίζειν ἑαυτούς, καὶ
ἅπαντ' ἀναβαλλομένους ἃ ἂν ᾖ δυσχερῆ πάντων ὑστερεῖν
τῶν ἔργων, (39) καὶ μηδὲ τοῦτο δύνασθαι μαθεῖν, ὅτι δεῖ

ΔΗΜΟΣΘΕΝΟΥΣ [4.40–2

τοὺς ὀρθῶς πολέμῳ χρωμένους οὐκ ἀκολουθεῖν τοῖς πράγμασιν, ἀλλ᾽ αὐτοὺς ἔμπροσθεν εἶναι τῶν πραγμάτων, καὶ
τὸν αὐτὸν τρόπον ὥσπερ τῶν στρατευμάτων ἀξιώσειέ τις ἂν
τὸν στρατηγὸν ἡγεῖσθαι, οὕτω καὶ τῶν πραγμάτων τοὺς
5 βουλευομένους, ἵν᾽ ἃ ἂν ἐκείνοις δοκῇ, ταῦτα πράττηται καὶ
μὴ τὰ συμβάντα ἀναγκάζωνται διώκειν. (40) ὑμεῖς δέ, ὦ
ἄνδρες Ἀθηναῖοι, πλείστην δύναμιν πάντων ἔχοντες, τριήρεις,
ὁπλίτας, ἱππέας, χρημάτων πρόσοδον, τούτων μὲν μέχρι
τῆς τήμερον ἡμέρας οὐδενὶ πώποτε εἰς δέον τι κέχρησθε,
10 οὐδὲν δ᾽ ἀπολείπετε, ὥσπερ οἱ βάρβαροι πυκτεύουσιν, οὕτω
πολεμεῖν Φιλίππῳ. καὶ γὰρ ἐκείνων ὁ πληγεὶς ἀεὶ τῆς
πληγῆς ἔχεται, κἂν ἑτέρωσε πατάξῃ τις ἐκεῖσε εἰσὶν αἱ
χεῖρες· προβάλλεσθαι δ᾽ ἢ βλέπειν ἐναντίον οὔτ᾽ οἶδεν οὔτ᾽
ἐθέλει. (41) καὶ ὑμεῖς, ἂν ἐν Χερρονήσῳ πύθησθε Φίλιππον,
15 ἐκεῖσε βοηθεῖν ψηφίζεσθε, ἐὰν ἐν Πύλαις, ἐκεῖσε, ἐὰν ἄλλοθί
που, συμπαραθεῖτε ἄνω κάτω, καὶ στρατηγεῖσθ᾽ ὑπ᾽ ἐκείνου,
βεβούλευσθε δ᾽ οὐδὲν αὐτοὶ συμφέρον περὶ τοῦ πολέμου,
οὐδὲ πρὸ τῶν πραγμάτων προορᾶτε οὐδέν, πρὶν ἂν ἢ γεγενη-
μένον ἢ γιγνόμενόν τι πύθησθε. ταῦτα δ᾽ ἴσως πρότερον μὲν
20 ἐνῆν· νῦν δ᾽ ἐπ᾽ αὐτὴν ἥκει τὴν ἀκμήν, ὥστ᾽ οὐκέτ᾽ ἐγχωρεῖ.
(42) δοκεῖ δέ μοι θεῶν τις, ὦ ἄνδρες Ἀθηναῖοι, τοῖς γιγνο-
μένοις ὑπὲρ τῆς πόλεως αἰσχυνόμενος τὴν φιλοπραγμοσύνην
ταύτην ἐμβαλεῖν Φιλίππῳ. εἰ γὰρ ἔχων ἃ κατέστραπται καὶ
προείληφεν ἡσυχίαν ἔχειν ἤθελε καὶ μηδὲν ἔπραττεν ἔτι,

31

ἀποχρῆν ἐνίοις ὑμῶν ἄν μοι δοκεῖ, ἐξ ὧν αἰσχύνην καὶ ἀνανδρίαν καὶ πάντα τὰ αἴσχιστα ὠφληκότες ἂν ἦμεν δημοσίᾳ·
νῦν δ' ἐπιχειρῶν ἀεί τινι καὶ τοῦ πλείονος ὀρεγόμενος ἴσως
ἂν ἐκκαλέσαιθ' ὑμᾶς, εἴπερ μὴ παντάπασιν ἀπεγνώκατε.
(43) θαυμάζω δ' ἔγωγε, εἰ μηδεὶς ὑμῶν μήτ' ἐνθυμεῖται 5
μήτε ὀργίζεται, ὁρῶν, ὦ ἄνδρες Ἀθηναῖοι, τὴν μὲν ἀρχὴν
τοῦ πολέμου γεγενημένην περὶ τοῦ τιμωρήσασθαι Φίλιππον,
τὴν δὲ τελευτὴν οὖσαν ἤδη ὑπὲρ τοῦ μὴ παθεῖν κακῶς ὑπὸ
Φιλίππου. ἀλλὰ μὴν ὅτι γε οὐ στήσεται, δῆλον, εἰ μή τις
κωλύσει. εἶτα τοῦτο ἀναμενοῦμεν; καὶ τριήρεις κενὰς καὶ 10
τὰς παρὰ τοῦ δεῖνος ἐλπίδας ἂν ἀποστείλητε, πάντ' ἔχειν
οἴεσθε καλῶς; (44) οὐκ ἐμβησόμεθα; οὐκ ἔξιμεν αὐτοὶ μέρει
γέ τινι στρατιωτῶν οἰκείων νῦν, εἰ καὶ μὴ πρότερον; οὐκ ἐπὶ
τὴν ἐκείνου πλευσόμεθα; "ποῖ οὖν προσορμιούμεθα;" ἤρετό
τις. εὑρήσει τὰ σαθρά, ὦ ἄνδρες Ἀθηναῖοι, τῶν ἐκείνου 15
πραγμάτων αὐτὸς ὁ πόλεμος, ἂν ἐπιχειρῶμεν· ἂν μέντοι
καθώμεθα οἴκοι, λοιδορουμένων ἀκούοντες καὶ αἰτιωμένων
ἀλλήλους τῶν λεγόντων, οὐδέποτ' οὐδὲν ἡμῖν μὴ γένηται
τῶν δεόντων. (45) ὅποι μὲν γὰρ ἄν, οἶμαι, μέρος τι τῆς
πόλεως συναποσταλῇ, κἂν μὴ πᾶσα, καὶ τὸ τῶν θεῶν εὐ- 20
μενὲς καὶ τὸ τῆς τύχης συναγωνίζεται· ὅποι δ' ἂν στρατηγὸν
καὶ ψήφισμα κενὸν καὶ τὰς ἀπὸ τοῦ βήματος ἐλπίδας

ἐκπέμψητε, οὐδὲν ὑμῖν τῶν δεόντων γίγνεται, ἀλλ᾽ οἱ μὲν
ἐχθροὶ καταγελῶσιν, οἱ δὲ σύμμαχοι τεθνᾶσι τῷ δέει τοὺς
τοιούτους ἀποστόλους. (46) οὐ γὰρ ἔστιν, οὐκ ἔστιν ἕνα
ἄνδρα δυνηθῆναί ποτε ταῦθ᾽ ὑμῖν πρᾶξαι πάντα ὅσα
5 βούλεσθε· ὑποσχέσθαι μέντοι καὶ φῆσαι καὶ τὸν δεῖνα
αἰτιάσασθαι καὶ τὸν δεῖνα ἔστιν, τὰ δὲ πράγματα ἐκ τούτων
ἀπόλωλεν· ὅταν γὰρ ἡγῆται μὲν ὁ στρατηγὸς ἀθλίων
ἀπομίσθων ξένων, οἱ δ᾽ ὑπὲρ ὧν ἂν ἐκεῖνος πράξῃ πρὸς ὑμᾶς
ψευδόμενοι ῥᾳδίως ἐνθάδ᾽ ὦσιν, ὑμεῖς δ᾽ ἐξ ὧν ἂν ἀκούσητε
10 ὅ τι ἂν τύχητε ψηφίζησθε, τί καὶ χρὴ προσδοκᾶν;
47. Πῶς οὖν ταῦτα παύσεται; ὅταν ὑμεῖς, ὦ ἄνδρες
Ἀθηναῖοι, τοὺς αὐτοὺς ἀποδείξητε στρατιώτας καὶ μάρτυρας
τῶν στρατηγουμένων καὶ δικαστὰς οἴκαδ᾽ ἐλθόντας τῶν
εὐθυνῶν, ὥστε μὴ ἀκούειν μόνον ὑμᾶς τὰ ὑμέτερ᾽ αὐτῶν,
15 ἀλλὰ καὶ παρόντας ὁρᾶν. νῦν δ᾽ εἰς τοῦθ᾽ ἥκει τὰ πράγματ᾽
αἰσχύνης ὥστε τῶν στρατηγῶν ἕκαστος δὶς καὶ τρὶς
κρίνεται παρ᾽ ὑμῖν περὶ θανάτου, πρὸς δὲ τοὺς ἐχθροὺς
οὐδεὶς οὐδ᾽ ἅπαξ αὐτῶν ἀγωνίσασθαι περὶ θανάτου τολμᾷ,
ἀλλὰ τὸν τῶν ἀνδραποδιστῶν καὶ λωποδυτῶν θάνατον
20 μᾶλλον αἱροῦνται τοῦ προσήκοντος· κακούργου μὲν γάρ ἐστι
κριθέντ᾽ ἀποθανεῖν, στρατηγοῦ δὲ μαχόμενον τοῖς πολεμίοις.
(48) ἡμῶν δ᾽ οἱ μὲν περιόντες μετὰ Λακεδαιμονίων φασὶ

Φίλιππον πράττειν τὴν Θηβαίων κατάλυσιν καὶ τὰς πολιτείας
διασπᾶν, οἱ δ᾿ ὡς πρέσβεις πέπομφεν ὡς βασιλέα, οἱ δ᾿ ἐν
Ἰλλυριοῖς πόλεις τειχίζειν, οἱ δὲ λόγους πλάττοντες ἕκαστος
περιερχόμεθα. (49) ἐγὼ δὲ οἶμαι μέν, ὦ ἄνδρες Ἀθηναῖοι, νὴ
τοὺς θεοὺς ἐκεῖνον μεθύειν τῷ μεγέθει τῶν πεπραγμένων καὶ   5
πολλὰ τοιαῦτα ὀνειροπολεῖν ἐν τῇ γνώμῃ, τήν τ᾿ ἐρημίαν
τῶν κωλυσόντων] ὁρῶντα καὶ τοῖς πεπραγμένοις ἐπηρμένον,
οὐ μέντοι γε μὰ Δί᾿ οὕτω προαιρεῖσθαι πράττειν ὥστε τοὺς
νοητοτάτους τῶν παρ᾿ ἡμῖν εἰδέναι τί μέλλει ποιεῖν ἐκεῖνος·
ἀνοητότατοι γάρ εἰσιν οἱ λογοποιοῦντες. (50) ἀλλ᾿ ἂν   10
ἀφέντες ταῦτ᾿ ἐκεῖνο εἰδῶμεν, ὅτι ἐχθρὸς ἄνθρωπος καὶ τὰ
ἡμέτερα ἡμᾶς ἀποστερεῖ καὶ χρόνον πολὺν ὕβρικε, καὶ
ἅπανθ᾿ ὅσα πώποτ᾿ ἠλπίσαμέν τινα πράξειν ὑπὲρ ἡμῶν καθ᾿
ἡμῶν εὕρηται, καὶ τὰ λοιπὰ ἐν αὐτοῖς ἡμῖν ἐστί, κἂν μὴ νῦν
ἐθέλωμεν ἐκεῖ πολεμεῖν αὐτῷ, ἐνθάδ᾿ ἴσως ἀναγκασθησό-   15
μεθα τοῦτο ποιεῖν, ἂν ταῦτ᾿ εἰδῶμεν, καὶ τὰ δέοντ᾿ ἐσόμεθα
ἐγνωκότες καὶ λόγων ματαίων ἀπηλλαγμένοι· οὐ γὰρ ἅττα
ποτ᾿ ἔσται δεῖ σκοπεῖν, ἀλλ᾿ ὅτι φαῦλα, ἐὰν μὴ προσέχητε
τὸν νοῦν καὶ τὰ προσήκοντα ποιεῖν ἐθέλητε, εὖ εἰδέναι.
   51. Ἐγὼ μὲν οὖν οὔτ᾿ ἄλλοτε πώποτε πρὸς χάριν εἱλόμην   20
λέγειν ὅ τι ἂν μὴ καὶ συνοίσειν πεπεισμένος ὦ, νῦν τε ἃ

γιγνώσκω πάνθ᾿ ἁπλῶς, οὐδὲν ὑποστειλάμενος, πεπαρρησίασμαι. ἐβουλόμην δ᾿ ἄν, ὥσπερ ὅτι ὑμῖν συμφέρει τὰ βέλτιστα ἀκούειν οἶδα, οὕτως εἰδέναι συνοῖσον καὶ τῷ τὰ βέλτιστα εἰπόντι· πολλῷ γὰρ ἂν ἥδιον εἶχον. νῦν δ᾿ ἐπ᾿
5 ἀδήλοις οὖσι τοῖς ἀπὸ τούτων ἐμαυτῷ γενησομένοις, ὅμως ἐπὶ τῷ συνοίσειν ὑμῖν, ἂν πράξητε, ταῦτα πεπεῖσθαι λέγειν αἱροῦμαι. νικῴη δ᾿ ὅ τι πᾶσιν μέλλει συνοίσειν.

# Commentary

## 1

*I. Proemium: D explains why he has risen to speak before the
older orators and asks for the audience's indulgence (§1)*

The author of the *Rhetoric to Herennius*, in discussing the function of the
proemium, points out that "we can by four methods make our hearers well
disposed: by discussing our own person, the person of our adversaries, that of
our hearers, and the facts themselves" (1.8). He goes on to note that we can
secure goodwill from a discussion of our own person by pointing out our past
conduct toward the audience. The scholion notes (Dilts, 1c) that this proemium
is taken οὐκ ἀπὸ τοῦ πράγματος, ἀλλὰ ἀπὸ τοῦ προσώπου, since some of the
elders would be annoyed that a young man has been the lead speaker, and D
must, therefore, point out that this is the first time that he has risen to speak
before his elders and explain why he has chosen to do so. D thus not only
projects the image of a young man who is modest, he also calls attention to the
fact that his advice will be very different from what the audience has heard
before (Carlier, 111). A proemium taken from the person of the speaker is most
commonly found in judicial oratory. Aristotle observes in the *Rhetoric* that most
deliberative speeches do not need a proemium, although he envisions situations, such as the need for the orator to justify his participation in the debate,
where one could be considered appropriate:

> The prooemia of deliberative rhetoric are copied from those of judi-
> cial, but in the nature of the case there is very little need for them.
> Moreover, they are concerned with what the audience [already]
> knows, and the subject needs no prooemion except because of the
> speaker or the opponents or if the advice given is not of the signifi-
> cance they suppose, but either more or less. Then it is necessary to
> attack or absolve and to amplify or minimize. (3.14.11)

Yunis cites this passage in his discussion of proemia in deliberative speeches
in general and in D in particular (247–57) and comments that in general
"Demosthenes' practice corresponds with the passage from Aristotle: his
demegoric preambles do not lay out the course of the argument and seldom
even broach the subject of the speech; but he does concentrate on promoting
himself at the expense of opposing speakers and on portraying the business at

hand as vitally important" (248). D thus puts himself prominently on stage at the outset of the speech, and he will stay there throughout: "Demosthenes portrays the Assembly as the scene of competition between himself, the good *rhêtor* who could save the *polis*, and his rivals, bad *rhêtores* who would inevitably harm it" (Yunis, 279). The prominence of the speaker, however, like the prominence of his art, can deflect attention from the issue under discussion: "But if the aim of the speaker is to deal with the matter, he must let his person and his art recede into the background" ("geht aber die Absicht des Redners auf die Sache, so muss er seine Person und Kunst zurücktreten lassen"; Blass, 213). And that may be a problem in this speech.

**1.1–8**   Its elaborately rhetorical nature (D's "Kunst"), specifically his tendency to use complex sentences that rely on repetition, contrastive arrangement, and suspense in order to highlight those ideas that are important to the orator, can be seen in the first sentence, which is composed of a present contrary-to-fact condition (Εἰ μὲν ... προὐτίθετο ... λέγειν) and a temporal clause with its conclusion (ἐπειδὴ δ᾽ ... τυγχάνειν). The second part of the sentence, the temporal clause and its conclusion, however, is shorter than the first. D has explained why, although he is young and inexperienced, he has risen to speak, and that is the main function of this section. There is no need to elaborate the second part of the sentence, and not to do so gives the impression of wanting to get down to business.

Hermogenes describes (288) this type of sentence as being a division (μερισμός). A division consists of a thought that is divided into two or more parts: "On the one hand, this student is bright; on the other, he is lazy" (238). Hermogenes points out, however, that it is possible to have divisions within divisions (292). If one of the parts of the division is itself divided, this produces what we might call a "double division": "On the one hand, this student is not only bright but also well trained; on the other, he is lazy." Hermogenes cites (292) the first sentence of this speech as being such a division.

The sentence is particularly complicated. First, each part consists of a subordinate clause and its conclusion: "If it were being proposed..., I would keep silent [or] I myself would try to say.../but since..., I think..." Second, there is a fairly lengthy participial phrase attached to the subordinate clause that introduces the first element in the division ("if...*having held back until...*") and a relative clause embedded in the one that introduces the second ("but since...*concerning those things that these men have often discussed before*"), thus creating a second level of subordination. The participial phrase represents the first conclusion to the condition that opens the sentence, since an aorist participle with ἄν can represent an aorist indicative with ἄν, in this case in the conclusion to a mixed contrary-to-fact condition (Smyth §2146). Here D is saying in effect: "If it were being proposed to speak concerning some new matter, I would have held back." Two other conclusions to this condition will follow (see below). This structure demonstrates D's ability to pack many thoughts into a single sentence, noted by

Hermogenes (375) as one of the elements that makes his style "forceful" (δεινός). Third, as noted above, what we have here is a "double division": the formal conclusion to the condition that opens the sentence is itself divided and each of the two possible conclusions is conditioned by a condition of its own: "if something said by them were pleasing to me, I would be keeping silent, but if not, I myself would be trying to say what I think." Thus, we have in this sentence what could be called a "primary" and a "secondary" division. The scholia say (Dilts, 1f–g) that some critics describe this sentence as a double division (διπλοῦν μερισμόν) and that others see it as consisting of a division and a subdivision (μερισμόν τε καὶ ὑπομερισμόν). Hermogenes does not use this terminology. He speaks (292) simply of divisions being inserted into divisions (ἔτι δ' οἱ μερισμοὶ ποιοῦσι μεστὸν <τὸν> λόγον, ὅταν τε αὐτοὶ αὐτοῖς ἐπεμβάλλωνται).

The sentence may be diagrammed as follows:

(1) Εἰ μὲν ... προὐτίθετο ... λέγειν, ἐπισχὼν ἂν ἕως ... ἀπεφήναντο,
    (2) εἰ μὲν ἤρεσκε ... ῥηθέντων,
        (3) ἡσυχίαν ἂν ἦγον,
    (4) εἰ δὲ μή, ·
        (5) τότ' ἂν ... ἐπειρώμην ... λέγειν·
(6) ἐπειδὴ δ' ὑπὲρ ὧν ... πρότερον συμβαίνει ... σκοπεῖν,
    (7) ἡγοῦμαι ... ἂν συγγνώμης τυγχάνειν.

The clauses of the secondary division (2–5 in my diagram) form a chiasmus. There is a long protasis (εἰ μὲν ἤρεσκέ τί μοι τῶν ὑπὸ τούτων ῥηθέντων), followed by a fairly short apodosis (ἡσυχίαν ἂν ἦγον), and then a short protasis (εἰ δὲ μή), followed by a long apodosis (τότ' ἂν αὐτὸς ἐπειρώμην ἃ γιγνώσκω λέγειν). This bracketing of short clauses by long ones allows D not only to vary the speed of the presentation but also to emphasize the thought in the first and the last clauses in the pattern: the older speakers have not come up with acceptable solutions to the problems facing the state; therefore, he feels justified in rising to speak. Demetrius notes (39) that the beginning and end of a unit of thought are the positions of emphasis (cf. Denniston GPS, 44–47).

There are other means by which D emphasizes, in the secondary division, the idea that he is rising to speak only because other politicians have failed to give good advice. First, he states it positively and negatively (εἰ μὲν ... / εἰ δὲ μή ...). In addition, he repeats the idea, already stated in the participial phrase, that normally he would not have risen to speak (ἡσυχίαν ἂν ἦγον = ἐπισχὼν ἄν). Second, he could have here omitted the second element in this division, thus creating what Hermogenes calls an unfinished or incomplete division (μερισμὸς ἀπόλυτος, 362), with no detriment to clarity. By saying "if something said by them were pleasing to me, I would be keeping silent," he could have simply implied the contrary ("but if not, I myself would be trying to say what I think"). He chooses, however, to state fully both the negative and the positive. This is similar to what he does in the primary division by contrasting a hypothetical situation (Εἰ μὲν περὶ καινοῦ τινος πράγματος . . .) with reality (ἐπειδὴ δ' . . .). Thus, the secondary division mirrors and restates the thought in the primary one. This recurrence of ideas in slightly different form, in order to emphasize them, is typical of D (Rowe SM, 361). Moreover, related to this repetition of ideas, although there is parallelism and antithesis in this sentence, D avoids, as he usually does, the sort of constrictive balance that one usually associates with the orator Gorgias (Rowe UL, 184–86). There is antithesis in the thought (e.g., speaking concerning a new matter as opposed to considering a topic on which others have often spoken before) but there is not exact parallelism in the language. Parallelism and antithesis can make the thought easier to follow; however, very exact, one-to-one balance, both in the thought and the language, can appear artificial and insincere.

The writer of the treatise *On Invention*, found in the works of Hermogenes but surely not by him, describes (175) this sentence as an ἀντίθετον, which he conceives of as a figure of thought that places side by side a hypothetical protasis and apodosis and the same structure referring to an actual situation. The first example that he gives is: "Since it is day, it is necessary to do this, for if it were not day but night, perhaps it would be necessary not to do it" (173). He argues (174) that no other figure is more compelling than ἀντίθετον, since the hypothetical situation creates an expectation among the audience for the actual one, particularly when the hypothetical precedes the actual, as here. Usher calls (43) this type of sentence a "hypothetical inversion" and notes that it is often found in proemia.

The contrast between the actual situation, described in the second element of the primary division (6–7 in my diagram) and the hypothetical situation developed in the first (1–5) gives this sentence the sort of rounded quality that Demetrius, relying on Aristotle, sees as being typical of periodic sentences (10 and 22). Moreover, Dionysius notes that the sort of embedding of subordinate clauses and phrases that delay the completion of the thought already begun, such as we see in the participial phrase and the secondary division in this sentence, is an approach that D uses frequently: "before rounding off the first idea (or clause if it should be so called), a second idea is introduced" (*On Dem.* 9). Longinus also points out that this tendency to "suspend the sense that he has begun to express" (22.4) is typical of D and tends to make the audience more attentive by creating suspense. In this speech D at times creates so much suspense and so breaks up the presentation to highlight the various parts that make it up that the approach may have lost some of its effect.

Although this sentence is complex, it is not sluggish. By means of the structure D adds suspense. When a Greek heard a μέν, he expected a δέ (or an ἀλλά), and D sets up that expectation twice in this sentence. The suspense is heightened by the fact that the second element of the primary division (6 and 7 in my diagram), what Hermogenes calls (291) the ἀνταπόδοσις, is delayed by the insertion of the secondary division (2–5), as Longinus notes in the passage quoted above. Hermogenes points out (284) that suspense is also created in this sentence by the fact that D gives the reasons that support a proposition (1–6 in my diagram) before giving the proposition itself (7).

Other elements keep the sentence from being sluggish. Although it is complicated, the clauses and phrases out of which it is constructed are relatively short and simple (Rowe UL, 186). It is these clauses and phrases, emitted one at a time, that the audience would hear. The sentence is composed of what one might call bricks rather than large stones. Dik points out that "as is the case with building structures in the real world, texts have to be planned and blocks must be presented in manageable quantities, preferably one at a time" (23). Moreover, in this sentence, except for the frozen phrase ὦ ἄνδρες Ἀθηναῖοι, there is no hiatus, or gaps caused by the meeting of two vowels, to slow down the delivery, and there may not be a hiatus even here, since spoken Attic probably did a synizesis of the two vowels (cf. Smyth §§60–61).

Nevertheless, the pace would not have been too quick. In this sentence, as elsewhere, D tends to avoid more than two short syllables in succession, particularly within a single word (Blass, 105). Most of the syllables are long, which would have given the delivery a steady, dignified effect, although ancient critics do not discuss the effect of avoiding more than two short syllables in succession (see the survey in McCabe, 17–21, and Dover, 175). In fact, there are almost twice as many longs as shorts. Thus, the sentence has momentum, but also a restraint that keeps it from moving too quickly, and this combination of lunging forward and holding back is typical of D. There is a tension between the smooth, forward impulse created both by the suspense and the lack of hiatus and the retarding effect of the long syllables.

It has been estimated that in the fourth century, out of a male citizen population of approximately 30,000, 6,000 would attend any given meeting of the Assembly (Hansen, 60). Why would D have opened a speech before a large audience, most of whom were ordinary people, with a sentence this complex? First, he wants to give his audience the impression that situations are often complicated but that he is the sort of man who can explain them in a comprehensible way. Second, as Dionysius points out (15) in his essay on D, a style that is too simple will alienate the intelligent; however, a complex style will not be understood by the ordinary man. Therefore, Dionysius concludes, an orator who wants to appeal to the largest possible audience must somehow combine the complex and the simple. This is particularly important at the very outset of the speech, since this is where the audience will get their first and, consequently, most important impression of the orator himself. Third, the complexity of the sentence, coupled with the suspense inherent in it, would tend to hold the audience's attention, and this is one of the major functions of the proemium (cf. Aristotle, *Rhet.* 3.7–8). Finally, the situation D is going to deal with is one that he considers to be unusual and important (cf. §10), and it should, consequently, be introduced by language that is more elevated than ordinary speech.

**1.1** A meeting of the Assembly would be called by the Council of Five Hundred. The council also set the agenda, which was published in advance of the meeting. Only matters on the agenda could be discussed; however, any citizen who wanted to address those matters could do so (Yunis, 7–8). Before the meeting, the Council would have passed a preliminary decree (*probouleuma*) that would have been either a concrete proposal worked out in detail on which the Assembly could vote or an "open" decree in which the Council simply proposed that a certain topic be discussed and that proposals be taken from the floor (Hansen, 138). In this case, regarding Philip, the Council had clearly passed on open decree. The imperfect in a present contrary-to-fact condition (προὐτίθετο) indicates that the action of "setting forth" certain topics for discussion is "regarded as continuing throughout the debate" (Davies, 47).

**1.1–2**   ὦ ἄνδρες Ἀθηναῖοι: D uses this apostrophe twenty-nine times in this speech. In each case the apostrophe comes early, usually in the second or third position, in the sentence, or very occasionally in an embedded subordinate clause (§§4, 13, 43), and creates a mild hyperbaton, separating a verb from its object (most often), a verb from its subject, a noun from the genitive with which it is construed, a conjunction from its verb, two parallel verbs, or two elements in an epanadiplosis (see under §5 for a fuller discussion of hyperbaton). This separation creates suspense, and this suspense calls attention to the element that is delayed and also to the first element, as Denniston notes (GPS) in speaking of hyperbaton in general:

> Separation gives full weight to each of the two terms. Striking colours, placed side by side, kill each other: divided by intervening neutral tints, each produces its full effect. Looking at the clause or sentence as a whole, we may say that the alternation of emphatic and unemphatic words produces "a sort of rhythm and melody." (50–51)

Similarly, in discussing the frequent use of vocative phrases in Attic oratory, Bers notes: "The principal motive, I suspect, was to combat inattention, but often the phrase interrupts a sentence in such a way as to suggest the speaker's emotional intensity" (201). Each of the sentences containing an apostrophe appears at the beginning of an important stage in the development of the speech, and every important stage in the development of the speech is so indicated, with the exception of the epilogue. One of the functions of an apostrophe is to gain contact with the audience (cf. Ronnet, 125). Perhaps D felt that by this stage in the speech he already had the audience's attention, or had lost it. Moreover, there is a solemn tone to the epilogue, and in solemn passages interruptions, such as apostrophes, which are associated with argumentation, are inappropriate (cf. Hermogenes, 251). There is an apostrophe, however, at the beginning of the proemium (§1), the preliminary argument (§2), the προδιόρθωσις (§13), the specific proposals (§16), and the resumption of general argument (§31). Within the argumentation and the specific proposals an apostrophe is used to indicate each stage in the development of the argument and each specific proposal, at what rhetoricians call an ἀπόστασις, an indication of a fresh start (cf. Hermogenes, 267). These direct addresses are often used in conjunction with particles, adverbs, or conjunctions that also indicate a new direction in the thought: ἀλλά (§§5, 8), γάρ (§§9, 27), δέ (§§4, 19, 31, 40, 42, 43, 49), ἔτι (§34), καίτοι (§35), μέν (§§1, 2, 16, 23, 30, 38, 49), μέντοι (§4), οὖν (§§1, 2, 3, 10, 47), and τοίνυν (§§7, 16). One of the techniques that D uses to indicate the introduction of a new point is an αἰτολογία, a question that the orator answers himself (cf. Lausberg §§771–72), and several times the direct address is combined with the answer to this type of question (§§2, 3, 47). D also uses an apostrophe with an emotional rhetorical question (ἐρώτημα), and epanadiplosis, to indicate a change in tone (§10). Several times the orator uses an apostrophe to introduce a summary conclusion, marking the completion of an argument (§§9, 27, 30, 33, 38). This speech well illustrates, therefore, the general conclusion of Ronnet, that apostrophes in D's speeches are used mainly to articulate the stages of the development of the argument (126).

Similarly, Eleanor Dickey (*Greek Forms of Address* [Oxford, 1996]) notes that apostrophes within orations "tend to mark key points, divisions, or emotional moments in the speech" (196) and, relying on Fraenkel's earlier study, that vocatives, which are normally postpositive, "within a sentence often come between two clauses or other distinct elements of the sentence and serve to separate them; when a vocative is found within a clause, it is usually positioned next to an emphatic word or phrase" (197). It is not, therefore, the use of apostrophes in this speech that is unusual, but their frequency, and this frequent use of apostrophe, like many other figures in this highly patterned speech, gives it a very insistent tone.

**1.2–3** τῶν εἰωθότων: sc. γνώμην ἀποφαίνεσθαι. D is here referring to those citizens active in politics who were known as "rhetors," "a recognizable 'set' of men who played a special role in the political life of the polis" (Ober, 107). This was a very small number, perhaps as few as ten or twenty at any one time, who came from an elite background, usually well educated and wealthy, and regularly spoke and proposed motions in the Assembly. There was, however, no legal distinction between the rhetor and ordinary citizens, since all citizens, unless specifically restricted, had the right to speak and make proposals in the Assembly (cf. Ober, 104–27). Socrates remarks, however, in the *Protagoras* (319c) that uninformed and unskilled speakers were hooted off the speaker's platform.

**1.5** ὑπέρ ὧν = ὑπὲρ τούτων ὑπὲρ ὧν. When a relative pronoun is used with the same preposition as its antecedent, the preposition with the relative is usually omitted (Smyth §1671); an antecedent that is a demonstrative is also often omitted (Smyth §2509). Thus, ὑπὲρ τούτων ὑπὲρ ὧν becomes ὑπὲρ τούτων ὧν and then ὑπὲρ ὧν. For the use of ὑπέρ in the sense of περί see LSJ, s.v., ὑπέρ, A.III. D may have used ὑπέρ simply for the sake of variety, since he had used περί in the corresponding phrase περὶ καινοῦ τινος πράγματος, which is similarly placed in its clause.

**1.7** καί indicates that the participle has adversative force (cf. LSJ, s.v., B.9): "even though I have risen first."

**1.8** ἐκ τοῦ παρεληλυθότος χρόνου: As Davies notes (47–48), we would say "in times past." Greek, however, often thinks of past time in terms of starting points, just as it thinks of future time as points of arrival (cf. εἰς αὔριον, "tomorrow").

**1.8–9** As is often the case in D, we find here a relatively short, straightforward sentence that repeats the gist of what has been said in the complex period that precedes. This gives the speech variety and is, as Dover notes, "a feature of Demosthenes' style which contributes much to the vigour of his work" (50). Demetrius says:

> My own personal view is that speech should neither, like that of Gorgias, consist wholly of a series of periods, nor be wholly disconnected like the older style, but should rather combine the two methods. It will then be simultaneously elaborate and simple, and draw charm from the presence of both, being neither too ordinary nor too artificial. (15)

Another advantage to this approach is that the orator can repeat, in simpler form, an idea that has already been developed in a more complex way. This not only emphasizes it but also assures that the audience has understood it.

There is some wordplay in συνεβούλευσαν, at the end of the subordinate clause, and βουλεύεσθαι, at the end of the main clause. Quintilian says (9.3.71) that this type of paronomasia, produced when the meaning of a word is substantially changed by the addition of a prefix, is a very emphatic and elegant way to draw a contrast between two different situations. Here D underlines the distinction, developed in the preceding period, between the failures of past policy and what he is proposing. This contrast between past and present is intensified by the word-play in τὰ δέοντα and ἔδει (cf. Quintilian 9.3.66, 71). The word βουλεύεσθαι leads nicely into the body of the speech, where the orator and his audience will deliberate about what to do. It marks off the end of the proemium.

D quite logically uses a mixed contrary-to-fact condition here: if speakers had given the proper advice in the past, it would not now be necessary to deliberate. ἄν is often omitted in the apodosis of a contrary-to-fact condition that contains a verb denoting obligation, possibility, or propriety (Smyth §2313). This is because it is not the obligation, possibility, or propriety that is being denied, but the action itself, which is usually expressed in an infinitive. If I say, for example, "If John committed this murder, he ought to be punished." I am not denying the obligation to punish murderers but rather that John is being punished. When, however, as here, it is the obligation, possibility, or propriety that is being denied, ἄν is used with the impersonal expression (Smyth §§2315–16).

## II. Preliminary Arguments (§§2–12)

A. First Topic: The Athenians should not be discouraged by the difficult situation, since they have done nothing to make it better, but should be encouraged by the examples of their ancestors and of Philip himself, who overcame formidable foes by taking vigorous action (§§2–7).

## 2

**2.10–11** D must convince his audience that the situation is dire enough that action must be taken; however, he must not let them think that matters have become so bad that there is no hope that they can get better. The preliminary argument, therefore, will consist of a mixture of encouragement and warning. Sections 2–9 are mainly encouraging; sections 10–12 are admonitory. This mixture of the positive and the negative can be seen in the very first sentence. D opens the sentence with an emphatic statement that the Athenians should not be discouraged but ends with a recognition that the situation is very bad. The author of the treatise *On the Method of Force*, found in the works of Hermogenes, remarks: "Deliberative oratory contains reproach and encouragement, the reproach chastising and instructing the minds of the audience, and the encouragement removing the sting from the reproach. All the *Philippics*, mingled together, are examples of this interweaving" (Rabe, 454).

The impersonal construction of the verbal adjective in –τέος, which often omits ἐστί, must be used with intransitive verbs such as ἀθυμέω. The construction thus formed is the equivalent of δεῖ with the accusative and infinitive (Smyth §§2149–52). If an agent is expressed it must be in the dative; if not, the construction is best translated by "one" or "we": "we must not be discouraged, gentlemen of Athens, by the present situation." The apostrophe allows D to emphasize the words οὐκ ἀθυμητέον, by pausing before he continues the thought and thus allowing these two words to linger in the minds of his audience.

**2.12–13** Before D explains why his audience must not be discouraged, he must ensure that he has their attention. He does this by means of a paradox, somewhat like a riddle, which reinforces the antithesis in the last sentence of the proemium between the past, on the one hand, and the future, on the other: "For what is worst of those things from the time gone by, this is best with regards to the future."[1] The phrase ἐκ τοῦ παρεληλυθότος χρόνου here harks back to the end of the proemium where the same phrase is used (23): what is worst from the past is that the Athenians have not been persuaded to do what was necessary, as D had stated at the end of the proemium. This antithesis between the past and the future is highlighted by chiastic order: (a) ἐστι (b) χείριστον... (c) τοῦ παρεληλυθότος χρόνου / (c) πρὸς τὰ μέλλοντα (b) βέλτιστον (a) ὑπάρχει.

To make sure that he has not lost contact with the audience and to clarify the paradoxical statement, D uses a short αἰτιολογία: τί οὖν ἐστι τοῦτο; Hermogenes points out (239) that these types of rhetorical questions produce an effect that he

---

[1] Cf. the discussion in E. Lounès, "Structures stylistiques et thématiques de l'exorde et de la péroraison dans les harangues de Démosthène," *Revue de philologie* 60 (1986): 263–64.

calls Distinctness (εὐκρίνεια). The major goal of Distinctness is to make clear to the audience what topic or topics the orator will discuss next. Here the topic is the explanation of the paradox, and to call attention to that D gives the beginning of the explanation (ὅτι οὐδέν, ὦ ἄνδρες) the same metrical configuration that we find at the beginning of the paradox (ὃ γάρ ἐστι χείριστον): ˘ ˉˉ ˉ˘ (Donnet, 415–16).

Lines 10–13 constitute an enthymeme. The major premise is that the situation is bad. The minor premise is that what is worst from the past is best with regard to the future. The conclusion is that the audience should not be discouraged. Although there is enthymematic reasoning in D, Blass notes (206–7) that he tends to rely on examples more than logic to make his point and that this reliance on examples gives the impression that D's presentation is soundly based in fact. Quintilian points out that some teachers argued that the example was more appropriate in speaking and the enthymeme in writing ("magistri παράδειγμα dicendo, ἐνθύμημα scribendo esse aptius tradiderunt"; 12.10.51).

**2.15** κακῶς . . . ἔχει: D, like all Greeks, frequently uses the verb ἔχειν plus an adverb as opposed to εἶναι plus an adjective. We see this construction three times in this section (cf. οὕτως εἶχεν below in line 7). Many of his speeches are calls to action and are based on the assumption that a situation can be changed. ἔχειν plus an adverb seems to indicate a situation that is dynamic, that is in the process of changing or at least that is capable of being changed (see the entries in LSJ, s.v., B.II.2). And that is exactly what D wants to convey to his audience.

**2.15–17** The end of the sentence demonstrates once again D's tendency to interrupt a thought that has been begun and his ability to express many thoughts in few words, a figure that Hermogenes (294) calls τὸ κατὰ συστροφὴν σχῆμα ("the figure that involves packing many thoughts into one sentence"), both typical of the highly contrived language frequently found in this speech (see discussion at 1.1–8). He begins to explain why he feels some optimism (ἐπεί τοι); however, he immediately interrupts this with a conditional clause (εἰ) that is itself interrupted by a genitive absolute (πάνθ' ἃ προσῆκε πραττόντων). The subject of the genitive absolute can be easily supplied from the ὑμῶν in line 15, where a genitive absolute is used that is very similar to the one here (ποιούντων ὑμῶν).

Throughout this section one sees D's ability to restate, for emphasis and clarity, the same point over and over, but to vary its presentation (ποικιλία). The idea that the situation is bad is stated three times: πάνυ φαύλως ἔχειν, κακῶς τὰ πράγματα ἔχει, and οὕτως εἶχεν, and the cause of that bad situation, the unwillingness of the Athenians to do their duty, is stated twice: οὐδὲν . . . τῶν δεόντων ποιούντων ὑμῶν and πάνθ' ἃ προσῆκε πραττόντων (negative in character since it is part of a contrary-to-fact condition, a particularly good example of ποικιλία). In keeping, however, with the mixture in this section of optimism and pessimism, encouragement and rebuke, the idea that the situation might improve is also stated three times: οὐκ ἀθυμητέον, πρὸς τὰ μέλλοντα βέλτιστον ὑπάρχει, and οὐδ' ἂν ἐλπὶς ἦν αὐτὰ βελτίω γενέσθαι (virtually positive since it is part of an unreal condition, another good example of ποικιλία). As Hermogenes points out (318), one of the most salient characteristics of D's style is his ability to seem to be passing quickly from one point to another, which holds the audience's interest and attention, while, in fact, lingering upon the same ideas, and thus making them very clear and emphatic (Wooten DH). The speed of the passage is produced by the short clauses and the tendency not to state what can be supplied from context (cf. the comments on the subject of πραττόντων in line 7).

Theon also pointed out D's tendency to repeat the same point but to vary it enough that the audience is not aware of the repetitions (*Progymnasmata* 1 in Leonardus Spengel, *Rhetores Graeci* [Leipzig, 1854–56], 2:64). Rowe notes that this approach in D is often not a "heavy repetition of ideas, but a subtle process of elaboration and development bringing to light new dimensions of meaning and sensation" (SM, 362).

The author of the *Rhetoric to Herennius* calls this approach, which he defines as "dwelling on the same topic and yet seeming to say something ever new" (4.42), *expolitio* ("refinement"). He recommends changes in delivery as one means of "refining." The importance that D attached to delivery is well known (Cf. Plutarch, *Life of Demosthenes* 7 and [Plutarch], *Lives of the Ten Orators* 845B). Judging from an anecdote told by Cicero (*de Orat.* 3.213), even Aeschines, D's political rival, who heard him speak on many occasions, attested to its effectiveness. It is impossible to say exactly what was the nature of his delivery. It seems, however, that it must have been varied. Dionysius, in his essay on D, after describing what effect a mere reading of one of his speeches had on him and wondering what effect it must have had on an audience when spoken by an orator who was best known for his delivery, argues that the text itself indicates how it would have been delivered:

> No one can pick it up and read it at will and for diversion, since the words themselves tell what actions must accompany their readings: the reciter must feign now irony, now indignation, now rage, now fear, now solicitude, now admonition, now exhortation; everything, in fact, which the words require, he must portray in his delivery. If, then, the spirit with which Demosthenes's pages are still imbued after so many years possesses so much power and moves his readers in this way, surely to hear him delivering his speeches at the time must have been an extraordinary and overwhelming experience (22).

Blass is surely right, therefore, when he talks about "his tremendously lively and varied delivery" ("seine ungeheuer lebendige und wechselvolle Action," 199).

**2.16** βελτίω: Some adjectives show two stems, one ending in ν, the other in σ. They both are used in certain cases, such as the neuter plural, where we find, for example, βελτίονα and βελτίοσα, which, when the intervocalic σ drops out and the ο and the α are contracted, produces βελτίω (Smyth §293).

3

**3.17–3**  D indicates to his audience that he is moving on to another point (ἔπειτα refers back to πρῶτον in §2). This new point will involve a specific historical example of how the Athenians improved a situation by taking action (see discussion at 2.12–13).

The historical precedent that D refers to may be Athens' involvement in the so-called Corinthian War of 395–86. In 396, a border dispute arose between Phocis and Locris. Thebes intervened on behalf of the Locrians, and it was clear that Sparta would take this opportunity to intervene on behalf of the Phocians and to humble the Thebans. Thebes accordingly made an alliance with Athens, and the allies defeated a Spartan force at Haliartus in 395. This victory was the stimulus for the creation of a larger alliance in central Greece whose aim was to confine Spartan influence to the Peloponnesus. The alliance was represented by a body of delegates, meeting permanently at Corinth, who directed policy. Fighting continued, inconclusively, in and around Corinth until the war was brought to an end by the King's Peace in 386. Their successes in the war encouraged the Athenians to pursue a more aggressive policy in international affairs. The Long Walls were rebuilt in 395/94, and the Athenians eventually recovered Lemnos, Imbros, and Scyros, which had been taken from them at the end of the Peloponnesian War in 404. (See Hammond, 457–65, and Sealey, 9–13. The most important ancient sources are Xenophon, *Hellenica* 3.5 and 4.8, and fragments of the *Hellenica of Oxyrhyncus*.)

Since, however, D imagines that there are people still alive who remember the events that he uses as a precedent here, it is more likely that he is referring to the invasion of Boeotia by Agesilaus in 378 when Athens came to the aid of the Thebans. In the winter of 379/78 a group of Theban exiles, who had been given asylum in Athens and who were tacitly supported by two Athenian generals with troops on the border, took Thebes and expelled the Spartan garrison that had been installed there by Phoebidas in 382. In response Agesilaus led an expedition into Boeotia in the summer of 378. The Athenians sent a large force, composed of five thousand hoplites and two hundred cavalry, under Chabrias, to help the Thebans. After inflicting some damage in minor skirmishes, Agesilaus retired to the Peloponnesus. (See Hammond, 483–84, and Sealey, 53–56. The major ancient source is Xenophon, *Hellenica* 5.4.34–41.)

Quintilian cites (6.5.7–8) sections 2–3 of this speech when he discusses D as an example of an orator who used good judgment (*consilium*) in the presentation of his argument. He says that D begins by pointing out to his audience that it is still possible to improve the situation that has been created by their negligence. Then, rather than openly attacking their lack of energy in defending their own interests, he praises the courageous policy of their ancestors. This, according to Quintilian, makes them favorably disposed to the speaker, and the pride that they feel in Athens' heroic past causes them to repent of their own unheroic behavior.

In this long sentence D inserts between the main verb and the indirect question dependent on it a long dative of agent construction (ὑμῖν must be understood with the two participles), a genitive absolute, and a temporal clause. These three subordinate constructions delay and thus call attention to the indirect question, where D develops the idea, essential to this and later speeches, that the Athenians fight in order to uphold their national traditions (Kennedy), but in addition to creating suspense, these subordinate constructions also give important information: the Athenians, in recent memory ("from which [time] there [is] not much time") fought against overwhelming odds ("when the Spartans once held such great power"), and the facts are beyond contestation ("[some of you] hearing from others and [others], the ones knowing it themselves, remembering"). Aristotle argues that when an orator says something like this "the listener agrees out of embarrassment in order to share in the [alleged] feelings of others" (*Rhet.* 3.7.7). Ober notes that "the statement that everyone knew something was also directly linked to egalitarian ideology" (150).

Ober explains one of the problems facing an orator speaking before a large crowd of often uneducated people:

> The difficulties faced by an orator who had to put on a good show, but avoid giving offense, are well illustrated by politicians' use of poetry and historical examples. Quotations of poetry and citations of historical precedent could enliven a speech and help to buttress the argument by the inspired wisdom of the poet and the authority of past practice. The technique held a certain risk for the speaker, however....[The orator] had to be very careful to avoid giving the impression that he disdained the educational level of his audience. The orator's role was, in its essence, a didactic one: he attempted to instruct his listeners in the facts of the matter under discussion and in the correctness of his own interpretation of those facts. But when using poetic and historical examples, the orator must avoid taking on the appearance of a well-educated man giving lessons in culture to the ignorant masses. (178–79)

D, who rarely quotes poetry, generally solves this problem when he cites historical parallels by making the reference fairly vague and by attributing it to common knowledge (Pearson HA).

**3.18–19** ἡλίκην ... ὡς: Double questions are unusual and awkward in English but not in Greek; cf. Davies, 49.

When D comes to the indirect question (19–3), he emphasizes the thought in it in several ways. First, he uses once again the figure κατὰ ἄρσιν καὶ θέσιν: "You did not do anything unworthy of the city but you endured the war against them on behalf of what was just." Second, he uses near-synonymity in the two adverbs at the beginning of the clause: καλῶς καὶ προσηκόντως. Blass says (97–98) that doublets in D usually have no other purpose than to allow the orator to linger on an idea (cf. Hermogenes, 284–86). When doublets are used by D, however, the second is often more precise and more restricted than the first. Here προσηκόντως denotes what is in accordance with Athenian national tradition and is defined more fully by the direct object that follows: οὐδὲν ἀνάξιον... τῆς πόλεως. It refers to a more restricted form, a special category, of what is καλῶς (see also discussion at 3.4 and 4.16). (We also see this tendency to become more precise in the arrangement of the two halves of the object clause: enduring the war against the Spartans is a particular example of doing nothing unworthy of the city.) The genitive τῆς πόλεως is separated from the noun with which it is construed and placed emphatically at the end of the clause. This is the institution by whose interests every action must be judged. Third, D calls attention to the thought in this object clause by using a chiastic order within it, putting what motivated Athenian policy more emphatically in the first and last positions and what the Athenians did in the middle: (a) οὐδὲν ἀνάξιον... (b) ἐπράξατε/(b) ὑπεμείνατε... (a) ὑπὲρ τῶν δικαίων. D ends this long period with a key word: πόλεμον. This word is paired with πόλεως placed in a similar position at the end of the first half of the object clause and having the same metrical configuration (˘ ˘‾), since as McCabe notes (129) a final syllable followed by a major pause is probably long. D's point is that it is through war that national character is preserved and national interests are protected.

Pearson discusses the sentence in lines 17–3 as an example of what he calls a "virtuoso passage" (Pearson VP). He defines these as "long, breathless sentences" (226) that overwhelm an audience: "The orator cannot pause or relax the tension anywhere in this sentence" (225). These very complex, often elliptical and artificially contrived sentences, which must have taxed the abilities of the audience to follow them, are more typical of this speech than of *Philippics* II and III, where D seems to have been more concerned with clarity than with conveying to his audience his own impatience and excitement.

**3.3–4**  ἵν' ἴδητε... καὶ θεάσησθε: θεάομαι is much more dynamic than εἴδω. D wants his audience not only to perceive the facts that he is relating but to contemplate them and their significance (cf. LSJ, s.v. θεάομαι, 2).

**3.4–6**  The indirect statement is divided and shows the mixture of encouragement and warning seen throughout the first part of this speech. The second clause (5–6) is given more weight. It is put in the more emphatic second position in the antithesis between being prepared and being negligent. Denniston sees the beginning as the "primary position of emphasis" (GPS, 47). It seems to me, however, that what is heard last lingers longer in the mind of the audience. Quintilian notes that "there is often a powerful significance in a single word; if this is then concealed in the middle of a sentence, it tends to escape attention and to be overshadowed by its surroundings, whereas if it is placed at the end it is impressed upon the hearer and fixed in his mind" (9.4.29). D emphasizes this clause because it contains what he sees as the real problem in Athens: the situation is bad because the Athenians do not do anything to make it better. D uses the periphrasis τοιοῦτον οἷον ἂν ὑμεῖς βού λοισθε ("such as you would wish") partially to make the clause longer and thus give it more weight. Vague expressions such as this, however, can also conjure up all sorts of ideas in the minds of the audience and thus expand the scope of the speech (cf. comments at 8.18–23).

**3.6–9**   D gives examples (παραδείγμασι) that prove or illustrate the general idea sketched out in the preceding two lines. In this part of the sentence the antithesis is reflected much more clearly in the structure than is usual in D. The two appositives to παραδείγμασι are strictly parallel: τῇ τότε ῥώμῃ τῶν Λακεδαιμονίων and τῇ νῦν ὕβρει τούτου. Each of the appositives is described by a relative clause, and these are also parallel: ἧς ἐκρατεῖτε and δι' ἣν ταραττόμεθα. Likewise, the reasons for success, on the one hand, and lack of success, on the other, are expressed in parallel articular infinitives: ἐκ τοῦ προσέχειν τοῖς πράγμασι τὸν νοῦν and ἐκ τοῦ μηδὲν φροντίζειν ὧν ἐχρῆν. Here D wants his audience to see as clearly as possible (cf. θεάσησθε above) the difference between earlier Athenian history and that of his own day, and he crystallizes this, consequently, into a neat antithesis, which, somewhat like a cadenza in music, brings to a close the argument in section 3 of the speech. What he wants to emphasize in particular, however, is the cause of Athens' success or failure. That is why he places the articular infinitive phrases at the end of each parallel group. Moreover, to emphasize the contrast between them, he not only makes them parallel in construction, he also gives them a similar length (eleven and ten syllables, respectively). Aristotle notes (*Rhet.* 2.24.2) that a compact and antithetical style gives a sentence an appearance of an enthymeme and thus renders it more persuasive.

D uses articular infinitives very often, particularly in the speeches before 346. They are concise, and the presence of so many in D's earlier speeches may show the influence of Thucydides (Ronnet, 35).

**3.9**   ἐκ τοῦ μηδὲν φροντίζειν ὧν ἐχρῆν: This phrase shows an unusual succession of nothing but long syllables. This is an appropriately weighty way to end the period and this section of argument. D ends other sections of argument with phrases composed of nothing but long syllables or all long syllables but one: §4.17, ἔχειν οἰκείως ἢ 'κείνῳ; §7.17, κἀκεῖνον τιμωρήσεσθε; §12.4, καὶ ταῖς παρασκευαῖς καὶ ταῖς γνώμαις.

μηδέν must be used adverbially here (Smyth §§1600–1611), since φροντίζω takes a genitive when it means "to take thought for, give heed to" (LSJ, s.v., II.2). The negative of the articular infinitive is regularly μή (Smyth §2712). ὧν ἐχρῆν = τούτων ἃ ἐχρῆν: When a relative pronoun is in the accusative and the antecedent is in the genitive or dative, the relative is normally attracted into the case of the antecedent, which, if it is an unemphatic demonstrative, is usually omitted (Smyth §2522).

In line 8 is the first mention of Philip, who is not referred to by name, but by the demonstrative pronoun τούτου, which imparts a contemptuous tone. The contempt shown for him is related to the encouraging tone of much of this part of the speech. If the Athenians could defeat the collective ῥώμη of the Spartans, surely they can overcome the individual ὕβρις of this unnamed man whom D describes in the *Third Philippic* (§31) as being nothing more than a "wretched Macedonian."

4

**4.9**    The δέ corresponds to the μέν at the beginning of section 2. To delay the second part of a division, as D does here, creates suspense, and this suspense tends to call attention to both halves of the division (see comments in the discussion of hyperbaton in §5).

Toward the end of section 3 D had used the example of the Athenians to prove that a state can defeat its enemies by paying attention to affairs (ἐκ τοῦ προσέχειν τοῖς πράγμασι τὸν νοῦν). In sections 4, 5, and 6, he will use the example of Philip to prove that same thesis, and he uses ring composition to mark off this argument clearly from the rest of the speech: the last sentence in section 6 also contains the phrase προσέχειν τὸν νοῦν.

Ian Worthington has demonstrated the importance of ring composition in the orators.[2] Although he uses Dinarchus as his example, he contends that ring composition, at all levels, using the repetition of words, phrases, or ideas, is common in all the orators. He argues that ring composition is used "as an aid to memory for the speaker and for repeating arguments and appeals in order to counteract wandering attention on the part of the listeners" (62). Blass had noted (222) long ago the importance of ring composition in D.

Section 4 consists of one long sentence, which takes the form of an epicheireme, a fully developed rhetorical syllogism, with reasons given to support each premise: Philip is a formidable foe because he has so much power, but we were formidable foes because we once had the same power. The conclusion, that the Athenians can regain their power, is understood. The two halves of the sentence, clearly articulated by the use of μέν and μέντοι, which create a much stronger contrast than μέν and δέ, which often mean little more than "A *and* B" (Denniston GP, 370), reflect the two premises of this argument as well as the mixture of optimism and pessimism seen frequently in this part of the speech. The encouraging part of the sentence (13–17), however, is emphasized. It is longer than the pessimistic part (four lines as opposed to three) and is put in the more emphatic final position. The unexpected conclusion (ὀρθῶς μὲν οἴεται), which is then corrected (λογισάσθω μέντοι), also calls attention to the correction. Moreover, D lingers upon the description of the favorable situation that existed for Athens before Philip began to intervene in Greek politics. First of all, he

---

[2] See "Greek Oratory, Revision of Speeches and the Problem of Historical Reliability," *Classica et Mediaevalia* 42 (1991): 55–74.

emphatically introduces the clause that describes these advantages with τοῦτο
(cf. Smyth §990). D also emphasizes the subject of the verb εἴχομεν with the
pronoun ἡμεῖς and the apostrophe ὦ ἄνδρες Ἀθηναῖοι, the second in this
sentence. Then the orator drags out the direct objects, partially by the use of
polysyndeton, but also by the presence of many long syllables: Πύδναν καὶ
Ποτείδαιαν καὶ Μεθώνην καὶ πάντα τὸν τόπον τοῦτον οἰκεῖον κύκλῳ. Of the
twenty-four syllables from Πύδναν to κύκλῳ only six are short. The detail here
also gives substance to the argument. D's speeches are filled with facts and
figures. His earliest critic, his political rival Aeschines, comments on how
effectively he uses them; cf. 2.153, 3.82, 98–100. The orator highlights Athens'
other advantages also by using polysyndeton (καὶ ... καί) to join the three
thoughts in the indirect statement: that Athens once controlled many of the
areas now in Philip's power, that many of his allies were once free, and that they
preferred to be on good terms with Athens rather than Philip.

The τις ὑμῶν indicates that D can imagine what members of the Assembly
might be thinking and thus creates a bond between himself and his audience
(cf. §44.14–15). Ober notes that the elite orator speaking before the people
must engage in a certain amount of role-playing: "When they addressed the
demos, or a fraction of it, the members of the educated elite participated in a
drama in which they were required to play the roles of common men and to
voice their solidarity with egalitarian ideals" (191). The scholion points out
(Dilts, 26b) that D here uses the figure called συνδρομή. This involves a partial
or provisional concession to an opponent's point of view. It projects an image of
the orator as a man who is fair and realistic (cf. Lausberg §856–57). It also
indicates that he is so confident in the strength of his own case that he can
admit the objections of his opponents and still win his point.

Yunis notes the potential problems that the sort of frankness seen in the
passage discussed above could create for D:

> Indeed, readers of Demosthenes quickly notice a remarkable feature of
> his political rhetoric—the utter bluntness with which he delivers his
> disagreeable advice. Yet the bluntness leads to a complication: though it
> is a key part of his persuasive strategy, it also entails the risk of alienating
> the decision-making audience. To counter-balance that risk Demos-
> thenes attempts to instruct the *dēmos* on the burdens of effective
> deliberation. (257)

In fact, D probably exaggerates the danger to some extent in order to justify the
serious measures that he is proposing: "Yet Demosthenes enhances the account
of the 'illness' (Philip) in order to make the 'illness' seem as dire as possible; this
enhancement, in turn, makes the 'bitter pill' (energetic, costly action) seem
absolutely urgent" (Yunis, 261).

τό τε πλῆθος ... τῇ πόλει: The phrase shows D's tendency not to use strict
parallelism. The first τό introduces a noun that is construed with a genitive

("the greatness of the power existing for him") and the second an articular
infinitive whose subject is τὰ χωρία πάντ' ("and the fact that all these places
have been lost for the city"). τῇ πόλει is a dative of disadvantage (see note at
12.19).

**4.16** Davies notes that ἐλεύθερα is stronger than αὐτονομούμενα, "denoting
complete independence of any foreign power" (49).

**4.17** ἢ 'κείνῳ: D generally avoids hiatus, and this makes his prose smooth. He
does not, however, avoid it as consistently as does Isocrates and, in fact,
sometimes seems to seek out a hiatus for effect.[3]

**4.15–18** This probably refers to the Illyrians and the Paeonians, who lived to
the north and northwest of Macedonia and who frequently overran Macedonia
itself. Philip defeated the Illyrians in 358 and the Paeonians in 356. (See
Hammond 537–38, Sealey 160–63, and Diodorus Siculus 16.4.2–7.)

## 5

In section 5, D develops, as the τοίνυν in line 17 indicates, the point that section
4 was leading up to, namely that Philip is an example that the Athenians should
emulate. The scholion notes (Dilts, 32a–c) that D praises Philip as a means of
reproaching the Athenians for not doing what he has done. D uses what is in
effect an a fortiori argument: if Philip, who was without resources, got the best
of the Athenians, who had so many advantages, surely the Athenians, who do
have resources, can get the best of Philip. D underscores the contrast between
the earlier advantageous position of the Athenians and Philip's lack of resources
by setting the participial phrases that describe each one side by side at the end
of the ὡς clause (lines 19–20). The description of the Athenians is long; that of
Philip is short and put emphatically at the very end of the clause, far separated
from the infinitive (πολεμεῖν) whose subject the phrase describes.

**5.18** ὁ Φίλιππος τότε ταύτην ἔσχε τὴν γνώμην: Dik, basing her conclusions
primarily on examples of main clauses from Herodotus, argues that marked
elements in Greek usually precede the predicate. The word in first position
(here Φίλιππος) has what she calls "Topic function"; it gives the point of
orientation, the general subject of the discussion. The word in the second
position (here τότε) gives the "Focus," the most salient piece of information
in the sentence, the most important for the addressee. The verb usually comes
in the third position, and everything else follows the verb. This schema well
describes the placement of emphasis in this clause. D has been discussing the

---

[3] Cf. Harvey Yunis, *Demosthenes, On the Crown* (Cambridge, 2001), 25–26.

advantages that the Athenians once had. He switches to a discussion of Philip and makes it clear that he is talking about the attitude of Philip toward Athens during this earlier period (τότε).

**5.19–20** ἐπιτειχίσματα τῆς αὑτοῦ χώρας refers to forts threatening Philip's lands placed in Athenian possessions or in the territory of the Athenian allies in the north, such as Pydna, Potidaea, and Methone, mentioned in section 4. χώρας is an objective genitive (cf. Smyth §1328) representing the dative that would normally be used after ἐπιτειχίζω: "holding so many *fortresses which command* his country" (LSJ).

**5.20–21** D states the apodosis of the condition forcefully. He puts the οὐδέν first and states the conclusion twice, first in a very general way and then more specifically (see comments at 6.3–5): "he would have accomplished nothing of what he has now done and he would not have obtained such great power." ὧν = τούτων ἅ: see note on 3.9. In the second half of the conclusion, the adjective τοσαύτην is emphasized by being separated from its noun in a mild hyperbaton. Denniston points out (GPS, 51–52) that what he calls "milder" forms of hyperbaton, such as the one here, particularly those in which a verb separates a noun and the adjective that agrees with it, are fairly common in all authors. (On hyperbaton in general see Denniston GPS, 47–59, and Lausberg §716.)

The determining factor in the effect produced by a hyperbaton is whether the first element in it arouses an expectation of some sort or not. When a word creates an expectation for something else, as with τοσαύτην above, and then that expectation is foiled by the intervention of some extraneous element, the hyperbaton thus created tends to give added weight to each of the three elements, the first because it lingers in the mind while the hearer waits for the element that completes it, the second because he focuses on it looking for what he has been alerted to expect, and the third because it is highlighted by the suspense that precedes it. If, for example, an adjective, which creates the expectation for a noun, is then followed by a verb phrase that separates the adjective from the noun, the hearer tends to hold the adjective in his mind until he hears the noun with which it is construed; however, he also scrutinizes the verb phrase looking for the noun that he has been led to expect and pays special attention to the noun when it comes because his appetite, so to speak, has been whetted for it. Devine and Stephens call this Y1 hyperbaton. They note (52) that the adjective is restrictive and contrastive and the noun backgrounded: "In Y1 hyperbaton, the Y1 adjective typically has strong focus and the Y2 noun is tail material" (88). They also argue that "Y1 hyperbaton exhibits not so much a different set of properties from simple modification as the same set of properties in an exaggerated form" (58). Dik, similarly, says that "in hyperbaton it is the adjective, the element we would expect to be the more salient one, that usually precedes the noun, with the intervening element mostly (almost 8 out of every 10 instances) being the predicate" (7).

When a word, however, that does not create an expectation for something else is separated from another word construed with it, it is really only the second word, which comes in unexpectedly, that strikes the attention of the hearer because of the surprise (cf. Gotoff, 164–65). When, for example, a noun, which does not necessarily create an expectation for an adjective, is separated from the adjective by a verb phrase, the adjective is the only element that is striking. Devine and Stephens put it thus: "the Y1 noun can be a topic and the Y2 adjective a weak focus" (88).

**5.21–22**  D repeats in a positive way the thought that has just been expressed negatively. The verb (εἶδεν), somewhat unusually, comes first (cf. Denniston GPS, 43), and the subject is at the end of the clause in a very emphatic position (ἐκεῖνος) to emphasize the difference between Philip and the Athenians. Dik notes (49) that the verb can take initial position, that is, that it can have Topic function. Here D is contrasting Philip's perceptiveness with Athenian foolishness. καλῶς is important. Earlier it had been applied to the Athenians (§3.1); now it is used to describe Philip's actions. Admittedly the adverb is used in a different sense ("well" as opposed to "nobly"), but the contrast is still pointed.

In this indirect statement D states the same idea, that people are successful who act and pay attention to their affairs, three times in slightly different ways. In the first expression of this idea he uses an image from sports.[4] The phrase ἆθλα... κείμενα ἐν μέσῳ is used to refer to prizes in an athletic contest (cf. Theognis 994 and Xen., *Ana.* 3.1.21). D is generally fond of athletic images, which are quite appropriate in the works of an orator who attaches so much importance to struggle and combat.

I do not understand the comma after χωρία in Dilts's text. It seems to me that ἆθλα is a predicate nominative and thus should not be set off from the rest of the text: "that all these places are prizes of war lying [exposed] in the middle." The hiatus between χωρία and ἆθλα could simply be used to emphasize the important word ἆθλα. Most editors, however, print χωρί᾽ ἆθλα.

The next two clauses deal with what D considers to be a general law of nature (cf. φύσει). They are brought into relief by means of antithesis, which is reinforced by a fairly strict parallelism. The neatness of the expression and the general nature of the thought create an aphoristic quality. In the first clause, τοῖς παροῦσι is contrasted with τῶν ἀπόντων, and in the second τοῖς ἐθέλουσι πονεῖν καὶ κινδυνεύειν with τῶν ἀμελούντων. D avoids perfect balance by adding the two infinitives πονεῖν καὶ κινδυνεύειν to the participle in the second of these two clauses. This also allows him to call attention to the two infinitives, which stand out not only because they break the parallel pattern but also because they both express more or less the same idea. And that idea is important because it is exactly what people do who act and pay attention to their affairs (προσέχειν τοῖς πράγμασι

---

[4] Cf. section 40 of this speech and see, for a general discussion of his metaphors and similes, Ronnet, 149–82.

τὸν νοῦν; §3.7–8). The two participles ἀπόντων and ἀμελούντων, placed at the end of each clause and highlighted by the strict parallelism and rhyming, express important ideas, already developed to some extent in the first part of the speech (cf. οὐδὲν . . . τῶν δεόντων ποιούντων ὑμῶν in §2 and ἂν ὀλιγωρῆτε in §3), and soon to be reinforced by the words εἰρωνείαν and ῥᾳθυμίαν in sections 7 and 8.

## 6

**6.3–5**  At the end of section 5 the discussion had become general. In section 6 D returns to the particular example of Philip. One of the ways in which D manages to recur to ideas already discussed, and thus to emphasize them without appearing to be repetitious, is to switch back and forth between the general and the particular (cf. Hermogenes, 278–79). The sentence that deals with Philip begins with καὶ γάρ τοι ("and in consequence"). This phrase is usually used to call attention to a point or to indicate a consequence, particularly at the end of a discussion (Smyth §§2819–20; Denniston GP, 113–14). Here D is concluding the argument in sections 4, 5, and 6 that Philip is an example that the Athenians should emulate.

**6.4**  τὰ μὲν ὡς ἂν ἑλών τις ἔχοι πολέμῳ: This compact phrase means: "[possessing] some, as anyone would possess them, having taken them in war." The participle ἔχων can be easily understood from the verb ἔχοι in the subordinate clause and also from the main verb ἔχει that precedes. The suppression of this participle allows D to keep the parallelism between τὰ μὲν . . . and τὰ δὲ . . . ποιησάμενος from becoming too strict. Philip's main military and diplomatic activity during the four years preceding the delivery of this speech was in Thessaly and Thrace (see the introduction and Sealey, 120–26).

**6.5–7**  Having discussed the particular example of Philip, D reverts to a more general discussion. He introduces this part of the sentence with καὶ γάρ, which calls attention to an explanation for what precedes (Smyth §2814; Denniston GP, 108–11). The last part of the first clause in this sentence falls into a dactylic hexameter: καὶ προσέχειν τὸν νοῦν τούτοις ἐθέλουσιν ἅπαντες ( ˉ ˘ ˘ | ˉ ˉ | ˉ ˉ | ˉ ˘ ˘ | ˉ ˘ ˘ | ˉ ). This rhythm is maintained at the beginning of the relative clause: οὓς ἂν ὁρῶσι παρεσκευ - ( ˉ ˘ ˘ | ˉ ˘ ˘ | ˉ ˉ ). Dover argues that D "developed his rhythmic preferences for prose in its own right, as if poetry did not exist" (172), and in general I would agree. In this section, however, D is making a gnomic pronouncement about what, in his opinion, constitutes heroic conduct, conduct in keeping with Athenian national traditions. It is reasonable, therefore, that, given the nature of the topic and the form in which it is expressed, he might, even unconsciously, have used such a poetic rhythm. οὓς ἂν ὁρῶσι, in keeping with the gnomic nature of the sentence, represents the protasis of a present general condition (cf. Smyth §2560).

The sentence ends with the theme that has been running through the speech up to this point, the main advice that D has to give his audience: they must be prepared to do whatever must be done (παρεσκευασμένους καὶ πράττειν ἐθέλοντας ἃ χρή). This is the sixth time in six sections of the speech that the idea of doing what requires doing has come up: τὰ δέοντα, ἔδει (§1, twice), οὐδὲν ... τῶν δεόντων, πάνθ᾽ ἃ προσῆκε (§2, twice), προσηκόντως οὐδὲν ἀνάξιον ὑμεῖς ἐπράξατε τῆς πόλεως (§3), and here. Having planted this idea firmly in the mind of his audience D will expand upon ἃ χρή in the next section of the speech.

7

D continues to switch back and forth between the general and the particular. The τοίνυν in line 10 marks "the transition from the enumeration of a general proposition to the consideration of a particular instance of it" (Denniston GP, 576). In section 6, D had described Philip as ταύτῃ χρησάμενος τῇ γνώμῃ. At the beginning of section 7, he envisions a situation in which the Athenians will ἐπὶ τῆς τοιαύτης ... γενέσθαι γνώμης. (The preposition is here used metaphorically, and the phrase means "to come to an opinion" [LSJ, s.v., A.I.3.c] or "to adopt an attitude.")

This whole section is taken up by one long sentence, by far the longest sentence in the speech so far and a good example of how form often reflects content in D. It is a grand, elevated call to action that sums up much of what has been argued up to this point. It is also typical of the demands made on the audience in this speech, stylistic demands but also demands of personal sacrifice. The first part of the sentence is the protasis to a condition whose conclusion is found at the end. The protasis is quite complicated and comprises about 75 percent of the sentence. What creates the complication is the fact that there is so much subordination within the protasis. One could diagram lines 10–15 as follows, indicating the two protases by letters and subordinate clauses within those protases by numbers:

ἂν τοίνυν ...

    (a) καὶ ὑμεῖς ... ἐθελήσετε ... νῦν,
        (1) ἐπειδήπερ οὐ πρότερον,
    (b) καὶ ἕκαστος ὑμῶν,
        (1) οὗ ... τῇ πόλει,
        (2) πᾶσαν ἀφεὶς τὴν εἰρωνείαν
        ἕτοιμος πράττειν ὑπάρξῃ,
        (3) ὁ μὲν ..., ὁ δ᾽ ἐν ...

**7.7–13** In each of these two initial clauses D uses elements that Hermogenes sees as producing Abundance, a style that expresses the thought in a full and expansive way. Of the techniques that Hermogenes recommends for creating Abundance, six appear in the protasis to this sentence: (1) the use of language that implies other thoughts: e.g., τοιαύτης implies thoughts that have been expressed in the preceding sentence; (2) division; (3) parenthesis: (4) κατὰ ἄρσιν καὶ θέσιν (νῦν, ἐπειδήπερ οὐ πρότερον); (5) coupling the general and the specific: "if you are willing to adopt such an attitude now... and each of you is ready to act where it is necessary and where he would be able to make himself useful to the city"; and (6) enumeration that breaks down a general idea into its component parts: "the one having money to pay taxes, the one in the prime of life to serve in the army." In this passage, having moved steadily from the general to the specific, D then breaks off the list of what individual citizens can do (συνελόντι δ' ἁπλῶς, "for [one] grasping [the situation] briefly") and reverts to the general in lines 13–15. Specific recommendations are thus bracketed by general considerations. This is similar to the general structure of the whole speech. W. Ross Winterowd, in fact, has argued that "the individual sentences that an author characteristically uses are a good place to begin a search for devices that will constitute, in the round, that writer's technique" (*Contemporary Rhetoric* [New York, 1975], 213).

**7.11** εἰρωνείαν, which is different from English "irony," implies that someone at first appears willing to do something but then hesitates (cf. LSJ, s.v., II). The most basic definition given in LSJ is *"ignorance purposely affected* to provoke or confound an antagonist." The Athenians pretend not to recognize the problem of Philip because they do not want to do anything about it.

**7.12–13** εἰσφέρειν is a technical term for paying the occasional war tax (εἰσφορά) that was levied on wealthy citizens and resident aliens (cf. LSJ, s.v., 2). After 347, however, it was not sporadic, but a regular annual tax of ten talents (Hansen, 112). A man needed to be worth about one talent to be in the "leisure class" (Ober, 128) on which this tax was levied, and it has been estimated that there were 1,200–2,000 citizens in this category. Men in this class were also liable to other financial obligations imposed by the state (see discussion at 36.27). During D's life *eisphorai* were paid by groups. The wealthy citizens were organized into a hundred "symmories" with about fifteen men per symmory, and each symmory was responsible for paying a certain quota of the tax. The richest of these citizens, however, worth three to four talents and probably numbering about 300 to 400, were required to pay the whole tax at once and then were allowed to reimburse themselves from other members of their symmory. These were known as *proeispherontes* or "advance payers" (Ober, 128; Hansen, 112–15). ἐν ἡλικίᾳ: In theory, Athenian citizens were liable to military service between the ages of eighteen and sixty; however, generally only those between twenty and fifty were called out.

**7.13–15** In this general summary, D first states the condition positively: "if you are willing to be your own masters" (γίγνομαι plus the genitive means to "be under the control of"; see LSJ, s.v., II.3.a). Then he states it negatively by stipulating what they must stop doing: "and you cease each one hoping that he himself will do nothing and that his neighbour will do all things on his behalf." Here, as earlier in the protasis (8–9), D couples the second person plural (παύσησθε) with the singular pronoun ἕκαστος. This allows him to pitch his appeal, not only to the Assembly as a whole, but also to each individual member of it.

**7.16–17**   The protasis is complicated and slow, filled with interruptions, qualifications, emphatic statements, all expressed in a very expansive style. In the conclusion, however, the structure becomes extremely straightforward, almost simple, and very regular. The protasis of this sentence describes the demands that will be made on the Athenians if they decide to defend themselves against Philip. These demands will be extensive, complicated, and drawn out, as is the structure of this part of the sentence. The conclusion, however, is simple and straightforward, and this indicates that the gains will be clear-cut if the Athenians will only act. There is thus a contrast between the complexity of the demands made on the Athenians and the clarity of the results that will follow. (For a discussion of this phenomenon in general in D see Wooten FO.)

> B.  Second Topic: Philip's position is not as sure as it seems, since his allies and subjects resent his arrogance; the Athenians should take advantage of the latter's animosity toward him (§§8–9)

8

**8.18–23**   The first sentence continues the positive, encouraging tone of sections 2–7, explaining more fully an idea that D had broached at the end of section 4 (15–18), that Philip's allies are not very loyal to him. In order to make his point as clearly as possible and to impress upon his audience how substantial Philip's disadvantages are, D uses a very simple style: three verbs, all of which have the same subject and object, joined by polysyndeton. The apostrophe allows the orator to emphasize the final verb by delaying it and gives some variety to the list. In dealing with someone who is successful envy is probably a more potent motivator than hatred or fear. In his discussion of the emotions in Book II of Cicero's *de Oratore*, for example, Antonius calls envy the strongest by far (*acerrimus longe*): "People are especially envious of their equals or inferiors, when they feel they have been left behind, and resent that those others have reached such heights. But often people are also fiercely envious of their superiors, all the more so if they become intolerably boastful, and use their pre-eminent status or fortune to overstep the bounds of fairness that apply to all alike" (209; translation by James May and Jakob Wisse [Oxford, 2001]).

Rather than continue the list of the various emotions that Philip evokes from people, D sums up with a general statement: καὶ ἅπανθ᾿ ὅσα περ καὶ ἐν ἄλλοις τισὶν ἀνθρώποις ἔνι, ταῦτα καὶ ἐν τοῖς μετ᾿ ἐκείνου χρὴ νομίζειν ἐνεῖναι. The generalizing expression (ἄπανθ᾽ ὅσα) and the alliteration and the jingle (καὶ ἐν ... ἔνι, καὶ ἐν ... ἐνεῖναι) give the sentence a gnomic quality. D is fond of these generalizing statements. They force the hearer to conjure up in his own mind many possibilities that the orator himself does not discuss, and in that respect they allow him to expand his argument while keeping his text brief. Ronnet makes the same point (23–24) about the use of the neuter of adjectives (cf. discussion at 42.2).

In lines 19–23 καί is used seven times. Four of these are copulative; three are intensifying adverbs. This conveys the impression that D is heaping up details, some of which he emphasizes, that pound home his argument that Philip is vulnerable. This accumulation of detail, often strung together in a fairly loose way, is typical of the orator. It gives "an impetus to the speech, a vigor that gives the impression of spontaneity and reveals an underlying emotion that drives the speaker relentlessly from one point to the next" (Wooten A, 504–5).

**8.19**  ἀθάνατα is used as a predicate adjective with πεπηγέναι (cf. Smyth §§1042–43). The perfect of πήγνυμι can be used intransitively to mean to "be irrevocably fixed, established" (LSJ, s.v., IV): "The present situation has not been irrevocably fixed for him, as for a god."

τις is here used in the general sense of "everybody" (cf. Smyth §1267).

δέδιεν: The second perfect of δείδω is less common in the singular, more common in the plural, than the first perfect δέδοικα (cf. Smyth §703); the perfect is used in a present sense (LSJ).

**8.22**  ἔνι is a shortened form of ἔνεστι.

**8.23–25**  D uses a metaphor to explain why these emotions hostile to Philip have not manifested themselves. They are like people who crouch down out of fear (καταπτήσσω) since they do not have anywhere to run for safety (ἀποστροφή). The sentence is a very straightforward example of the analytical period that D prefers.[5] The main verb is placed at the beginning of the sentence (κατέπτηχε) in a short clause that consists of little more than a verb, its subject, and an adverb. The ramifications of this main thought are then explored in short, simple, straightforward phrases and clauses. There is first the reason why these passions have not erupted (οὐκ ἔχοντα ἀποστροφήν). Then there is an explanation of why there is no place of refuge (διὰ τὴν ὑμετέραν βραδυτῆτα καὶ ῥᾳθυμίαν). And finally there is the claim that the orator makes based on these considerations (ἣν ἀποθέσθαι φημὶ δεῖν ἤδη).

The really important thought comes at the end of the participial phrase: διὰ τὴν ὑμετέραν βραδυτῆτα καὶ ῥᾳθυμίαν. This idea, that Athenian slowness and indifference in responding are at the root of most of Athens' problems, is one of

---

[5]  Cf. Wooten CP, 34–35.

the recurring themes that hold this speech together. Similarly, D elsewhere uses medical language to show that Philip is simply a symptom of an underlying disease (cf. Wooten UM). At the end of the sentence D appends what Hermogenes calls (250) an "added value judgment" (ἐπίκρισις). These "added value judgments," according to Hermogenes, convey an impression of sincerity and conviction, since they seem to be spontaneous comments on a thought that has just been enunciated (361–62). The tone of the last sentence in section 8 is insistent and peremptory (cf. the synonymity in διὰ τὴν ὑμετέραν βραδυτῆτα καὶ ῥᾳθυμίαν), indignant (cf. ἣν ἀποθέσθαι φημὶ δεῖν), and impatient (cf. the final ἤδη), and this makes an effective transition to the tone of the next four sections, which are more critical, both of the Athenians and of Philip, than those that precede. D is modulating from rational to emotional argument. Jaeger (130–33) comments on the sense of crisis and urgency in D's speeches against Philip, the idea that the Athenians have been presented with an opportunity that they must not miss.

## 9

The section numbers, added in Bekker's edition of 1823, sometimes do not reflect the development of the thought. This section is closely related to the one that precedes. ὁρᾶτε γάρ indicates clearly that it gives the reason why people cower before Philip and hate and fear him, and this forms part of an enthymeme. A more logical division would have come before κατέπτηχε in line 23. D gives as his proof, however, not how Philip treats his allies, but how he deals with the Athenians, and the contemplation of his outrageous conduct toward Athens evokes the anger that motivates the passionate outburst in sections 10–12.

**9.1**  ἀσελγείας, meaning something like "outrageous conduct," is a partitive genitive with the adverb οἷ: "to what degree of outrageous conduct the man has come." ἀσέλγεια is often associated with ὕβρις (cf. the first words of D's speech Against Meidias: Τὴν μὲν ἀσέλγειαν, ὦ ἄνδρες δικασταί, καὶ τὴν ὕβριν), and D has already described Philip's conduct as ὕβρις in section 3 (τῇ νῦν ὕβρει τούτου). Moreover, the idea of his ὕβρις is developed in the rest of the sentence. Philip uses words that are ὑπερήφανοι, an adjective that is often used in conjunction with ὕβρις (cf. Aristotle, Rhet. 2.16.1: ὑβρισταὶ γὰρ καὶ ὑπερήφανοι), and is never content with what he has, always grasping after more (οὐχ οἷός ἐστιν ἔχων ἃ κατέστραπται μένειν ἐπὶ τούτων, ἀλλ' ἀεί τι προσπεριβάλλεται). This emphasis on Philip's always grasping after more explains why D highlighted the idea of envy in line 20.

**9.1–6**  The relative clause that describes ἄνθρωπος makes its point by using the figure κατὰ ἄρσιν καὶ θέσιν twice: οὐδ'... ἀλλ'... οὐχ... ἀλλ'. In the paired negative and positive clauses, the positive element uses much stronger language than the negative with which it is coupled and in each case is put in the more emphatic second position. In addition, the last clause is the most vivid. D there uses two strong verbs to refer to Philip's activities: he is always surrounding himself with some new addition (προσπεριβάλλεται) and surrounding the Athenians with nets, as a hunter surrounds his prey (περιστοιχίζεται). Philip is described by means of verbs that denote activity, of which he is the subject, and they contain as many shorts as they do longs: he acts, decisively and quickly. The Athenians, on the other hand, are the direct object, described by means of the participles of verbs that denote inactivity. They are acted upon. Moreover, the words used to describe the Athenians contain many more longs than shorts, indicating their slowness: μέλλοντας ἡμᾶς καὶ καθημένους.

As we have seen, D uses the figure κατὰ ἄρσιν καὶ θέσιν frequently in the *Philippics*. One of its advantages is that it "can adorn every thought," as the author of the treatise *On Invention* notes (175) about ἀντίθετον. Like ἀντίθετον also it can be used to arouse the expectation of the audience. In an ἀντίθετον the orator usually puts the hypothetical situation first, which makes the audience wonder what the actual situation is. Similarly, when D uses κατὰ ἄρσιν καὶ θέσιν, he usually puts the negative before the positive. When a member of the audience hears what something is not, he begins to wonder what it is.

Hermogenes also points out that D was "eager to give Grandeur and dignity to his speeches" (289). Of the types of style that produce Grandeur only Abundance, which can be created by the figure κατὰ ἄρσιν καὶ θέσιν (293), is able to be used almost everywhere: "But not even in public speeches [which give greater opportunity for stylistic variation than private speeches] is it possible to use the other styles such as Solemnity or Asperity or Vehemence or Brilliance or Florescence as often as one uses Abundance" (290).

**C. Third Topic: Philip has grown great only because of Athenian negligence and carelessness; they will never be able to defeat him if they are unorganized and unprepared (§§10–12)**

## 10–11

**10.6–8** The strong language and antitheses in section 9 indicate a heightened emotional tone. This becomes even more pronounced in section 10 (see the introduction). The purpose of this section is to arouse the audience's attention before D makes his specific proposals beginning in section 13. The dramatic presentation, with its use of direct speech (*oratio recta*), is engaging. It adds variety to the presentation, and variety is one of D's favorite techniques for engaging his audience: "OR [*oratio recta*] constitutes a modulation, a shift from the surrounding utterance. Like other shifts in an utterance, say from proem to narration in a court speech, OR stimulates attention" (Bers, 224). In addition, D uses other techniques of effecting closer contact with his audience. The short rhetorical questions at the beginning, the first one using epanadiplosis and apostrophe, convey to the audience his impatience and anger: πότ᾽ οὖν, ὦ ἄνδρες Ἀθηναῖοι, πότε ἃ χρὴ πράξετε; ἐπειδὰν τί γένηται; The scholion supposes (Dilts, 52) that the second πότε would be pronounced more deeply (βαρυτέρᾳ φωνῇ) than the first. Longinus cites section 10 of this speech as an illustration of the fact that "emotion is always more telling when it seems not to be premeditated by the speaker but to be born of the moment; and this way of questioning and answering one's self counterfeits spontaneous emotion" (18).

The writer of the treatise *On the Method of Force* says (Rabe, 425–26) that a question that involves a supposition that cannot be denied (ἀναντίρρητον), what he calls a πεῦσις, takes three forms, being addressed either to the audience or to one's opponents or by the orator to himself. If it is addressed to the audience, it involves reproach, as does this passage, which the author of the treatise cites as an example; if to the opponents, refutation. Such a question that the orator addresses to himself has two functions: it attracts the attention of the audience and shows that the orator has confidence in what he is saying, since he would never ask himself a question that he could not answer. The technical rhetorical term for this use of short questions and quick responses is *hypophora*; see Bers's discussion (195–96).

**10.7**   γένηται is the verb in what is, in effect, the protasis to a future more vivid condition (cf. Smyth §2561) with πράξετε understood as the conclusion. The same is true of ᾖ in the next line.

**10.8**   τί is an adverbial accusative, in effect, an accusative of respect: "in respect to what" = "how" (cf. Smyth §§1600–1611).

**10.8–10**   The key word (ἀνάγκη) in the imaginary reply, emphasized by the νὴ Δία that precedes it, allows D to move to the next stage of his argument, where, by defining what constitutes necessity, he demonstrates that the situation envisioned by his imaginary interlocutor already exists. Before he does this, however, he makes sure that he maintains the lively tone of the exchange by inserting another question (νῦν δὲ τί χρὴ τὰ γιγνόμενα ἡγεῖσθαι;), which he then proceeds to answer himself. Dover points out (62–65) that oaths and other colloquial elements such as the demonstrative affix -ί appear more often in D than in earlier orators and indicate a "change towards informality, no doubt very carefully calculated, in the middle of the fourth century" (63).

The reply to this question is more extended than the brief exchanges that we have seen so far in this section, and D calls attention to it in that there is clear patterning for the purpose of emphasis. The predicate of the indirect statement (τοῖς ἐλευθέροις μεγίστην ἀνάγκην) and the subject (τὴν ὑπὲρ τῶν πραγμάτων αἰσχύνην) have about the same number of syllables (eleven and ten, respectively). Each ends with a word of three syllables (ἀνάγκην, αἰσχύνην), and these two words rhyme. This calls attention to the most important words in the sentence and to the fact that one is here presented as almost the definition of the other (ἀνάγκην =

αἰσχύνην). When it is necessary to distinguish the subject from the predicate, Greek uses the definite article with the former but not with the latter (Smyth §1150). The motivation seems here to be internalized rather than to be produced by the fear of discovery or the hope of praise, as is often the case in a shame culture; see the discussion of this passage in Bernard Williams, *Shame and Necessity* (Berkeley, 1993), 81–82 and 195–96. Harvey Yunis, drawing on an earlier discussion by Stuart Hampshire in *Public and Private Morality* (Cambridge, 1978), describes this attitude well as "the assertion of a moral imperative not because of any moral injunction, rational principle, or utilitarian consideration, but as the expression of a way of life, an ideal way of life, that will not be abandoned or sacrificed" ("Politics as Literature: Demosthenes and the Burden of the Athenian Past," *Arion* 8 [2000]: 109).

As the scholion points out (Dilts, 54a), there is no δέ that corresponds to the μέν in the phrase ἐγὼ μὲν γὰρ οἴομαι. This produces an unfinished division, which indicates the kind of spontaneity appropriate to an angry passage.

**10.10–13**  In the second half of this section D repeats the approach that he has taken in the first half. First, in order to maintain close contact with his audience, he asks them a question (ἢ βούλεσθε . . . περιόντες αὐτῶν [=ὑμῶν αὐτῶν; see Smyth §1230] πυνθάνεσθαι . . .;) and, in this case, inserts an imperative (εἰπέ μοι) into the question. The question is plural, but the imperative is singular. This must have made every member of the Assembly feel that D was talking to him individually. Longinus says: "By appearing to address not the whole audience but a single individual . . . you will move him more and make him more attentive and full of active interest, because he is roused by the appeals to him in person" (26). He answers the question himself, for the sake of greater liveliness, with another question (γένοιτο γάρ . . . διοικῶν;). Third, he answers the question by playing on a key term in it, here καινόν. The first use of καινόν, in a conversational sentence, has the meaning "new"; however, in D's reply it takes on the additional meaning "strange" or "unusual." There is at the end of the question a striking juxtaposition of a noun and the participles that describe it, and this brings out clearly the unusual nature of the situation: an unnamed Macedonian (Μακεδὼν ἀνήρ) successfully making war (καταπολεμῶν) on the Athenians and managing the affairs of the Greeks.

**10.12–13**  διοικῶν probably refers to all of Philip's successful operations against the Athenians since 357, when they had declared war on him, including the capture of Potidaea in 356 and of Pydna and Methone in 354. Philip's involvement in the Sacred War in in 351 and 352 had allowed him to meddle in the affairs of central Greece, and his attack on Heraion Teichos in 352 had threatened to cut off Athenian grain routes from the Black Sea.

**11.13–18**  The tone becomes harsher in the next piece of dramatic dialogue. The preceding dialogue had demonstrated ignorance or dispassionate observation of the news on the part of the Athenians; this one shows self-deception. The presentation here is also livelier. There are now three participants rather than two. One Athenian asks whether Philip has died. Another replies that he is not dead but ill. D asks, what difference does it make? This leads up to the really striking paradox that none of this matters. If Philip dies, D argues, the Athenians will create another one, since it is not Philip, but the attitude of the Athenians that is the real problem. This idea allows D to return to the leitmotif developed earlier in the speech, that the Athenians have caused their own problems (cf. §2), and thus creates a ring that brings to a conclusion the section of the speech preceding the specific proposals. The section concludes with a parallel antithesis that neatly sums up the thought that D has been developing since section 3: οὐδὲ γὰρ οὗτος παρὰ τὴν αὑτοῦ ῥώμην τοσοῦτον ἐπηύξηται ὅσον παρὰ τὴν ἡμετέραν ἀμέλειαν. Quintilian points out (8.5.11) that this sort of sententious, generalizing expression is a good way to conclude an argument. When it is used to sum up a long train of thought, such a statement is called an *epiphonema* (cf. Lausberg §879, and §5.1–2).

**11.16–17** παρά with the accusative can express cause (cf. LSJ, s.v., C.III.7): "not so much because of his own strength as because of your negligence."

## 12

Section 12 is a transitional passage, between the preliminary argument in sections 2–11 and the specific proposals that begin in section 13. The καίτοι at the beginning indicates that D is introducing a new idea (Smyth §2893; Denniston GP, 559–61). In this speech D usually develops only one argument at a time, and he frequently passes quickly from one to another without indicating to his audience exactly where the general argument is leading, thus conveying an impression of spontaneity and underlying emotion, which drives the orator from one point to another (Pearson DD, 96; cf. Wooten A, 494–95). In spite of this, it is usually easy for the reader or hearer to see where the argument is going. The transition here, however, is quite abrupt, as indicated by the elliptical and generic introduction καίτοι καὶ τοῦτο. D passes quite unexpectedly from a general consideration of why Philip has grown great to envisioning a future situation in which Athens might have the opportunity to regain its power. This abrupt transition indicates D's emotion and impatience to get to the specific proposals.

In his earlier discussion of the past and the present in sections 2–11, D had used a mixture of encouragement and criticism. He takes the same approach here in contrasting the future with the present. He is encouraging with reference to the future (18–2) but critical with reference to the present (2–4). The juxtaposition of ὅπως βούλεσθε διοικήσαισθε and ὡς δὲ νῦν ἔχετε brings out this contrast well. In section 4, D had pointed out that Philip now holds the power that the Athenians had once held. In section 12, he argues that in the future the

Athenians can regain this power. Philip now manages the affairs of the Greeks (τὰ τῶν Ἑλλήνων διοικῶν, §10); in the future the Athenians could manage the situation as they wish (ὅπως βούλεσθε διοικήσαισθε, §12). The use of the same verb in each instance is significant, and the reference to the future is a good way to make a transition to the specific proposals. The last words of this section describe the Athenians in striking terms: ἀπηρτημένοι καὶ ταῖς παρασκευαῖς καὶ ταῖς γνώμαις. Vince describes the phrase as being "vigorous but untranslatable" (74). The sense, however, is clear: "detached [from the possibility of acting] both by your preparations and by your basic policies."

**12.19**  τὰ τῆς τύχης: D is fond of the neuter article with the genitive (cf. §32, τὸ τῶν πνευμάτων ἀσφαλές, "the [blowing] of the winds [is] steady"). This construction, like the use of the articular infinitive, which D uses more often than any other orator, shows the influence of Thucydides (Blass, 87–88). As in Thucydides, such a construction, which is abstract in nature, elevates the style (Denniston GPS, 36–40), which is quite appropriate in a reference to divine forces. Moreover, a vague expression like τὰ τῆς τύχης can conjure up all sorts of thoughts in the mind of a listener and thus can expand the scope of a speech (cf. comments on 8.19). As Demetrius points out (241), it is forceful to convey much meaning in a few words. ἡμῖν is a dative of advantage (cf. Smyth §1481) with ἐξεργάσαιτο: "should accomplish even this for us."

**12.19–20**  This is somewhat elliptical. The full form would be ἥπερ ἀεὶ βέλτιον ἡμῶν ἐπιμελεῖται ἢ ἡμεῖς ἡμῶν αὐτῶν ἐπιμελούμεθα: "and the [workings] of fate, which always takes better care of us than we do of ourselves." In general, Athenian orators, unlike tragedians, see the divine forces in the universe as being beneficent and favorably disposed to the city. Human beings, they argue, fail to attain their objectives only when they do not take advantage of the opportunities offered to them, which is exactly the point that D is making here.[6]

**12.2**  ἐπιστάντες: ἐφίστημι with the dative means to "*give attention to*" (LSJ, s.v., VI): "paying attention to all the situation that has been thrown into confusion."

**12.3**  διδόντων τῶν καιρῶν: The genitive absolute forms the protasis of a future less vivid condition (= εἰ οἱ καιροὶ διδοῖεν; cf. Smyth §2067). καιρός in the plural usually means "the times, i.e. the state of affairs" (LSJ, s.v., III.4): "even if the state of affairs should offer [it]."

---

[6] Cf. J. D. Mikalson, *Athenian Popular Religion* (Chapel Hill, N.C., 1983), 58–60, and R. Parker, "Gods Cruel and Kind: Tragic and Civic Theology," in *Greek Tragedy and History*, ed. C. Pelling (Oxford, 1997), 143–60.

### III. Specific Proposals (§§13–30)

### A. Partition: D outlines the subjects that he will discuss and requests a fair hearing (§§13–15)

This speech is quite different from most deliberative orations from the fourth century, which Ober describes as being "highly crafted speeches in which discussion of substantive proposals did not predominate" (124). Sections 13–15 form the introduction to two specific proposals. First, D suggests that the Athenians equip fifty triremes and enough transport ships to carry half the Athenian cavalry (§§16–18). This is reminiscent of proposals that he had made three years earlier in his first deliberative speech, *On the Symmories*, and is basically a defensive measure to protect Athenian possessions in the Aegean. Second, he argues that the Athenians should outfit a standing force that will harass Philip in the north (§§19–30). This is an offensive measure, which D considered more important and to which he devotes more space and about which he gives more details. It also figures more prominently in the general discussion that follows the specific proposals. The failure of his speech *On the Symmories* had indicated that the Athenians were unlikely to add considerably to their fleet.

It has been argued that this plan was too expensive and would not have caused Philip much harm anyway. D is careful, however, to try to minimize the costs (see below), and Athenian troops near Macedon could have surely inflicted damage on Philip's territory. If nothing else, they would have given confidence to Athenian allies in the north (Carlier, 116–17)

George Kennedy has pointed out, in discussing some of the common features seen in classical literature:

> ...the tendency, existing already in the Homeric poems and found in virtually every literary form throughout antiquity, to organise incidents, scenes, or speeches into antithetical or chiastic patterns much like the arrangement of figures in pedimental sculpture. To us, symmetry and proportion, in extreme cases perhaps even mathematical proportion in the number of lines used, seems central to Classical composition, and there is a corresponding tendency for the climax, or at least the most significant thought, to come near the center of the work, with some fall-off of intensity thereafter.[7]

This is an excellent description of the structure of this speech. After a brief proemium (§1), there is a part consisting of general arguments about the situation, trying to prove that some action must and can be taken (§§2–12). Then there is a part that includes argument and proposals, with specific arguments tailored to demonstrate the necessity of the specific proposals that

---

[7] *The Cambridge History of Literary Criticism*, vol. 1 (Cambridge, 1989), xiv–xv.

D makes (§§16–30). This is the central segment of what Kennedy calls the pediment. After this there is a part (§§31–50) in which D returns to general arguments, picking up many of the ideas discussed in the part of the speech between the proemium and the specific proposals, which lie more or less at the center of the speech (Blass, 302). This part of the speech demonstrates, not so much that some action is necessary, but that the action that D is proposing will solve the problems outlined earlier in the speech, before the specific proposals. Finally, there is an epilogue that is as brief as the proemium (§51). The result is a chiastic order, ringing the specific proposals, that could be diagrammed as A [§1] – B [§§2–12] – C [§§16–30] – B1 [§§31–50] – A1 [§51]. The proportions, however, are not mathematical. Parts B and C are about equal in length (3.5 and 4 pages, respectively). Part B1, however, is longer than either (7 pages). This seems quite reasonable: it was important for D to outline general considerations before making his specific proposals, in hopes of making his audience receptive to them, but it was also important to impress these general considerations on them toward the end of the speech, before they vote, particularly to demonstrate how the specific proposals would solve the problems outlined in part B. There is also a distinct difference in the tone of these various parts of the speech. The proemium and epilogue are calm and reflective. Part C, dealing with the specific proposals, is tightly organized and carefully reasoned. Parts B and B1, on the other hand, the general arguments that support the specific proposals, are lively and emotional. They are more loosely organized than Part C and often involve quick transitions from one topic to another, as one would expect in emotional passages. In part B1 in particular arguments are loosely strung together.

## 13

**13.5–7** D indicates clearly to his audience that a major section of the speech is finished by giving a short recapitulation of what he has been arguing. Here he also projects to his audience an image of the ideal auditor who will listen to these specific proposals, a man firmly convinced that he must now do his duty to the state, "a model of what the rhetor would have his real audience become" (Black, 113). He tells his audience, in effect, how they should have reacted to the first part of the speech and thus holds out to them a "beckoning archetype" (Black, 119) to which he hopes that they will conform.

The first ὡς introduces an indirect statement dependent on ἐγνωκότων ὑμῶν καὶ πεπεισμένων. The second indicates that the genitive absolute that it introduces is causal in nature (cf. Smyth §2086d). Synonymity makes the passage emphatic. In addition to the two participles above, compare also ἐθέλοντας ὑπάρχειν . . . ἑτοίμως: "Therefore, since you have recognized and been persuaded that it is necessary that you all be ready, willingly, to do what is necessary, I cease speaking."

**13.7–12**   Having given a résumé of what he has proved in the first twelve sections of the speech, D in the second sentence indicates what he will demonstrate in the next major part (§§16–30). He neatly juxtaposes the conclusion of the preliminary argumentation (παύομαι λέγων), seen at the end of the first sentence in section 13, and the beginning of the specific proposals (τὸν δὲ τρόπον τῆς παρασκευῆς), seen in the first position of the second. In fact, the second sentence of section 13 reads almost like a list, similar to a partition, outlining the various aspects of the proposed standing force that he will discuss: τὸ πλῆθος ... πόρους ... καὶ τἆλλα ....

This sentence has other functions as well as creating Distinctness. At the very outset, for example, D continues the encouraging tone that he has employed in the first part of the speech. The measures that he is proposing, he states, will free the Athenians from their troubles: ἀπαλλάξαι ἂν τῶν τοιούτων πραγμάτων ἡμᾶς. He also adopts a fairly modest tone, in an attempt to make his proposals more palatable to his audience, by indicating that they are his opinion: οἴομαι ... ὡς ἄν μοι ... δοκεῖ. Toward the end of section 15 (21–22) he will invite other members of the audience to offer other proposals (μὴ κωλύων εἴ τις ἄλλος ἐπαγγέλλεταί τι). By showing some hesitation about whether his proposals are actually the best, he uses an approach that Hermogenes (350) calls Modesty (ἐπιείκεια), the purpose of which is to make it easier for the average man in the audience to identify with the speaker (345).

The verb πειράσομαι picks up the modest tone seen earlier in the sentence and leads into the request at the end: δεηθεὶς ὑμῶν, ὦ ἄνδρες Ἀθηναῖοι, τοσοῦτον. In rhetorical terms this request is called a προδιόρθωσις or a προθεραπεία. Its purpose is to prepare the audience to receive an idea that they might normally find offensive, strange, or shocking (Lausberg §786.1). The structure of the sentence calls attention to the phrase δεηθεὶς ὑμῶν, ὦ ἄνδρες Ἀθηναῖοι, τοσοῦτον. Up until this point in the sentence D has used the same pattern twice: a long object followed by a simple verb with a form of λέγειν dependent on it: Ὡς μὲν ... παύομαι λέγων/ τὸν δὲ τρόπον ... πειράσομαι λέγειν. The phrase introduced by δεηθείς breaks this pattern and thus calls attention to itself, as does the apostrophe embedded in it.

**13.8**   ἄν should be taken with the infinitive, which represents a potential optative in direct discourse (cf. Smyth §1845). ἥν (sc. παρασκευήν) is the subject of the infinitive: "which I think would free us from such great troubles."

**13.11–12**   τοσοῦτον here means "only so much" (Davies, 54).

14–15

**14.13**   προλαμβάνω here means "prejudge" (LSJ, s.v., II.8.b).

**14.13–14**   παρασκευή generally means "preparation" but is frequently used in a military sense to refer to "armaments" (LSJ, s.v., II.2). καινὴν παρασκευήν refers to the standing force that will harass Philip in the north. Before D actually reveals what this will be, however, he begins to defend his proposal. To put the reasons for supporting a proposal before actually stating the proposal itself creates a certain amount of suspense, which is meant to arouse the audience's interest and attention (cf. Hermogenes, 284), which is essential just before the specific proposals.

**14.14**  ἀναβάλλειν must mean "to put off" although when the verb has this meaning it is usually used in the middle (cf. LSJ, s.v., A.II.1 and B.II.1).

**14.16**  τῇ νυνὶ βοηθείᾳ: "by dispatching levies now" (Davies, 54). The article, as Davies notes, is hard to explain. He postulates that the phrase may mean "the levy implied by those who cry ταχύ." A βοήθεια is an expeditionary force sent to meet a particular crisis, as opposed to the παρασκευὴ συνεχής that D is proposing (cf. §32). D may be referring here to supporters of Aristophon (Cawkwell, 50).

**14.14–15.20**  D describes who does and who does not give good advice, making his idea emphatic by stating it both positively and negatively. The οὐ . . . οἱ sets up an expectation for ἀλλ᾽ οἱ. D, however, switches to the singular (ἀλλ᾽ ὅς). This underlines the contrast between those who want immediate action and the one speaker, D, of course, who advises differently. He also breaks up the parallelism by inserting between the two parallel clauses a parenthesis that delays and thus calls attention to the important second one, which outlines what sort of advice a good advisor would give in this situation. This parenthesis (οὐ γὰρ ἂν τά γ᾽ ἤδη γεγενημένα τῇ νυνὶ βοηθείᾳ κωλῦσαι δυνηθεῖμεν) explains why there is no need for haste, and it does so in a very striking way. Sandys notes that there is a "rhythmical correspondence" (84) between the last two phrases in the parenthesis, τῇ νυνὶ βοηθείᾳ and κωλῦσαι δυνηθείημεν ( ‾ ‾ ˘ ‾ ˘ ‾ ‾ ), as well as internal assonance in the -ηθειη- in the same position in each phrase. The many long syllables at the end of the parenthesis also slow down the speed and thus delay even more the clause that the hearer has been expecting. The clause thus highlighted (ἀλλ᾽ ὅς ἂν δείξῃ) picks up the ideas, in lines 17–18, already outlined by D earlier in section 13.

**15.17**  ὅς ἂν δείξῃ functions as the protasis of a present general condition whose apodosis (εἰς δέον λέγει) must be understood from what precedes.

**15.17–18**  D outlines what a speaker who speaks to the point (εἰς δέον) would discuss. Earlier, in section 13 (7–9), he had indicated what he himself would discuss. There is a close correspondence between the two. τίς πορισθεῖσα παρασκευή corresponds to the phrase τὸν δὲ τρόπον τῆς παρασκευῆς in the middle of section 13. πόση picks up the idea of τὸ πλῆθος ὅσον, and πόθεν corresponds to πόρους οὕστινας χρημάτων. This allows D to repeat what he will discuss after having begged indulgence from his audience and attacked his opponents.

**15.18–20**   Decisive action will bring clear-cut results. The two possibilities are expressed in the two very straightforward parts of the ἕως clause. In each of these the verb is put in the first position. Both verbs have the same number of syllables, the same ending (-ώμεθα), and the same metrical configuration (˘ ˘ ˘ - ˘ ˘). The many short syllables at the beginning of each part of the clause may indicate the speed with which results will follow action.

**15.20**   τοῦ λοιποῦ is a genitive of time within which (Smyth §1444).

**15.21**   μή: We would expect the participle to be negated by οὐ (Smyth §2728). It is construed, however, with the infinitive λέγειν, which, since it is not in indirect discourse (unlike ἔχειν), would be negated by μή (Smyth §2713). Often when a participle is construed with a verb that either has μή or would have it if negated, the participle itself is thus negated, although normally we would expect οὐ (Smyth §2737).

**15.21–23**   In the second half of section 15, D brings to a close this introduction to the specific proposals. He projects an image of confidence (οἶμαι τοίνυν ἐγὼ ταῦτα λέγειν ἔχειν) but also invites the cooperation of his audience (μὴ κωλύων εἴ τις ἄλλος ἐπαγγέλλεταί τι). ἐπαγγέλλω, particularly in the middle, means to "offer of one's free will" (LSJ, s.v., 4). D's hope is that he has persuaded his audience to participate, not only in action, but also in the formulation of policy (note the emphatic position of ἑτοίμως in line 6). He then uses an epigram of sorts (cf. Quint. 8.5.11), drawing on the familiar distinction between λόγος and ἔργον: ἡ μὲν οὖν ὑπόσχεσις / τὸ δὲ πρᾶγμα. He has made large claims and submits these to the judgment of his audience: κριταὶ δ' ὑμεῖς ἔσεσθε. This is similar to the ending of Lysias's speech *Against Eratosthenes*. In keeping with the judicial tone, Sandys notes (85) that the phrase τὸν ἔλεγχον δώσει involves a "forensic metaphor." He translates it "the performance (of my promise) will supply the test" or "proof." He also notes that the three "short and sharp" sentences that end this part of the speech express confidence on the part of the orator. This famous sentence was frequently used by writers on rhetoric in their introductions; cf. Hermogenes, 217, and H. Rabe, ed., *Prolegomenon Sylloge* (Leipzig, 1931), no. 15, p. 234, lines 12–13.

**15.21**   ἔχω with an infinitive means to "be able" (LSJ, s.v., A.III.1.a).

**B. First Proposal: The Athenians must equip fifty triremes and enough ships to transport half the cavalry, so that Philip will know that they are prepared to act (§§16–18)**

## 16

In this section, D enumerates three specific recommendations: Πρῶτον . . . ,
εἶτ᾽ . . . πρὸς δὲ τούτοις . . . Hermogenes (235) describes the procedure that D
uses in such passages: "Distinctness is primarily concerned with the approach
of the speech. It is the function of Distinctness to determine what aspects of the
case the judges should consider first and what they should consider second and
to make that clear to them." The first and the third of these recommendations
are for materiel: fifty triremes and enough ships to convey half the cavalry. The
second, however, picks up the theme that D has been hammering on throughout the first fifteen sections of the speech: that the Athenians must change their
attitude and be willing to take action themselves. This is emphasized by the two
uses of the intensive pronoun toward the beginning and the end of the second
half of the first sentence in section 16: αὐτοὺς[ sc. ὑμᾶς] οὕτω τὰς γνώμας ἔχειν
ὡς, ἐάν τι δέῃ, πλευστέον εἰς ταύτας αὐτοῖς[ sc. ὑμῖν] ἐμβᾶσιν. By putting this
reference to the need for citizens to participate in the campaign together with
the two specific recommendations for supplies, D reminds his audience that no
amount of provisions will solve the problem unless the Athenians are willing to
use them. πλευστέον[ sc. ὄν], as Davies notes (55), can be seen, by comparing it
with similar expressions elsewhere, to be an accusative absolute (cf. Smyth
§2078) correlative with οὕτω. This construction puts more emphasis on the
reality of the need for the Athenians to embark on the ships themselves: "that
you yourselves thus make up your minds, since you yourselves must embark on
them and sail."

**16.24–25** τριήρεις πεντήκοντα: D tells us in the speech *On the Symmories*
(§13) that in 354 the Athenians had 300 ships. Here, however, he is talking only
about the ships that will be outfitted immediately and that will be manned by
citizens. In the same passage from *On the Symmories* he also tells us that the
Athenians had a thousand cavalry; thus, half of them (τοῖς ἡμίσεσιν τῶν ἱππέων)
would be five hundred.

**16.3** πλοῖα were merchant ships or transports that were not generally used as
ships of war (LSJ, s.v.).

## 17–18

In order to inject some excitement into the presentation, so as not to lose the
audience, after presenting an analysis that is lengthy, calm, and at times dry, D
uses an interruptive, disjointed sentence, in which the orator's emotion drives
him to pile one thought on top of another and to dart off in different directions.
Such sentences, which make great demands on the audience, are found fairly
often in this speech (cf. §3.17–3). In this analytical period there are five levels of

linear, progressive subordination (a γάρ explanatory clause, an indirect statement, a purpose clause, a genitive absolute, and a condition), each of which
depends upon and naturally grows out of the one that precedes. In addition to
these linear levels of subordination there is also one instance of embedded,
interruptive subordination (within the indirect statement) and two parentheses, one separating two levels of subordination (the indirect statement and
the purpose clause) and one embedded, interrupting the development of the
thought within the first element of the purpose clause. The sentence could be
outlined as follows:

ταῦτα μὲν δεῖν ὑπάρχειν ...

   (1) δεῖ γὰρ ...
      (2) ὡς ... {ὥσπερ ... Πύλας} ... ὁρμήσαιτε (οὗτοι ... ἐστιν)
         (3) ἵν᾽ ἢ ... (εἴσεται ... δέοντος) ... ἔχῃ ἢ ... ληφθῇ
           (4) μηδενὸς ... ὑμῖν
           (5) ἂν ... καιρόν.

ταῦτα μέν ἐστιν ... (§19.16)

Dilts puts a mark of parenthesis before the clause introduced by δεῖ γάρ. That
seems to me to be unnecessary. The clause is closely related to what precedes,
giving the reason why it is necessary that preparations be made (ταῦτα μὲν
οἴομαι δεῖν ὑπάρχειν). It seems more logical, as I have indicated in my diagram,
to put a mark of parenthesis only before οὗτοι in line 10, since this introduces a
statement that really is parenthetical. Because of the complicated nature of the
sentence, D summarizes it at the beginning of section 19, as I have indicated.
The ταῦτα μέν here repeats the same phrase at the beginning of section 17.

This sentence might be labeled what the writer of the treatise *On Invention*
calls (191) a τάσις, a period actually longer than what the breath of a speaker
could produce. It is impossible to know what the relationship was between the
delivered and published version of this speech. It is difficult to imagine,
however, that a sentence such as the one in sections 17 and 18 could be
successfully delivered before a large audience of average men, and it is tempt-
ing to speculate, therefore, that the delivered version of the speech, at least in
these sections of it, would have been simplified. Other passages (cf. §3.17–3)
invite the same conclusion.[8] D was the first Athenian politician to publish his
own deliberative speeches. He seems to have done so mainly to influence

---

[8] For a general discussion of the publication of speeches, particularly forensic speeches, see
K. J. Dover, *Lysias and the Corpus Lysiacum* (Berkeley, 1968), 151–54 and 168–74, and S. Usher,
"Lysias and his Clients," *Greek, Roman, and Byzantine Studies* 17 (1976): 31–40. Yunis has a very
good discussion (241–47) of the relationship between the delivered and published versions of D's
speeches. His general conclusion, with which I agree, is that "Demosthenes' published speeches
are realistic and more or less genuine representations of actual speeches on particular questions of
communal concern" (247). Milns comes to the same general conclusion; R. D. Milns, "The Public
Speeches," in Worthington, 207–9.

public opinion, which, during much of his career, was opposed to his policies. This aim seems to be confirmed by the fact that he ceased publishing his speeches in 341 when the people began to support him and to recognize him as the leading statesman in Athens (Hansen, 7).

In the first part of this sentence (§17) D uses specific examples from history to prove that the Athenians have suffered in the past from Philip's swift and unexpected attacks on Athenian possessions and also from the inability, or unwillingness, of the Athenians to respond to those attacks. He amplifies the latter idea by giving some examples of when the Athenians did, in fact, successfully take action. Pearson points out the extensive use of narration as one of the characteristics of judicial oratory that D transferred to deliberative speeches, especially in the *Philippics* and the *Olynthiacs*. However, "his object is no longer, as in a simpler forensic speech, to describe what has happened but 'to show the kind of thing that has happened and will happen again unless certain measures are taken' " (AD, 64).

These two problems are closely related, and in order to indicate that relationship D uses a similar structure to introduce them. First, there is an expression of necessity: ταῦτα μὲν οἶμαι δεῖν ὑπάρχειν (4) and δεῖ γὰρ ἐκείνῳ τοῦτο ἐν τῇ γνώμῃ παραστῆσαι (6–7). After this, there is a definite article followed by a word that is essential to understanding the problem under discussion, and this key word is followed by a demonstrative adjective. The article and the demonstrative thus bracket the emphatic word: τὰς ἐξαίφνης ταύτας (4) and τῆς ἀμελείας ταύτης (7–8). Each key word (ἐξαίφνης, ἀμελείας) is followed by a phrase that completes its meaning: ἀπὸ τῆς οἰκείας χώρας αὐτοῦ στρατείας (5) and τῆς ἄγαν (8). Then there are specific examples, highlighted in each case by the use of polysyndeton, of (a) when Philip attacked Athenian possessions (εἰς Πύλας καὶ Χερρόνησον καὶ Ὄλυνθον καὶ ὅποι βούλεται) and (b) when the Athenians roused themselves from their lethargy and did, in fact, take action in order to defend their interests (ὥσπερ εἰς Εὔβοιαν καὶ πρότερόν ποτε φασιν εἰς Ἁλίαρτον καὶ τὰ τελευταῖα πρώην εἰς Πύλας). The first example given of Philip's aggressions against Athens is Thermopylae (εἰς Πύλας), and the last example given of when the Athenians defended their interests is Thermopylae (εἰς Πύλας). Thus, the phrase εἰς Πύλας neatly brackets negative and positive events in the recent Athenian past.

**17.4–5** ἐπὶ τὰς ἐξαίφνης ταύτας ... στρατείας: Davies notes (56) that the demonstrative may be inserted between the article and its substantive when a word that describes the substantive follows the article and precedes the demonstrative (cf. τὰς ἐπιστολιμαίους ταύτας δυνάμεις in §19).

**17.5** εἰς Πύλας: Attributive phrases such as this can be added without the article "(a) when the words following the substantive are so closely connected with words preceding it that they form practically a single attribute, and (b) when the substantive has a distinctly verbal character and the attribute is adverbial in form" (Davies, 56).

As is usual in this speech, D here is careful to temper warning with encouragement, the positive with the negative, and in order to highlight the encouragement he emphasizes that the Athenians have taken appropriate action even in the recent past (πρῴην), when, in 352, the year before the delivery of this speech, Athens joined a coalition of Greek states to prevent Philip from marching from Thessaly through Thermopylae into Boeotia after the defeat of the Phocians at the battle of the Crocus Field. (See Sealey, 122, and Hammond, 544. The major ancient source is Diodorus, 16.35–38).

D continues (§18) with an explanation of the advantages of being prepared. The style becomes somewhat disjointed, as he switches construction and changes the thought several times. There is first a parenthesis (οὗτοι... ἐστιν), which gives the impression that this idea has occurred to him on the spur of the moment. Then he attaches a purpose clause that picks up the logic of the γάρ clause that begins in line 6 (ἵν' ἤ... ληφθῇ). Before this is completed, however, there is another inserted thought, this one quite long and emphatic, bringing out the idea that traitors are a cause of Athenian problems (εἴσεται γὰρ ἀκριβῶς· εἰσὶ γὰρ... πλείους τοῦ δέοντος). The idea is highlighted by the epanadiplosis in εἰσὶ γάρ, εἰσίν and πλείους τοῦ δέοντος at the end of the parenthesis. The latter phrase involves an ἐπίκρισις, a common technique in D for calling attention to what precedes.

All of the elements discussed above are typical of a style that Hermogenes calls (352–63) sincere (ἀληθινὸς λόγος), a style that should be used when the speaker is animated or angry. As Hermogenes points out (358), in such passages the emotion or vehemence of the speaker disturbs the natural sequence of the sentence, causing him to use anacolutha or to interject comments that occur to him on the spur of the moment. It is important, however, for the orator not to give the impression that he is completely overcome by emotion and to keep the sentence clear in spite of the emotional interruptions. Here, if one removes the two interjected parentheses in lines 10–11 and lines 12–14, there is an orderly analytical period, built up of clauses that are generally short and straightforward and that are arranged in a logical order. The clarity of the organization of the sentence moderates the emotional tone of the interruptions.

**17.5–7**　This passage refers to Philip's military operations in 352/51. Having been checked at Thermopylae after the defeat of the Phocians (see above), Philip intervened in Thrace where war had broken out between king Cersobleptes and two Greek cities (see the introduction). Soon after his return from Thrace, Philip made threatening gestures toward Olynthus, which had concluded a peace with Athens in 352/51 (Sealey, 124, 137, and Hammond, 542–47). When Philip had agreed to hand over Potidaea to the Chalcidean League in 357/56, a treaty was concluded between the two parties according to which each agreed not to make a separate peace with Athens. Several years later, however, when Philip had grown much more powerful than he had been in 357, the League became apprehensive about having an ally who could easily take advantage of them and concluded a peace treaty with Athens, probably late in 352 or early in 351. To show his displeasure at their violation of the treaty with him, Philip made an incursion into the territory of the League in the spring of 351. The dispute, however, was settled diplomatically when the League agreed not to make an alliance with Athens, and Philip did not insist that the peace treaty be revoked (Griffith, 296–99).

**17.7** παραστῆσαι means to "place beside" (LSJ, s.v., I) and thus "to set before the mind" or suggest.

**17.8–9** εἰς Εὔβοιαν: sc. ὡρμήσατε; εἰς Ἁλίαρτον: sc. ὑμᾶς ὁρμῆσαι.

**17.8–10** In 357, civil strife broke out in Euboea. One side called in the Thebans, who sent troops. Athens was thus faced with a Theban presence just north of Attica. The Athenians acted swiftly and sent a fleet to Euboea within days of learning that the Thebans were on the island, and within thirty days the Thebans had withdrawn, which "shows that the Athenians could act quickly and efficiently to repel a strategic threat in the neighborhood of Attica" (Sealey, 103). (The major ancient sources are D's speeches: 8.74, 18.99, 21.161, 22.14.) For a discussion of the battle of Haliartus see section 3. In order not to offend his audience by appearing to be too much more knowledgeable than they are, D uses the word φασίν to indicate how he knew about it and is somewhat vague about when exactly (ποτέ) it took place (cf. Pearson HA).

**18.10** A potential optative with ἄν is used in a protasis only when the optative is in fact the apodosis to some other protasis that is expressed or understood (Smyth §2353). Here Davies reconstructs (57) the understood protasis thus: εἰ οὕτω διακεῖσθε ὥστε οὐκ ἂν ποιήσαιτε (sc. εἰ δέοι).

**18.11** εὐκαταφρόνητόν ἐστιν: Davies remarks that the expression here is "decidedly obscure" (56). D's general meaning, however, is clear enough: the knowledge that the Athenians are prepared to act, even if they don't, will probably deter Philip to some extent. Emotional people do not always express themselves clearly or draw logical connections tightly.

**18.12** εὐτρεπεῖς: sc. ὄντας.

**18.14** πλείους is nominative from πλείοσες (see comments on βελτίω in §2).

παριδών: παρεῖδον can mean to look past or beyond to the point of overlooking or disregarding (LSJ, s.v., II.1).

**18.15–16** μηδενός could be either masculine or neuter. μή is used rather than οὐ, since the construction depends upon a verb (ληφθῇ) which, if negated, would use μή (cf. comments on 15.21). The subject of ἐνδῷ is probably Philip.

C. Second Proposal: The Athenians need to station a standing force
in the north to harass Philip; D discusses the nature of this force
(§§ 19–22)

19

**19.16–20**   D first signals the conclusion to the proposal concerning a defensive force (16–17). ταῦτα, referring to what precedes (cf. Smyth §1245), sums up the proposals that have been discussed in sections 16–18. The repetition seen in the closely parallel and nearly synonymous phrases πᾶσι δεδόχθαι φημὶ δεῖν and παρεσκευάσθαι προσήκειν οἴομαι brings this section to an emphatic halt. The phrase πρὸ δὲ τούτων at the beginning of the next sentence indicates a transition to a new topic and the δύναμιν makes clear at the outset what that topic will be.

**19.17**   δεδόχθαι: δοκέω usually means, as here, to "seem good" in the sense of to "decree or resolve" (LSJ, s.v., II.3); a dative of agent (πᾶσι) is often used with passive verbs in the perfect (Smyth §1488). A resolution ordering the construction of ships would have had to be passed (δεδόχθαι) before the ships could be constructed (παρεσκευάσθαι). Davies notes the force of the perfects: "the resolution must be *maintained* and the preparations *kept up*" (57).

**19.20–24**   Before describing in more detail the force that he is proposing, D anticipates the reaction of his audience, using a figure of speech called πρόληψις (cf. Lausberg §855). Many of Athens' problems in the past had been caused by the use of mercenaries, who did not follow their general when they were not paid, and the Athenian tendency to vote extravagant measures that were then never carried out.

That citizen soldiers should fight alongside mercenaries will be an important idea in the rest of the speech. When he first touches on this idea here, the tone becomes animated. The abbreviated nature of the sentence (some imperative such as εἴπητε must be understood with ξένους) reveals his impatience. The metaphorical expression in τὰς ἐπιστολιμαίους ταύτας δυνάμεις ("paper armies") shows how ridiculous the situation has become. And the violent hyperbaton in ἢ τῆς πόλεως ἔσται, which is far separated from its antecedent δύναμιν, indicates rising emotion. Longinus points out: "Just as people who are really angry or frightened or indignant... often put forward one point and then spring off to another with various illogical interpretations, and then wheel around to their original position, while, under the stress of their excitement, like a ship before a veering wind, they lay their words and thoughts first on one tack then another, and keep altering the natural order of sequence into innumerable variations— so, too, in the best prose writers the use of hyperbaton allows imitation to approach the effects of nature" (22).

The emphasis created by the polysyndeton, anaphora, and repeated direct objects in the condition in lines 22–23 reveals the intensity of the orator's belief that the army should follow whomever the city chooses to command it. The repetitions are, to use an image of Longinus (20), like the blows of a boxer that strike the mind of the audience one after another in quick succession: κἂν ὑμεῖς ἕνα κἂν πλείους κἂν τὸν δεῖνα κἂν ὁντινοῦν χειροτονήσητε στρατηγόν ("whether you appoint as general one or many or this one or that one"). Dover says of similar features in a sentence from Xenophon that they "are meant to have the effect of table-thumping in an argument" (155). The synonymity in the conclusion to the condition (πείσεται καὶ ἀκολουθήσει) also highlights the idea that the army must follow the man whom the city has set over it as general. That will not happen, however, unless the soldiers are supported. Thus, D ends this section with the brief and emphatic sentence: καὶ τροφὴν ταύτῃ πορίσαι κελεύω.

## 20

**20.24–2** This sentence functions as another partition, outlining the structure of the speech in the next ten sections. D, however, does not follow exactly the order outlined in this brief introductory section. He discusses the first and third topics and then the second. Not following precisely the order outlined makes the presentation seem more natural and spontaneous (cf. Hermogenes, 362–63).[9] In sections 20–27 he will deal with the nature of the force that he is proposing: τίς ἡ δύναμις καὶ πόση. In these sections he will also discuss the third topic announced here, how this force will be willing to do what must be done: πῶς ταῦτ᾽ ἐθελήσει ποιεῖν. In sections 28 and 29 he will deal with providing for it: πόθεν τὴν τροφὴν ἕξει.

**20.2–7** The ξένους at the beginning of the third sentence in this section corresponds to and begins to answer the question τίς ἡ δύναμις at the beginning of section 20. In order to appear more spontaneous, however, and to underline the dangers of relying too much on mercenaries, D abruptly switches construction and shifts from proposal to argument, using a figure that Hermogenes calls aposiopesis and that he sees as giving an impression of spontaneity, which is typical of Sincerity (361). ὅπως plus the future indicative may be used without any main clause to convey an urgent exhortation or warning (Smyth §2213). In the negative it often denotes a desire to avert something (Smyth §1921). All the manuscripts read the subjunctive ποιήσητε. ὅπως μή plus the subjunctive, however, which is quite rare, is used either in cautious assertions or expressions of fear, which do not seem to fit here; see W. W. Goodwin, *Syntax of the Moods and Tenses of the Greek Verb* (Boston, 1890), §283.

---

[9] The author of the treatise *On Invention* also comments (128–29) on the rearranging of headings and gives an example from D's speech *On the False Embassy* (182).

The warning that D makes here revolves around the discrepancy in Athenian policy, frequently noted in this speech (cf. §§16 and 30), between intention and action. The sentence beginning with πάντ' is neatly constructed. ἐλάττω is the second and also the next to the last word; between these repetitions comes a contrast between τὰ μέγιστ', which the Athenians intend (αἱρούμενοι), and τὰ μικρά, which they actually do (ποιεῖτε), as well as one between τοῖς ψηφίσμασιν and τῷ πράττειν. The juxtaposition of αἱρούμενοι and ἐπὶ τῷ πράττειν points up the contrast between intention and action. If there is hiatus here, it would have the same function. Pearson has argued that hiatus occurs, not only within a clause, but also "at comma or colon," that is, at pauses within a sentence, in which cases the hiatus normally indicates a short break without breath (H, 142–43). Such a hiatus, according to Pearson, often "underlines a contrast or contradiction between two clauses or phrases" (152), which would be the case here. Dover, however, raises doubts (178–79) about whether hiatus actually exists in such positions. D also uses a chiastic structure in lines 17–18 in order to reinforce this contrast between intention and action, particularly between the words at the end of the frame: (a) τὰ μέγιστ' (b) ἐν τοῖς ψηφίσμασιν / (b) ἐπὶ τῷ πράττειν (a) οὐδὲ τὰ μικρά.

**20.4**  ψηφίσμασιν: The fourth century drew a sharp distinction between νόμοι and ψηφίσματα, both of which could be translated "law." The former were "laws of a general nature and of permanent standing that had been passed by a lawmaker of the past (e.g., Solon) or by one of the new boards of Lawmakers [set up between 405 and 399 to review old laws and establish new ones]" whereas the latter were decrees passed by the Assembly that "dealt with immediate issues and did not necessarily establish legal precedent" (Ober, 96). Hansen explains the difference somewhat more theoretically: a νόμος was a "general norm without limit of duration" whereas a ψήφισμα was "an individual norm which, once carried out, was emptied of its content" (162).

**20.5**  ἐπὶ τῷ πράττειν: As Davies points out (58), ἐπί here has a local sense, "when it comes to action."

## 21–22

**21.7**  τοὺς πάντας στρατιώτας: In the attributive position πᾶς denotes "the whole regarded as the sum of all its parts (the *sum total*, the *collective body*)" (Smyth §1174). In the predicate position it denotes the individuals that make up a whole.

**21.8**  δισχιλίους: D's speeches are filled with facts and figures, which give the impression of an orator who has done his homework. Blass notes (207) that this extensive documentation, as opposed to the more theoretical discussions that one finds, for example, in the speeches in Thucydides, is an indication of the more pragmatic nature of Greek politics in the fourth century as opposed to the more intellectual considerations of the fifth. It is possible, however, that these differences derive simply from the fact that the ones are real speeches and the others are in a historical work. In a section filled with so many facts and figures the main problem is how to avoid seeming tedious. D accomplishes this in two ways. First, although he is giving what is really a list, he varies the way in which he presents his material, which Hermogenes sees (316) as being typical of Rapidity (γοργότης). The first sentence in section 21 (λέγω δὴ ... ἀλλήλοις), for example, is quite long, adding to the main thought one qualifying phrase after another, as is typical of many of D's periods. The second is very brief (τοὺς δ' ἄλλους ...). The length of the two sentences reflects the importance of the thoughts that they express. The citizen soldiers, who are essential to D's proposal, are described in great detail. The mercenaries are then dismissed with six words.

**21.9**  ἐξ ἧς ... τίνος ... ἡλικίας: ἧς and τίνος go together: "from whatever age category." ἄν is used with the subjunctive because the clause forms a conditional relative in a future more vivid condition (δεῖν εἶναι = future), as does ὅσον ἂν δοκῇ καλῶς ἔχειν in line 11 (cf. Smyth §§2565, 2326).

Each year officials would draw up a list of young men admitted to citizenship at 18 and thus eligible for military service. When troops were needed, certain years, indicated by the eponymous archon of that year, would be called out.

**21.10**  χρόνον τακτόν: an accusative of extent of time (Smyth §1582). In other words, these troops would serve for a fixed period, unlike those who served on βοήθειαι, which lasted only as long as the crisis endured.

**21.12–15**  In the second half of section 21 D speeds up the presentation by leaving out governing verbs, which can easily be supplied from the context, and by using very short clauses, which are really little more than phrases. This very brief exposition is the second factor that keeps a section like this from being tedious. In section 22 he varies his presentation of information, combining here, however, both the variety and the speed that one sees in section 21. First, rather than simply stating what needs to be done, he uses two short rhetorical questions: τί πρὸς τούτοις ἔτι; and πόθεν δὴ τούτοις ἡ τροφὴ γενήσεται; The first of these is combined with a quick answer (ταχείας τριήρεις δέκα), a technique that Hermogenes also sees as being characteristic of Rapidity (313). Moreover, unlike the information presented in the preceding section, which is stated with no explanation, he expands these two recommendations by appending to the first a reason why his proposal is necessary (δεῖ γὰρ ...) and to the second an explanation of when he will answer the question that he has just posed (ἐγὼ καὶ τοῦτο φράσω καὶ δείξω ...). These short rhetorical questions are a good way to regain close contact with the audience, whose attention may have strayed during the presentation of these specific proposals.

**22.15**   ταχεῖας τριήρεις are fighting ships, unlike the triremes referred to in section 16, which would be used for transport (see comment on §16.3).

**22.17–20**   The last two sentences in section 22 foreshadow the next topics that the orator will discuss: why such a small force is sufficient, including why citizen soldiers should form a part of it (διότι τηλικαύτην ἀποχρῆν οἶμαι τὴν δύναμιν καὶ πολίτας τοὺς στρατευομένους εἶναι κελεύω) and how this force will be supported (πόθεν δὴ τούτοις ἡ τροφὴ γενήσεται;). The former topic will be discussed in sections 23–27; the latter, in sections 28 and 29. He thus outlines, once again, as he did in section 20, the topics to be discussed in the remaining sections of the specific proposals.

**22.20**   στρατευομένους would seem to refer to the whole force, only part of which was actually composed of citizens. Either D is being careless or there is a manuscript problem.

### D. D explains the reasons for the size and composition of the force that he has proposed (§§23–27)

### 23

D makes a brief reference to what he has already proposed (τοσαύτην) as a way of signaling to his audience that the description of the size of the force is over. He then foreshadows what he will discuss next with the phrase διὰ ταῦτα. These three words (τοσαύτην ... διὰ ταῦτα) create, in very abbreviated fashion, the main clause of an analytical period. Here one sees the extreme conciseness, first pointed out by Aeschines (2.51), for which D was famous (Wooten A). There are no wasted words, only enough to provide the necessary information before moving on to the next point, which is an explanation of why he has proposed such a force.

**23.21**   τοσαύτην: sc. (from the preceding sentence) δύναμιν ἀποχρῆν οἶμαι.

**23.22**   παραταξομένην: The future participle probably expresses purpose (cf. Smyth §2065). παρατάττω in the middle usually means to "draw up in battle order" (LSJ). ἐκείνῳ is a dative of hostile association (Smyth §1523): "to provide a force to draw up in battle order against him." Davies notes (59) that the future participle of purpose often uses a definite article where to us the reference seems indefinite.

**23.22–23**   λῃστεύειν seems to refer to what we would call "guerilla warfare" as opposed to fighting pitched battles (παρατάττομαι).

**23.24**   τὴν πρώτην, probably with ὥραν or ὁδόν understood (cf. LSJ. s.v. πρότερος, B.III.1), has the same meaning as πρῶτον.

αὐτήν = δύναμιν. ὑπέρογκος is a two-termination adjective. Most of these are compounds (Smyth §288–89).

## 24

**24.26–2**   The next topic to be discussed is clearly indicated by the first words (πολίτας ... παρεῖναι) in this section, which will deal, not with the size of the force, but its composition. Using another analytical period, similar to the one that begins section 23, D makes his proposal and then states the reasons for doing so (... κελεύω, ὅτι ...). Repeating the pattern of argument makes it easier for the audience to follow the presentation. Here, as in section 17, he proves his point by adducing historical parallels. (These events took place during the so-called Corinthian War from 394 to 387; see discussion under §3. ποτ’ ἀκούω: see discussion at §17.) The really important idea, the one that D wants to stress, comes at the end of the description of the force that was stationed in Corinth: καὶ αὐτοὺς ὑμᾶς συστρατεύεσθαι. This expresses the same idea as the phrase πολίτας παρεῖναι at the beginning of the sentence, but it expresses it in a more forceful way because of the intensive pronoun and the prefix on the verb (αὐτοὺς ὑμᾶς συσ-).

**24.27 & 3**   ἀκούω ... ἀκούων: see comments at 3.17–3.

**24.1**   Very little is known about Polystratus. Iphicrates was famous for having defeated a *mora* (600 troops) of heavily armed Spartan hoplites with a squadron of more lightly armed troops in 390 during the Corinthian War (Sealey, 12).[10] Chabrias succeeded Iphicrates as general in the Corinthian War but was to achieve greater fame by his defeat of the Spartan fleet at Naxos in 376 (Davies, 60).

**24.3–10**   In the next sentence, to stress the cooperation, or interlocking, of mercenary troops and citizens, D uses chiasmus: μεθ’ ὑμῶν ἐνίκων οὗτοι οἱ ξένοι καὶ ὑμεῖς μετ’ ἐκείνων. Then (4–7) he contrasts this situation in the past with the current one, and to do so he uses a paradoxical antithesis. Troops supported by Athens attack Athenian allies, and the enemies of Athens have become greater, a point that Isocrates also makes in *On the Peace* (46). This ridiculous situation, part of what Rowe calls (SM) the "satiric mode" in this speech, is

---

[10] R. Seager, however, comments: "But for all of its short-term psychological effect and its place in the orator's roll of the triumphs of Athens the defeat of the *mora* was of little real importance. Spartan losses had not been great ... and the Spartans retained control of Lechaeum"; "The Corinthian War," in *The Cambridge Ancient History*, vol. 6, ed. D. M. Lewis, J. Boardman, S. Hornblower, and M. Ostwald (Cambridge, 1994), 111.

summed up by the strikingly short clause put at the end of the next sentence: ὁ δὲ στρατηγὸς ἀκολουθεῖ. This is a ludicrous inversion of the reasonable situation envisioned at the end of section 19 (κἂν ὁντινοῦν χειροτονήσετε στρατηγόν, τούτῳ πείσεται καὶ ἀκολουθήσει [ἡ δύναμις]). Sandys notes that the unusual three successive short syllables seen in the phrase στρατηγὸς ἀκολουθεῖ "may perhaps be defended on the ground of the satirical character of the passage" (94).

D makes a surprising comment on this sentence: εἰκότως. The comment allows the orator to return to an idea that he has developed earlier (§20), that the troops must be paid, since he must explain why he thinks that the situation that he has just described is reasonable. The last sentence in this section ends with the phrase μὴ διδόντα μισθόν. Sandys points out that this phrase has the same metrical configuration as οὐ γὰρ ἔστιν ἄρχειν that immediately precedes it ( ˘ ˘ ˘ ¯ ¯ ) and that this "symmetry of form gives fresh point to the epigram" (94). Quintilian recommends epigrams as a good way to conclude a section of argument: "Even common sayings and popular beliefs may be useful. All these are in a sense testimonies, but they are actually all the more effective because they are not given to suit particular Causes, but spoken or given by minds free of prejudice and favour for the simple reason that they seemed either very honourable or very true" (5.11.37).

**24.5**  αὐτὰ καθ᾽ αὑτά: "*by themselves, separately*" (LSJ, s.v. κατά, II.1); ὑμῖν is a dative of interest or advantage (Smyth §1474).

**24.6**  According to LSJ (s.v., III) an ἐχθρός is "one who has been φίλος but is alienated" whereas a πολέμιος is simply "one who is at war." Davies argues (61), more to the point, that ἐχθροί here implies fundamental and natural hostility rather than simply the existence of a state of war.

**24.7**  παρακύπτω, meaning to "*peep out of* a door or window," is often used in Aristophanes (cf. LSJ, s.v., II.2). Davies points out that it "suits the satirical character of the passage" (61).

**24.8**  πρὸς Ἀρτάβαζον: During the Social War between Athens and some of her allies in the Athenian League who had revolted in 357/56, Chares was one of the Athenian commanders, and when Artaxerxes III Ochos, for reasons that we do not completely understand, ordered the satraps along the coast to dismiss their mercenary troops, Chares enrolled ten thousand of them into his army, although he could not pay them. When, consequently, Artabazus, the satrap of Hellespontine Phrygia, who was in revolt against Artaxerxes, again for reasons that we do not understand, invited Chares to fight with him against the Great King, Chares's men forced him to accept. After defeating a large Persian force, Artabazus gave Chares money to pay his troops (Sealey, 104–5; Hammond, 515–16; Diodorus 16.22.1).

**24.9** μή is used with the participle since it has conditional force (Smyth §2728); διδόντα describes the understood subject of ἄρχειν (στρατηγόν): "it is not possible that [the general] command if he does not give pay."

## 25

**25.10–13** μισθόν and στρατιώτας οἰκείους pick up ideas developed in sections 23 and 24 respectively. To these ideas, however, D adds a new dimension, as he often does when he reverts to an idea already discussed. He will return to this new dimension in section 33: these citizen-soldiers will be overseers (ἐπόπτας), as it were, of what goes on in the campaign. This sentence grows steadily and has a real momentum. The second participial phrase (12–13), in fact, which contains the important new idea, is almost as long as the rest of the sentence. Understand ὑμᾶς as the subject of ἀφελεῖν (and see comments on §23).

One of the most striking aspects of this speech is the constant modulation in tone—D's ability to move quickly from exposition and argumentation to discussion of historical precedents to sarcastic criticism of his audience. These quick changes in the nature of the presentation are intended to keep the audience alert, but they must have also made the speech somewhat difficult to follow.

The presentation thus far in this section and the two that precede it has been expository in nature. The next sentence, however, makes a transition to the sarcastic tone of the end of the section. The key word is γέλως ("an occasion of laughter, food for laughter"; LSJ, s.v., II). The short dialogue characterizes the Athenians, as so often in this speech, as people who talk but do not act. These short dialogues have several functions. They convey D's scorn for how the Athenians carry on their foreign policy. They characterize the audience by letting them speak for themselves. And they enliven the presentation with a short dramatic interlude (cf. Quintilian 9.2.30 and the *Rhetoric to Herennius* 4.65). Here the short dialogue serves to regain the audience's attention, which may have been flagging after a fairly lengthy presentation of recommendation and explanation, filled with facts and figures.

**25.12** ὥσπερ is often used to apologize for a strong metaphor (LSJ, s.v., II). ἐπόπτης usually refers to an overseer or an inspector, not a role generally associated with a soldier vis-à-vis his general.

**25.12–13** στρατηγουμένων is probably neuter: "the things done by the general" (LSJ, s.v., f).

**25.16** Φιλίππῳ πολεμοῦμεν: This had been the case since 357 when Philip seized Amphipolis (Hammond, 538–39).

26

**26.16–18**  D continues in this section the scornful tone seen at the end of the previous one. The first sentence is a rhetorical question in the true sense, because the answer is obvious. Such a question (ἐρώτημα or ἐρώτησις), which can be answered only by a "yes" or a "no," shows impatience and strong feeling (cf. Quintilian 9.2.8 and Lausberg §§767, 770).

The imperfect ἐχειροτονεῖτε must refer to repeated past action: "Have you not been in the habit of electing?" Tarbell argues that it refers to the period during which the Athenians had been at war with Philip (60). The abrupt switch to the present that follows (τί οὖν οὗτοι ποιοῦσιν) would be in keeping with the emotional and excited tone of this passage.

In 507 Cleisthenes had divided the citizen body into ten tribes (*phylai*), each of which consisted of three geographically distinct areas, one from the city, one from the coast, and one from the inland region. Each tribe had to supply one regiment (*taxis*), commanded by a taxiarch, for the hoplite force, commanded by a general, and one squadron (*phylê*), commanded by a phylarch, for the cavalry (Hansen, 106), which was commanded by the two hipparchs (Arist., *Ath. Pol.* 61.6). Davies notes: "The supervision of the στρατηγοί and (for cavalry) the ἵππαρχοι was in earlier times exercised jointly, but recently separate provinces had been assigned to the several στρατηγοί, so that here we find one only in charge of the war" (62). Most magistrates in Athens were selected by lot, but military officials were always elected (Hansen, 52). Elections, like voting on decrees, were by show of hands. Citizens proposed candidates for election, and a citizen could propose himself. Those attending the Assembly voted for each candidate until the requisite number of officials had been selected. (Most offices in Athens were held simultaneously by more than one person.) Then any new candidate could be proposed to replace one already elected, and the ensuing vote would be between these two. Proceedings went on until no more opposition candidates were proposed (Hansen, 234–35).

**26.18–20**  The rhetorical question in line 18 (τί οὖν οὗτοι ποιοῦσιν;) is technically a πύσμα, a question that cannot be answered with a "yes" or a "no" but requires a more detailed explanation (Lausberg §770). The explanation allows D to pass from the reasonable expectation to the ridiculous reality. ἑνός is contrasted with the many officials, emphasized by polysyndeton and homoioteleuton, listed in the first sentence of this section and framed by δέκα and δύο. Likewise, within this sentence, ἑνὸς ἀνδρός is contrasted with οἱ λοιποί and the phrase ἐκπέμψητε ἐπὶ τὸν πόλεμον with τὰς πόμπας πέμπουσιν. The repetition of π and σ in τὰς πόμπας πέμπουσιν produces a harsh sound that is appropriate to convey D's scorn.[11] Moreover, every syllable in this phrase is long, and this

---

[11] For the effect produced by these consonants, see Dionysius of Halicarnassus, *On Composition*, 14 and 22, plus the comments of Usher in the introduction to his translation (p. 8).

allows D to linger upon it, just as the Athenians linger upon the activity. In the phrase ἐπὶ τὸν πόλεμον, however, every syllable but one is short. In order to reinforce the contrast between festivals, to which tremendous resources are devoted, and preparations for war, which are neglected, there is also a play on words in ἐκπέμψητε and πέμπουσιν.[12] The contrast will be developed more fully in sections 35 and 36. The phrase μετὰ τῶν ἱεροποιῶν, placed at the end of the sentence, highlights the absurdity of the situation, in which these military officers spend their energies associating, not with soldiers but with civilian officials. ἱεροποιῶν refers to a board chosen by lot to supervise most of the festivals in Athens (cf. Arist., *Ath. Pol.* 54.6).

**26.20**  ὑμῖν: see note at 24.5.

**26.20–22**  D sums up the argument in this section with a striking comparison of the Athenians to people who fashion clay puppets, useless except for show. Like his use of verbs relating to hunting at the end of section 9, this is an indication of his ability to sum up an argument with a memorable image. In the rest of this sentence he repeats the contrast seen in the preceding one by placing εἰς τὴν ἀγοράν at the beginning of the main clause and ἐπὶ τὸν πόλεμον at the end.

27

**27.23–1**  D repeats the key idea from section 26: ταξιάρχους παρ᾽ ὑμῶν, ἵππαρχον παρ᾽ ὑμῶν (cf. ἐξ ὑμῶν αὐτῶν). The homoioteleuton underlines how important citizen commanders are to D's proposal. In order to reinforce this idea, he repeats it in the summary phrase ἄρχοντας οἰκείους. In section 19, at the beginning of the part of the speech dealing with the standing force, D had insisted that it must truly represent the city (ἣ τῆς πόλεως ἔσται). Here at the end of this part of the speech he returns to the same idea, using the same phrase, by pointing out that in the past this has not been the case: ἵν᾽ ἦν ὡς ἀληθῶς τῆς πόλεως ἡ δύναμις. The use of the indicative ἦν in the purpose clause indicates that the purpose was not or could not have been fulfilled in the past (cf. Smyth §2185c). Similarly, the use of the imperfect ἐχρῆν at the beginning of the sentence indicates that the action in the dependent infinitive was not realized (Smyth §1774; cf. ἔδει in line 4).

**27.1–5**  Having discussed the problem of native commanders in general terms, D concludes this argument with a specific example. The native hipparch

---

[12] Cf. the discussion of paronomasia in Lausberg §§637–39, particularly 638.1.a, where he discusses this particular type of paronomasia, which he calls *annominatio per adiectionem vel detractionem*.

sails to Lemnos, seemingly for ceremonial purposes.[13] Thus, Menelaos, apparently a mercenary commander, has taken charge of the Athenian cavalry who are actually fighting on the city's behalf (ὑπὲρ τῶν τῆς πόλεως κτημάτων ἀγωνιζομένων). τὸν παρ' ὑμῶν ἵππαρχον, unnamed since he does not exist as far as military operations are concerned (and that is all that matters to D), is contrasted with Μενέλαον, who appears not to have been an Athenian, but a Pelagonian (cf. CIA II.55). D ends this section about citizen commanders with the most basic point that he has made in it: ὑφ' ὑμῶν ἔδει κεχειροτονημένον εἶναι τοῦτον, ὅστις ἂν ᾖ.

**27.1** ὡς ἀληθῶς: The ὡς does not really affect the meaning ("in the true way, really"; LSJ, s.v. ἀληθής, III.b).

**27.3** ἱππαρχεῖν is here used in the general sense "to command the cavalry," in which sense it usually is followed by a genitive, rather than in the technical sense of "to be hipparch."

**27.5** ᾖ: After ἔδει we might expect the optative; D, however, retains the subjunctive of the original statement, probably to emphasize that this is a general truth (cf. the discussion at 51.21).

### E. D gives an estimate of expenses and discusses the source of funds (§§28–29)

## 28

**28.6–8** Having argued since section 24 that native troops and native commanders should be used in the war against Philip, D now makes specific proposals for funds to support them. But first of all he signals that one argument is over: Ἴσως δὲ ταῦτα μὲν ὀρθῶς ἡγεῖσθε λέγεσθαι. He also makes it clear to his audience what topic he will treat next: τὸ δὲ τῶν χρημάτων. In fact, he calls attention to this by dividing the general concept into its component parts: πόσα καὶ πόθεν. He will deal with the former topic in sections 28 and 29, with the latter in the πόρου ἀπόδειξις that will be read into the record. This was a memorandum of ways and means drawn up by D and his political allies or some members of a financial board (cf. δεδυνήμεθ' εὑρεῖν, §30). Having promised that he will deal with finances (τοῦτο δὴ καὶ περαίνω), he repeats briefly the topic that he will discuss: χρήματα τοίνυν.

There is a striking effort here to get the attention of the audience and their goodwill. D tries to put himself in their place by imagining what is going on in their minds (and to some extent by telling them what should be going on there),

---

[13] In the work attributed to Aristotle (*Ath. Pol.* 61.6), the author says that an Athenian hipparch was sent to Lemnos to command the cavalry there. The context here, however, would suggest that the hipparch in question was sent for religious purposes.

not only what they have come to accept but also what questions they are pondering. Speakers often use the speech itself to try to create the sort of audience who will react favorably to what they are saying (Black, 119). In this respect the phrase ποθεῖτε ἀκοῦσαι in lines 7–8 is particularly noteworthy. This is a very important part of the speech, the real point of everything that precedes, and D does not want to continue with it until he has the audience's undivided attention.

**28.8–15**   This section is filled with factual detail. A part of the speech such as this, which in many ways is simply a list, could be very dull. Therefore, D packs all the factual information into one sentence. In order to keep this sentence clear, he uses the same basic pattern for each expenditure: dative/amount of money/justification. In order to keep from being too tedious, however, he varies the pattern, particularly the justification for each expenditure. Hermogenes recommends (315) such variations in a list, known as ἐξαλλαγή, as an appropriate figure to keep a passage from being flat.

**28.10**   πρός: adverbial, "besides" (LSJ, s.v., D). The small amount in addition to ninety talents, as will be clear from the tabulations below, comes to two talents.

Vince, in a note on this passage, sets out (84–85) how this money would be spent. The sum total of ninety-two talents is based on a year's expenditure.

**28.10–11**   There was a crew of 200 on each trireme, and the proposed pay for each marine is two obols a day, thus a need for 4,000 obols per day for the crews of the ten ships. Since there were sixty minai in a talent, a hundred drachmas in a mina, and six obols in a drachma, forty talents would come to 1,440,000 obols, or 4,000 obols per day for 360 days. Twenty minai per ship (εἰς τὴν ναῦν; cf. Smyth §1120f) would be 12,000 obols each month (τοῦ μηνός) or 144,000 obols per year, which multiplied by ten ships would also give 1,440,000 obols.

**28.12–13**   D is proposing two obols a day, which comes to sixty obols or ten drachmas per month, for infantry. This is half what hoplites were normally given. D makes it clear, however, that he is proposing money only for rations (σιτηρέσιον μόνον), not for pay, which was normally another two obols. As Tarbell notes (62), ἔστι μὲν ἡ τροφή leads one to expect ἔστι δ' ὁ μισθός. The corresponding clause, however, is a statement that no money needs to be raised for wages: εἰ δέ τις οἴεται μικρὰν ἀφορμὴν εἶναι... οὐκ ὀρθῶς ἔγνωκεν (29.15–17). D has implied earlier that the troops can make up their pay by looting Philip's land (cf. §23), and he makes that idea explicit in section 29 (18–20). If each soldier receives ten drachmas per month, there is a need for 20,000 drachmas per month, or 240,000 drachmas per year to pay the 2,000 hoplites. 240,000 drachmas is 2,400 minai, which is forty talents.

**28.13–15**   Cavalry normally received two drachmas or twelve obols a day, but, as with the hoplites, D will cut this in half, which will require 1,200 obols a day, 36,000 a month, 432,000 a year for the cavalry. 432,000 obols is 72,000 drachmas, which is 720 minai or twelve talents.

Vince points out that "to appreciate these sums, it should be noted that an unskilled labourer at Athens received 3 or 4 obols a day" (85). Hansen reckons (115) that a talent represented what an ordinary Athenian would earn over the course of more than ten years. He also points out (316), in commenting on the financial burden that military activity put on Greek states, that the entire income of Athens early in the fourth century was only 130 talents a year. By 340 it had risen to 400 and after the peace with Philip it rose to 1,200. But 92 talents out of 1,200, and certainly out of between 130 and 400, is a very significant expenditure, and D is trying to keep the amount as low as possible.

29

**29.15–20**   Before leaving the specific proposals, D inserts a section of argument to prop up the last proposal that he has made and introduces this argument by imagining that someone in the audience has found his proposal insufficient. In his reply to the imaginary objector, D reverts to an idea that he developed at the beginning of the part of the speech that deals with the standing force, using ring composition to signal that this part of the speech is over and to emphasize an important idea by repeating it. μικρὰν ἀφορμήν recalls τὰ μικρὰ ποιήσαντες in section 20, where the argument was that even small measures are better than no measures at all. In fact, μικρὰν ἀφορμήν coupled with προσποριεῖ τὰ λοιπά in the next sentence essentially reproduces the thought seen in section 20: τὰ μικρὰ ποιήσαντες καὶ πορίσαντες τούτοις προστίθετε.

**29.16**   LSJ takes ἀφορμήν in this passage to mean "a small *inducement*" (s.v., 2). I would take it, rather, to mean "*the means with which one begins* a thing" (LSJ, s.v., 3) and then construe the indirect statement that follows as an appositive to ἀφορμήν: "But if anyone thinks that the means with which we begin the campaign are small, namely, that there exists money to buy grain [only] for the ones making the expedition." This seems easier to me than taking ἀφορμήν as part of the indirect statement, as Davies does (64). Dilts's punctuation would indicate that he also sees the indirect statement as an appositive.

**29.17**   τοῦτ' = σιτηρέσιον

**29.20–21**   This sentence illustrates the style that Hermogenes calls sincere. Prayers and oaths (and this sentence is similar to an oath), particularly when they come without any advance indication that the orator is going to use them, create, as Hermogenes argues (354–56), a spontaneous tone and reveal deep feelings, in this case, confidence. Aristides says (1.95) that it lends credibility to a speech when the orator envisions punishment for himself if what he says is not true, and he gives this sentence as an example. In his analysis of the famous oath by those who died at Marathon in the speech *On the Crown* (208), Longinus discusses (16) how effectively D could use emotional figures of speech as confirming arguments.

**29.21**  ἕτοιμος: sc. εἰμί (cf. Smyth §§944–45).

**29.21–23**  After this emotional outburst, the αἰτιολογία at the end of this section changes the tone back to the expository one seen earlier and introduces the memorandum of ways and means. πόθεν picks up πόθεν in the first sentence of section 28 and brings this part of the speech dealing with finances (§§28 and 29) to a conclusion. The question introducing a topic, followed by a statement such as τοῦτ᾽ ἤδη λέξω, is typical of this part of the speech (cf. §§20, 22, 28), which is tightly organized and clearly marked to make it easier to follow.

Dionysius (*Letter to Ammaeus* 1.10) had a manuscript that showed the speech ending here, and he treats sections 30–51 as a separate speech. This division is not accepted by modern scholars who maintain the unity of the speech as we have it (see Davies, 65). To break the speech into two here would mean (a) that the first speech has no peroration and the second has no proemium, and (b) that ταῦτ᾽ in the first sentence of section 30 would have no antecedent.

## 30

### F.  D concludes the part of the speech about specific proposals (§30)

The first sentence of this section signals an end to the immediately preceding discussion about finances, the second brings to a conclusion this whole part of the speech dealing with specific proposals. ταῦτ᾽ in the first sentence refers narrowly to the financial matters outlined in the memorandum of ways and means; γνώμας, however, must refer to the entire set of proposals (γνώμη = motion; LSJ, s.v., III.b.2). The section preceding the discussion of the specific proposals had ended with γνώμαις (§12), and the reference to γνώμας in this section concludes the ring that brackets them.

Davies has problems with this passage, since he sees γνώμας as referring to all the proposals that would be presented to the Assembly, "my own and others which may be made" (65). D, however, has made two separate proposals (see discussion of §§13–15), and I do not see why γνώμας cannot refer to them. On this interpretation ἐπιχειροτονέω, meaning "*sanction* or *confirm by vote* of the Assembly" (LSJ, s.v., 1), would make perfect sense. At meetings of the Assembly, which probably met thirty to forty times a year for a few hours each (Hansen, 133–36, 313), voting was by a show of hands. An exact count of the votes was probably not undertaken, but officials presiding over the Assembly would estimate the vote (Hansen, 147). According to Hansen (332), any citizen who was not convinced by the assessment of the presiding officers could file a sworn complaint, and the show of hands would be repeated.

In the fifth century the Assembly had been presided over by the *prytaneis*, the fifty members of the Council of Five Hundred from each tribe that also formed the executive committee of the Council, each of the ten groups acting as *prytaneis* for a tenth of the year. In the fourth century, however, possibly to avoid bribery, these were replaced by nine *proedroi*, one member from each tribe not serving as *prytaneis*, selected by lot just before the meeting of the Assembly and serving for only one day. A second selection by lot would choose their leader (*epistates*), who was primarily responsible for controlling and directing the discussion (Hansen, 140–41).

**30.1**   ἡμεῖς refers to D and his political allies; he does not use the first person plural to refer to himself.

The first half of the purpose clause in the second sentence of this section essentially repeats one of the most important ideas that appears earlier in this part of the speech, the contrast between Athenian preparations and actions. τοῖς ψηφίσμασι ... πολεμῆτε recalls the phrase τὰ μέγιστ᾽ ἐν τοῖς ψηφίσμασι αἱρούμενοι of section 20, and ταῖς ἐπιστολαῖς πολεμῆτε recalls the ἐπιστολιμαίους δυνάμεις of section 19. D concludes this part of the speech with a contrast with which he had begun it (cf. the first sentence in §13, which ends with the word λέγων), that between words and deeds, and the section ends with a word that sums up what has been stressed throughout this part of the speech, τοῖς ἔργοις, and which resonates in the mind of the audience as D turns to the next major unit in the speech.

### IV. Resumption of General Argument (§§31–50)

A. First Topic: Geographical and climatic considerations make a standing force in the north attractive (§§31–32)

### 31

D returns, rather abruptly, to a general consideration of the situation, already delineated in sections 2–12. This abrupt turn in the argument is similar to the one seen in section 12, at another division between major parts of the speech, and is probably intended to indicate an eagerness to get on with the business at hand.

**31.7–10**   D makes it clear at the outset that his arguments here are closely related to the first two major parts of the speech. I would take περὶ τοῦ πολέμου to refer to the general discussion of the hostilities between Philip and Athens in sections 2–12 and ὅλης τῆς παρασκευῆς to refer to the specific proposals in sections 16–29. The sentence takes the form of a future less vivid condition, envisioning a possible but unlikely situation, quite in keeping with the pessimistic view of his audience seen elsewhere in this speech (see the introduction). ἄν... βουλεύσασθαι = the optative plus ἄν (cf. Smyth §1845); τόπον = "the geographical position" (Davies, 65).

**31.10–13**   In this section, as in those preceding, D projects the image of himself as someone who is well informed, who knows about geography and weather and has considered what effects they have on Athenian affairs. In the sentence as a whole, as often in Demosthenic periods, there is a steady movement from the general to the particular, from τὸν τόπον... τῆς χώρας to winds and seasons and then to Etesian winds and winter. The result of all this is stated emphatically in the indefinite temporal clause at the end of the sentence, which is the main point that D wants to make (ἡνίκ᾽ ἂν ἡμεῖς μὴ δυναίμεθα ἐκεῖσ᾽ ἀφικέσθαι). Greeks normally suspended naval operations in the winter, when the weather in the Aegean can be stormy. In the summer the Etesian winds often blow from the northwest, thus making it difficult to sail from south to north. Philip takes advantage of these situations (φυλάξας τοὺς ἐτησίας ἢ τὸν χειμῶνα).

The ἡνίκα clause represents the apodosis of a future less vivid condition with an implied protasis such as εἰ δέοι. μή is used instead of οὐ because the temporal clause refers to action that "occurs in the indefinite future" and "recurs an indefinite number of times" (Smyth §2392). The abrupt switch in time is only apparent, since ἐπιχειρεῖ, a generalizing present, can be seen as referring also to the future (cf. Smyth §§1877, 1879).

One of the articulating principles in the sentence is a chiasmus in the long protasis that makes up most of it (8–13). Here we have a direct object (τὸν τόπον... τῆς χώρας) followed by the verb on which it depends (ἐνθυμηθείητε) plus a verb (λογίσαισθε) followed by the indirect statement that depends on it (ὅτι... ἐπιχειρεῖ). This allows D to repeat his basic point by framing the two verbs that have similar meanings with objects that refer to the same idea, one stated generally, the other more specifically. There is also a chiasmus near the end of the sentence, and it sums up D's point: διαπράττεται Φίλιππος/ἡμεῖς μὴ δυναίμεθα, in which the factual reality is put in the indicative and is contrasted with frustrated potential, in the optative. The verb διαπράττω is carefully chosen; it means to do thoroughly, to carry out to the desired end, exactly what the Athenians have failed do.

## 32

**32.13–15**   ταῦτ᾽ ἐνθυμουμένους connects this sentence with the preceding section (ἐνθυμηθείητε). If his audience will take weather and geography into account, they will see why past policies have failed and D's policy will succeed. D's own proposal of a standing force, which will solve these problems, is then placed emphatically at the end of the sentence, having been delayed by an expression of how they should not fight (μὴ βοηθείαις) and by a parenthesis (ὑστεριοῦμεν γὰρ ἁπάντων).

The theme of being too late to take advantage of opportunities is one that D will return to and develop more fully in sections 35–37 (cf. ὑστερίζειν τῶν καιρῶν, §35.24; οἱ δὲ τῶν πραγμάτων οὐ μένουσι καιροί, §37.11). The theme of καιρός, therefore, which is so important in D (cf. Jaeger, 130–33, 138), forms a ring that brackets the first major part of the speech following the specific proposals, the discussion of how the expeditionary force will operate to Athens' advantage, delineated in sections 31–37. This discussion is amplified by contrasting military preparation and festivals in sections 35–36. Comparison or contrast, what Quintilian calls *per comparationem incrementum* (8.4.9), is a common technique of giving a topic more weight (cf. Arist., *Rhet.* 1.9.38–39).

**32.13–14**   sc. ὑμᾶς as the subject of πολεμεῖν.

**32.15–18**   The sentence is filled with polysyndeton, which emphasizes not only how many places could serve as bases for winter operations but also how many advantages each of these offers. The places and their advantages are ringed by ὑπάρχει, placed emphatically at the beginning and end of the sentence. This is a strong verb that indicates something that is already actually in existence (cf. LSJ, s.v., B.2). It is a verb of which D is fond and which he uses frequently in this speech (cf. §§2, 4, 5, 7, 13, 17, 29, 33, 37).

In his Oxford text of 1903, S. H. Butcher marked the text at the end of the section as corrupt. ῥᾳδίως is difficult to construe with ἔσται, since an adverb is not usually used with this verb, and it is not completely clear what is the subject of ἔσται. These points, however, are not decisive, and most editors, like Dilts, have accepted the manuscript reading. Adverbs are used with εἶναι (cf. LSJ, s.v., C.I), and the subject δύναμις could fairly easily be supplied from context. Taking πρός with the dative in the sense of "near to" (cf. LSJ, s.v., B.1), we would thus get the translation "it [the force] will easily be near the land itself and the mouths of his harbors." The future indicative (ἔσται) at the end of this section contrasts nicely with the optative (δυναίμεθα) at the end of the preceding one. There the expeditionary force could not arrive; here the standing force will already be present.

**32.15–16**   There are many datives in this sentence. ὑμῖν should be construed with ὑπάρχει: "it is possible for you." Λήμνῳ, etc., are the objects of χρῆσθαι (Smyth §1509), and χειμαδίῳ is an appositive to them (singular because only one will be used). δυνάμει is a dative of advantage: "to use as winter quarters for the force Lemnos, etc."

**32.16–17**  Lemnos and Thasos had been allied with Athens since the Corinthian War; Sciathos had been a member of the Athenian League (Sealey, 10–11, 59).

**32.19**  ὥραν refers to the *"fitting time* or *season* for a thing" (LSJ, s.v., B.1), in this case sailing.

B.  Second Topic: The general in charge will decide how exactly the force is to be deployed, but this force will deprive Philip of his ability to harass Athenian shipping and possessions and thus of a major source of revenue (§§33–34)

### 33

**33.22–6**  Before proceeding with the argument in these two sections, which comes only at the beginning of section 34, D sums up some of the ideas developed in the specific proposals relating to the force that he has proposed: the need for a commander appointed by the Athenians themselves (ὁ τούτων κύριος καταστὰς ὑφ' ὑμῶν; cf. §27: ὑφ' ὑμῶν ἔδει κεχειροτονημένον εἶναι), the need for the Athenians to vote funds for the standing force (τὰ χρήματα ... καὶ τἄλλα παρασκευάσαντες; cf. §25: μισθὸν πορίσαντας καὶ στρατιώτας), the need for native soldiers who will keep an eye on what the commander does (αὐτοὶ ταμίαι καὶ πορισταὶ γιγνόμενοι; cf. §25: ὥσπερ ἐπόπτας τῶν στρατηγουμένων παρακαταστήσαντας), and, above all, the need to act rather than simply plan (παύσεσθε ... βουλευόμενοι καὶ πλέον οὐδὲν ποιοῦντες; cf. §20: ταῦτ' ἐθελήσει ποιεῖν). ταῦτ' ἐστὶν ἀγὼ γέγραφα gives D an opportunity to repeat, in the next sentence, the gist of the specific proposals that he has made earlier: χρήματα, στρατιώτας, τριήρεις, ἱππέας, which he then sums up in ἐντελῆ πᾶσαν τὴν δύναμιν. D makes it clear that money is the most basic requirement, reflecting the emphatic position of the discussion of finances at the end of the specific proposals (§29). Here, consequently, the topic is given a prominent position: τὰ χρήματα πρῶτον ... εἶτα καὶ τἄλλα.

**33.22**  ἅ means "in respect to what" or "how"; see comments on the adverbial accusative at 10.8.

**33.22–23**  παρὰ τὸν καιρόν literally means "alongside of the right moment," so "when occasion arises" (Davies, 67).

**33.24**  γέγραφα: γράφω is used here in its technical sense, to "*write down* a law to be proposed" (LSJ, s.v., II.6), hence simply to propose.

**33.3**  νόμῳ κατακλείσητε is a strong and vivid expression, meaning "to lock up by means of the law." It is another example of D's ability to convey his thought in a striking way through the use of metaphorical expressions.

**33.4** The ταμίαι were treasurers appointed to control receipts and expenditures. The πορισταί were members of a financial board appointed to raise money in times of crisis.

**33.5** λόγον ζητοῦντες: The conduct of public officials was formally examined once their term of office was over. This is a less technical way of saying what is described more technically in section 47 (13–14).

## 34

**34.6–8** Having reminded his audience of points already made earlier in the speech and thus prepared them to receive new information, D introduces at the end of the sentence a topic not developed before (καὶ ἔτι πρὸς τούτῳ), that Athenian action will deprive Philip of his greatest source of revenue. The hiatus between καί and ἔτι marks off this part of the sentence for special attention (Pearson H, 148; to be sure, D regularly allows hiatus after καί). The use of πρὸς τούτῳ twice in this section (καὶ ἔτι πρὸς τούτῳ, ἔπειτα τί πρὸς τούτῳ;) is indicative of the way in which arguments are loosely strung together in this part of the speech, which is only to be expected given the emotional tone of much of it.

**34.9** ἄγων καὶ φέρων: idiomatic for "harrying, ravaging" (LSJ, s.v. ἄγω, 1.3).

**34.10–17** In the preceding parts of the speech, D has clearly set up the contrast between Philip, who acts, and the Athenians, who talk and vote. This contrast will be developed at length in the rest of section 34 and the three sections that follow. As usual in this speech Philip is dealt with fairly briefly (see the introduction); the Athenians, the real object of D's attack, are dealt with much more fully.

Lines 12–16 describe how Philip acts. The section is filled with verbal forms (eight in four lines). Moreover, much action is packed into each clause, and the clauses are all relatively short. The first, for example, has three verbal forms (ἐμβαλών, ᾤχετ᾽, ἔχων), all of which denote action, motion, or possession, characteristics that D associates with Philip (cf. §9). The accumulation of detail, particularly the use of proper names and references to specific occasions, gives the section credibility and vividness; the piling up of so many transgressions against the Athenians, in such a short space, is also intended to evoke an emotional response from the audience.[14] In addition, the clauses are connected in asyndeton, and their structure varies. The predominant rhythm here is trochaic (cf. ἀμύθητα χρήματ᾽ ἐξέλεξε: ˘ | ˉ ˘ | ˉ ˘ | ˉ ˘ | ˉ ˘), and there is no hiatus. All of these are characteristics that Hermogenes associates with Rapidity (319–20). This reinforces the idea that Philip acts and that he acts quickly, frequently, and unpredictably.

---

[14] Cf. Cecil Wooten, "Cicero and Quintilian on the Style of Demosthenes," *Rhetorica* 15 (1997): 185–86, for a discussion of Quintilian's analysis of D's ability to accumulate detail to evoke emotion.

The second part of this last sentence (16–17) shifts back to the Athenians, and the style changes abruptly. Here D uses Abundance, a style that is quite suitable to describe their slowness and lack of energy. First, there is the unnecessary but emphatic pronoun ὑμεῖς. Second, there is polysyndeton in the οὔτε . . . οὔτε, and the negation of action clearly contrasts with the assertion of it earlier, in the sentence discussing Philip. Third, there is synonymity, since both the οὔτε clauses really say the same thing (cf. Hermogenes, 284–86). Fourth, the insertion of the subordinate clause οὓς ἂν προθῆσθε, delaying the infinitive that completes the thought, also creates a halting effect (cf. Hermogenes, 288). Finally, this part of the sentence contains more longs than the preceding part, being composed of cretics and spondees (cf. κωλύειν οὔτ᾽ εἰς τοὺς χρόνους; ˉ ˘ ˉ| ˉ ˘| ˉ ˘ ˉ), and this also slows down the speed of the passage.

**34.10–11**   τοῦ πάσχειν αὐτοὶ κακῶς ἔξω γενήσεσθε: As Sandys notes (106), the adverb κακῶς is separated from the infinitive with which it is construed, partially to emphasize it and partially to avoid hiatus between αὐτοί and ἔξω: "you yourselves will be outside (beyond the reach of) suffering harm."

**34.11–12**   οὐχ ὥσπερ τὸν παρελθόντα χρόνον: As Davies points out (67–68), this involves an ellipsis. The full form would be something like οὐκ (ἐν τῷ κακῶς πάσχειν) ὥσπερ (ἦτε) τὸν παρελθόντα χρόνον (ὅτε).

**34.12**   These raids from Macedonia probably took place in 351, not long before the delivery of this speech (cf. Hammond, 548; Sealey, 155; Aeschines 2.72). These events confirm D's statement, made in section 22, that Philip has a fleet.

**34.13**   Geraestus was on a promontory at the south end of Euboea and was a regular port of call for ships traveling to the north Aegean or the Black Sea.

**34.14–16**   τὰ τελευταῖα εἰς Μαραθῶνα ἀπέβη καὶ τὴν ἱερὰν ἀπὸ τῆς χώρας: Sandys notes (107–8) that this part of the sentence is dominated by anapaests (˘ ˘ ˉ| ˘ ˘ ˉ| ˘ ˘ ˉ| ˘˘˘ ˉ| ˉ|˘˘ˉ|˘˘ˉ| ˉ ˉ). This, he argues, gives an impression of "measured advance." The end of this clause (ᾤχετ᾽ ἔχων τριήρη) uses a "swift dactylic and trochaic movement" (ˉ ˘ ˘ | ˉ ˘ | ˉ ˘). He also notes that the mention of a landing at Marathon would have evoked a strong response from the audience. This is our only reference to this emotional incident.

   Athens had several sacred triremes that were used for public business, particularly for transporting religious embassies. The most important of these were the *Salaminia* and the *Paralos*. This reference is probably to the latter, which seems to have stopped periodically at Marathon to receive a blessing from the priest of Apollo there (cf. Tarbell, 65, and Plato, *Crito* 43d).

**34.15–16**   τὴν ἱερὰν . . . τριήρη: Ronnet points out (42–43) that the most common type of hyperbaton in D's early political speeches is the one that involves

separating an adjective from the noun that it qualifies and putting the adjective
before the noun (cf. ὑμετέρων ὑμῖν πολεμεῖ συμμάχων in line 9). Although this
type of hyperbaton is common in all authors, it usually involves the interposi-
tion of only one word between the adjective and the noun (Denniston GPS,
51). Here five words intervene. Devine and Stephens, citing this example, note
(132) that most cases like this involve a verb of motion and a participle (see the
general discussion of hyperbaton at §5.20–21). The adjective at the beginning
of the clause and the noun at the end also bracket the whole phrase and thus set
it off from the actions that precede. Its final position in the list of Philip's
transgressions also calls attention to it. D is underlining once again Philip's
hybris, his lack of respect for men or gods, associated with him from the first
time he is mentioned in the speech (§3) and recurring at other points in the
argument (cf. §§9 and 49).

   C. Third Topic: There is a striking contrast between the careful
   way in which festivals are organized and the haphazard manner
   in which military objectives are carried out (§§35–37)

35

In the next three sections, which continue to describe the Athenians, the style
remains very full and is used to convey the lavish attention that the Athenians
pay to domestic affairs as opposed to foreign policy. The passage contains many
elements that Hermogenes associates with Abundance. The inserted parenthesis in the first sentence of section 35, using polysyndeton (ἄν τε ... ἄν τε), is a
good example of extraneous detail (278), as is the parallelism (284). The next
four clauses use the figure called ὑπόστασις, the use of grammatical constructions that require subordination and thus imply other thoughts (290):
τοσαῦτα ... ὅσα ... τοσοῦτον ... ὅσην. The enumeration (ἀπαρίθμησις) at the
end of the sentence produces the same effect (287). Here also D mentions
the undefined (τοὺς ἀποστόλους πάντας) as well as the defined (τὸν εἰς Μεθώνην
etc.), and this also creates Abundance according to Hermogenes (278). As
Sandys notes (110), D departs from chronological order here so as to be able
to mention Potidaea, the most important of these losses, last. Philip took
Methone in 353, Pagasae in 352, and Potidaea in 356.
   There is also a fair amount of hiatus in section 35, particularly in the middle of
the sentence, between γίγνεσθαι and ἄν and between ἰδιῶται and οἱ in line
20, between ἐπιμελούμενοι and εἰς and τοσαῦτα and ἀναλίσκεται in line 21 and
between χρήματα and ὅσα in line 22 and ὅσα and ὀνς̄ in the same line. Pearson
argues (H, 153) that D uses hiatus to slow down the delivery when, as here, he is
dealing with arguments that he particularly wants to impress upon his audience.
   In this section there is a contrast, similar to the discussion in section 26,
between festivals, to which D, like the Athenians, devotes a lot of attention
(seven lines) and military expeditions, which are treated very briefly (two lines).

In the discussion of the festivals there is much polysyndeton and hiatus; in dealing with the military operations D uses asyndeton (τὸν . . . , τὸν . . . , τὸν . . .) and no hiatus.

**35.17**  καίτοι τί δήποτε: The question shows great impatience: "and yet why in the world" (LSJ, s.v. δήποτε, 3). It is D's anger that motivates the abrupt transition from Philip's military activity to Athenian handling of festivals.

**35.18–19**  The Panathenaea was celebrated in August in honor of Athena. The great procession associated with it, which is depicted on the Parthenon frieze, culminated on the Acropolis, where sacrifices were made to the goddess. Every four years Athena was presented with a new Panathenaic embroidered robe and musical and athletic competitions were added. The Dionysia referred to here is probably the City Dionysia, celebrated in March, which included a procession, sacrifices, and the presentation of plays.[15] Παναθήναια and Διονύσια are adjectives that describe ἱερά, which is understood.

**35.19**  τοῦ καθήκοντος χρόνου: We might have expected a dative of time when rather than a genitive of time within which, but Greek does not always make such a clear distinction between the two (cf. Smyth §1543).

**35.20**  δεινοί and ἰδιῶται refer, respectively, to people who hold public office or take part in public affairs and people who are private citizens, similar to the distinction that we make between professionals and amateurs (cf. Ober, 109–12). These terms, however, are not official classifications. λαγχάνω refers to obtaining an office or position by lot as opposed to being elected (LSJ, s.v., I.2). Since the verb often functions as the passive of κληρόω (Smyth §1752), it frequently is followed by a predicate nominative: "whether public office holders or private individuals are chosen by lot [to be] the ones in charge of each."

**35.21**  ἑκατέρων ἐπιμελούμενοι: It is unusual to find in D two successive words that begin with three short syllables. If we read ἐπιμελησόμενοι, as does one manuscript, this phrase has exactly the same metrical configuration as the opening phrase in section 36: ὅτι ἐκεῖνα μὲν ἅπαντα νόμῳ ($\smile\smile\smile$|$\smile\smile\smile$|$\smile\smile\smile$). In any case, whether the metrical similarity is exact or only approximate, D calls attention to the importance of these phrases and the connection between them through the unusual piling up of so many short syllables and through the similarity in meter (Blass, 110).

The Eponymous Archon was in charge of the Dionysia, and ten appointed commissioners supervised the Panathenaea.

---

[15] For basic information about these Athenian festivals see the entries under "Dionysia" and "Panathenaea" in the *Oxford Classical Dictionary*, 3rd ed., ed. Simon Hornblower and Antony Spawforth (Oxford, 1996).

**35.22**    Davies translates (69) ὄχλον as "fuss."

**35.23**    οὐκ οἶδ' εἴ τι τῶν ἁπάντων ἔχει: ἔχει must be used as the verb in the relative clause, with the antecedent ἅ understood, and as the verb in the correlative ὅσην clause: "[which] have such a great crowd and such great preparation as I do not know whether anything in the world has." The exaggeration reveals D's frustration.

**35.24**    ὑμῖν is probably a dative of disadvantage, which is often best translated as if it were a possessive genitive (cf. Smyth §1481).

## 36–37

**36.25–4**    The abundant style continues in the first sentence of section 36. The next sentence describes preparations for war. It is half the length of the sentence that precedes and contains none of the detail seen there. In the adjectives at the end of the sentence, nine syllables out of fourteen contain an alpha: ἄτακτα, ἀδιόρθωτα, ἀόριστα ἅπαντα. This creates a striking repetition of similar sounds that calls attention to the phrase. Three of these are formed with alpha-privatives, and this underlines how little attention is given to preparations for war. There is a pointed contrast between warfare, where everything is unplanned (ἄτακτα ... ἅπαντα), and festivals, where everything is carefully regulated (ἅπαντα ... τέτακται). Moreover, depending on how quickly these adjectives were spoken together, this could be a really remarkable example of hiatus, not only between the adjectives themselves but also between the string of adjectives and παρασκευῇ. Just as the presence of hiatus in prose can imply a lack of polish (cf. Hermogenes, 232, 308), its presence here may be used to reflect a lack of organization and preparation. Or, it may be used primarily to call attention to a phrase or word (Demetrius, 299). In any case, the jerky, jolting effect produced by this phrase would be striking and conveys the emotional state of the speaker.

**36.27**    χορηγὸς ἢ γυμνασίαρχος: Athens imposed on its wealthiest citizens public services or contributions known as "liturgies." One of these was the recruitment and training of a chorus for performances at festivals.[16] Similarly, each year one gymnasiarch was appointed from each of the ten tribes to organize torch races and to train the runners. Another liturgy was the outfitting of a ship for the Athenian navy (a "trierarchy") and often being the captain of the ship (cf. what D says in lines 4–5 below). The outfitting of a ship fell only to citizens; resident aliens could

---

[16] Cf. Peter Wilson, *The Athenian Institution of the Khoregia: The Chorus, the City, and the Stage* (Cambridge, 2000).

perform festival liturgies. The generals chose those who would outfit ships; the men assigned festival liturgies were chosen either by the archons or by the members of their tribe. A festival liturgy might cost only a few hundred drachmas; the outfitting of a ship as much as a talent. Thus, the latter liturgy tended to be imposed only on the very richest of the leisure class. During the lifetime of D, in each year there were about a hundred festival liturgies, and as many as four hundred trierarchies, which could be shared by two citizens. A man could not be obliged to perform more than one liturgy per year (Hansen, 110–12). After 358, rich men were divided into twenty symmories of about sixty men each, and the trierarchies were performed by groups. Wrangling over how exactly the tax burden would be spread over the members of the symmory created delays that hampered the Athenians' ability to respond quickly to crises. In 340, therefore, D had passed in the Assembly a decree that the richest men in each symmory would be primarily responsible for the funds demanded of each group (Hansen, 112–15; cf. the discussion of *eisphorai* at 7.12).

If a man was appointed to perform a liturgy but felt that someone else was richer, and thus more capable of performing it, he could propose that the second man either accept the liturgy or exchange property with him. If the man so challenged refused to accept either option, the case went to trial (cf. 5 below). This procedure was known as *antidosis*. Although we know of many such cases that came to court, not a single example of an actual exchange of property has been attested (Hansen, 112).

**36.4–37.9** D gives the consequences of what he has described (τοιγαροῦν). He uses a remarkable string of short clauses loosely connected by five examples of καί. One brief action follows another in a seemingly endless stream with no real goal in sight. Demetrius compares such a style to "stones that are simply thrown about near one another and not built into a structure" (13). In such sentences "the clauses seem thrown one on top of the other in a heap without the connections or buttressing or mutual support which we find in periods" (12). The long sentence in section 35, however, which takes the form of an analytical period, is well organized. Demetrius says of such sentences: "The clauses in the periodic style may in fact be compared to the stones which support and hold together the roof which encircles them" (13).

The anaphora with the repeated εἶτ' in lines 7 and 8 highlights the idea that the Athenians make the same mistake over and over again. μέλλεται sums up what he has been saying ("while these delays are going on") and brings the series to a close.

**36.7** Metics were foreigners who lived in Athens but did not have Athenian citizenship. The τοὺς χωρὶς οἰκοῦντας probably refers to freedmen, former slaves who "live apart" from the masters who once owned them (Davies, 70), although Hansen argues (121) that this phrase refers to slaves who lived in their own houses, worked for themselves, and gave part of their income to their masters. These slaves, of course, often eventually bought their freedom. ἀντεμβιβάζειν means to "put substitutes on board." These would either be slaves or people hired to fill in for those called up for service.

**37.8** μέλλω used without an infinitive means to "delay, put off" (LSJ, s.v., III).

**37.9** προαπόλωλεν is an intensive perfect, which denotes "an action rather than a state resulting from an action" and is the equivalent of a "strengthened present" (Smyth §1947).

**37.10–11** τῶν πραγμάτων, as Davies notes (70), could be either a subjective genitive ("opportunities offered by events") or an objective genitive ("opportunities for action"). The long hyperbaton that separates οἱ from its noun καιροί calls attention to the latter word, which is important in D (see discussion of §12). Moreover, the placement allows D to draw a strong contrast between καιροί and βραδυτῆτα and εἰρωνείαν, which are put emphatically at the end of the sentence.

**37.12** εἰρωνείαν: see note at 7.11.

**37.13–14** οἷαί τ᾽ οὖσαι: This is a supplementary participle with ἐξελέγχονται (οἷός τε means "*fit* or *able* to do"; LSJ, s.v. οἷος, III.2): "are proved to be able to do nothing at the times of the crises themselves."

**37.14–15** Meanwhile, as the Athenians spend all their efforts on festivals and develop their war plans only in a sporadic and disorganized way, Philip has acted. The ὁ δ᾽ in the last sentence of section 37 comes in abruptly and unexpectedly, as does Philip himself. Moreover, this sentence, unlike the long and involved sentences that precede, is direct and to the point. It has an energy and a vigor that the sentences describing the Athenians lack.

We do not know what was in the letter that Philip addressed to the towns in Euboea, but we assume that it pointed out that Athens was an unreliable ally and that the Athenians were not even concerned with protecting their own interests. Philip probably pointed out also that he could protect the Euboeans from domination by either Athens or Thebes (Griffith, 310). David Mirhady has argued that D, as compared with earlier orators, makes a greater use of supporting documents in his judicial speeches: "In particular, his success was due to his employment of the various forms of documentary evidence that were available to Athenian logographers, documents such as laws, witness testimony, contracts and challenges" ("Demosthenes as Advocate," in Worthington, 182). The use of documentary evidence, such as this letter from Philip, is also characteristic of the *Philippics*, where the abundance of specific information lends credibility and substance to the presentation.

## 38–39

**D. Fourth Topic: Statesmen must tell the truth, even if it is unpleasant to hear; otherwise the city will never be prepared to act (§§38–39)**

D's reaction to Philip's letter (16–18) allows him to return to a general discussion of the relationship between words and deeds, one of the recurring motifs in this speech, which takes the form of a divided supposition (cf. Hermogenes, 287–88), similar to the first sentence in the speech, which envisions two possibilities: if pleasant words will make the situation more pleasant, an orator should speak to please; if, however, pleasant words are actually harmful, the orator must tell the truth. The first possibility is stated in two lines (19–21); the second, and its implications, in ten (21–6). The latter is clearly the correct analysis of the situation.

The second half of the division (21–22) is generally parallel to the first (19–21) up until the clause αἰσχρόν ἐστι φενακίζειν ἑαυτούς. Then, like an analytical period, it begins to grow and expand, exploring all the consequences and ramifications of the thought stated in the clause just cited. There is only one infinitive dependent on the impersonal verb in the first half of the division (δεῖ . . . δημηγορεῖν). In the second half, however, there are three, and they are joined together with polysyndeton (φενακίζειν . . . καὶ . . . ὑστερεῖν . . . καὶ μηδὲ . . . μαθεῖν). Moreover, the infinitive phrases become longer and longer. The first consists of only two words (φενακίζειν ἑαυτούς). The second is a little over a line long. The third, when one includes the ὅτι clause dependent on μαθεῖν and the subordinate clauses embedded in it, runs for six lines. This sort of swelling sentence, in which D piles one bit of information on top of another, is meant to overwhelm the listener and win him over to D's position (cf. Wooten A, 504–5, and Pearson VP, 226).

There are other instances of recurrence in this passage in addition to the discussion of the discrepancy between talk and action. In the second infinitive phrase (22–24), for example, D picks up a theme that he had developed at length in sections 32 and 37: the Athenians delay doing anything that is difficult (ἅπαντ' ἀναβαλλομένους ἃ ἂν ᾖ δυσχερῆ) and consequently lose the opportunity to act (πάντων ὑστερεῖν τῶν ἔργων). The latter phrase is almost exactly the same as the one that he uses in section 32: ὑστεριοῦμεν γὰρ ἁπάντων.

**38.18**  ὡς οὐκ ἔδει contains a brief but pointed criticism of the audience. The phrase "as was not fitting" is a shortened way of saying, "You should not have allowed them to get to this point." οὐ μὴν ἀλλ' means "nevertheless, notwithstanding" (Smyth §2767). It is usually assumed that this is an elliptical phrase that requires something to be supplied from the context before ἀλλά, although it is sometimes difficult to say exactly what must be supplied. Here, for example, the full phrase could have been "not [false] to be sure (μήν) but perhaps not pleasant to hear." The phrase, which is used more often by D than most prose writers, is strong and "normally denotes that what is being said cannot be gainsaid, however strong the arguments to the contrary" (Denniston, GP 28).

**38.22**   ἑαυτούς is here the equivalent of the reflexive of the second person (Smyth §1230).

**39.1–2**   D indicates the stark choice by using two parallel phrases that have nine syllables each: οὐκ ἀκολουθεῖν τοῖς πράγμασιν/ἔμπροσθεν εἶναι τῶν πραγμάτων. The latter phrase means "to be in front of" in the sense of to control events as much as possible. The οὐκ must be construed with δεῖ rather than with the infinitive, which would take μή. There is no difference in meaning, however (cf. Smyth §§2693, 2714b). D ends the sentence with the same contrast, in reverse: ταῦτα πράττηται καὶ μὴ τὰ συμβάντα ἀναγκάζωνται διώκειν.

**39.3–5**   A comparison is a common way to amplify a passage. Much of the structure of the second half of the comparison must be supplied from the first: ὥσπερ τῶν στρατευμάτων ἀξιώσειέ τις ἂν τὸν στρατηγὸν ἡγεῖσθαι and οὕτω καὶ τῶν πραγμάτων (ἀξιώσειέ τις ἂν) τοὺς βουλευομένους (ἡγεῖσθαι). The comparison allows D to repeat the point made earlier (cf. §19) that generals should lead their troops: "just as anyone would demand that a general lead his armies, so also would anyone demand that the ones who give advice direct affairs."

E. **Fifth Topic: Athenian policy has been reactive rather than proactive, but this is no longer possible (§§40–41)**

40

**40.6**   The emphatic ὑμεῖς δέ, emphasized by being separated from the rest of the sentence by the apostrophe that follows, introduces a passage that examines how the Athenians measure up to the general considerations sketched out in the preceding sentence.

**40.6–9**   First, their advantages are enumerated. These are contrasted, however, with the manner in which they use them—or don't use them. Moving quickly through the catalogue of their assets, which are listed in asyndeton, D slows down when he comes to his main point, that the Athenians don't take advantage of these assets. The hyperbaton involved in separating τούτων from the dative with which it is construed (οὐδενί) creates suspense and thus calls attention to this part of the sentence. Moreover, the full expression τῆς τήμερον ἡμέρας and the strength that πώποτε gives to οὐδενί all slow the sentence down and thus emphasize the verb at the end.

**40.9** εἰς is here used to express purpose (LSJ, s.v., A.V.2): "for anything necessary."

**40.10–14** Having made his point, D reinforces it with the famous comparison of the Athenians to a barbarian boxer who reacts only when he has been hit but never takes measures to prevent a blow. This illustrates very well the last phrase in the preceding section: τὰ συμβάντα ἀναγκάζωνται διώκειν. This tendency to cap a section of argument with an image that sums it up is seen elsewhere in D (cf. *Phil.* §3.69; see Ronnet, 176–82, for a discussion of D's use of similes). Barbarian boxers, particularly if the barbarians referred to are Persians, may have been considered ineffective simply because they did not have athletic training, which the Greeks considered to be distinctively characteristic of themselves (cf. Plato, *Symp.* 182b). Michael Poliakoff points out that the two founding fathers of Greek boxing, Onomastus and Pythagoras, were Ionians, from an area often associated with effeminacy, and adds:

> But at the same time this refined Ionian heritage also demonstrates a major element of Greek boxing—the triumph of skill and intelligence over brute force. When Demosthenes chides the Athenians for fighting Macedon by relying on superior strength rather than strategy he maintains that they fight "as barbarians box—when one of them is hit he follows the punch, and if you hit him on the other side, there are his hands. He neither knows how nor cares to put up his guard or watch the opponent."[17]

In keeping with the satiric mode in this speech the implication is that Philip, a barbarian, fights like a Greek.

**40.10** οὐδὲν ... ἀπολείπετε: I would take οὐδέν as an adverbial accusative ("you fail in no way").

**40.12** ἔχω in the middle with a partitive genitive means to "cling to": "*claps his hand on* the place struck" (LSJ, s.v., C.1).

**40.13** προβάλλω in the middle means to "*hold before oneself* so as to protect" (LSJ, s.v., B.III.1).

In sections 38–40, D has made one basic point, that foreign policy should be proactive rather than reactive. He has made this point in several ways. Sections 38–39 deal with the idea generally and theoretically. The first half of section 40 looks at the particular example of the Athenians. In the second half of this section he makes his point by means of a simile.

---

[17] *Combat Sports in the Ancient World* (New York, 1987), 82. I am grateful to Professor Hugh Lee for pointing out this reference to me.

41

**41.14–16**   In this section, D applies the simile to the actual historical situation in Athens. The anaphora (ἂν ἐν Χερρονήσῳ, ἐὰν ἐν Πύλαις, ἐὰν ἄλλοθί που) and the parallelism (ἂν . . . ἐκεῖσε . . ., ἐὰν . . . ἐκεῖσε) emphasize the regularity with which the Athenians act like the boxer who cannot defend himself because he is always a step behind his opponent. Their expeditions are like his hands, going only to areas that have already been struck. To underline the similarity, D uses the same word to describe where they move (ἐκεῖσε, §40.12). Like the boxer, the Athenians do not know how to take defensive or precautionary measures. In order to highlight this idea, D uses very similar language to describe how the boxer fights (προβάλλεσθαι . . . οὔτ᾽ οἶδεν οὔτ᾽ ἐθέλει, §40.13–14) and how the Athenians conduct their foreign policy (πρὸ τῶν πραγμάτων προορᾶτε οὐδέν).

After ἂν ἄλλοθί που D breaks the pattern that he has set up. The hearer has been led to expect another example with ἐκεῖσε. Instead, he generalizes and sums up. A dash should be put after που. Breaking off a sentence this way normally reveals passion, in particular anger (Quint. 9.2.54), since the orator is so overwhelmed with emotion that he cannot pursue the logical structure that he has begun (Hermogenes, 357–58).

**41.16**   In addition to the comparison with the boxer, D also uses very vivid language to make his point. The verb συμπαραθέω, typical of the compounds that D employs when he wants to be vivid (cf. προσπεριβάλλεται, §10), indicates clearly how the Athenians act: they run (θέω) with Philip (συμ) alongside of him (παρα). The phrase ἄνω κάτω ("to and fro") reinforces the idea that the Athenians have no goal or purpose. The passive στρατηγεῖσθ᾽ ὑπ᾽ ἐκείνου is also quite striking, since an enemy is normally not one's στρατηγός. Inverted situations such as this, like the general who follows his soldiers (§24), help to create the portrait of a world where nothing is where it should be, the surprising reality that is so vividly contrasted in this speech with what one would expect the situation to be. Athenians acting like barbarians convey the same idea (Rowe SM).

**41.17–20**   D has presented in various ways the idea that Athenian foreign policy has been reactive and therefore ineffectual when dealing with someone like Philip. He restates this point in straightforward language, by way of summary, before moving on to a new idea in section 42. This summary statement signals to the audience that one part of the speech is finished and that they should be ready to receive a new argument, which is introduced, as is usual in this speech, without any other preparation.

42

F. Sixth Topic: Some god seems to be goading Philip on in the hope that his aggressions might arouse the Athenians from their torpor (§42)

**42.21–23**   As he nears the end of the speech, D begins to hark back to points developed earlier. In the first sentence of section 42 he recalls the idea seen in section 9 that Philip is guilty of hybris. Here he implies that the gods are leading him on, afflicting him with *ate*, because of the shame that they feel at what is happening, even if the Athenians do not. Earlier in the speech (§10), D had discussed the idea of shame as the factor that motivates free men to act; he had also developed the thesis (§12) that the divine forces in the universe look after the Athenians better than they look after themselves. He is using here an a fortiori argument: if the gods are concerned about the welfare of Athens, surely the Athenians should be. The arguments that I have mentioned were first introduced about a fifth of the way into the speech. They are here repeated about a fifth of the way from its end. D is reminding his audience of ideas that he developed earlier in the speech and signaling to them, by reverting to ideas already presented, that the speech is drawing to a close.

**42.23–4**   This passage is organized around a division that contrasts a hypothetical situation (εἰ γάρ), described in lines 23–2, with reality (νῦν δέ), which is described in lines 3–4. Each of the two parts of the sentence has the same general structure and contains harsh criticism of the audience, placed at the end of each half, for emphasis: ἐξ ὧν αἰσχύνην καὶ ἀνανδρίαν καὶ πάντα τὰ αἴσχιστα ὠφληκότες ἂν ἦμεν δημοσίᾳ and εἴπερ μὴ παντάπασιν ἀπεγνώκατε.

**42.1**   ἄν should be taken with ἀποχρῆν after δοκεῖ. The subject of δοκεῖ is the understood antecedent of the relative ὧν in the next clause: "[things] from which . . . seem to me would be satisfactory to some of you," or, as LSJ translates it (s.v. ἀποχράω, 2.c), "methinks *it would have satisfied* some of you."

**42.2**   αἴσχιστα: Ronnet points out that the use of substantived adjectives in the neuter is fairly common in D. She argues that if they refer to positive qualities, their "vagueness, moreover, allows [the orator] to wrap the thing evoked in a sort of mystery that enlarges it" ("imprécision permet d'ailleurs d'envelopper la chose évoquée d'une sorte de mystère qui l'agrandit," 23). τὰ σαθρά in section 44 (15) would be a good example. If, as in the passage above, such adjectives refer to negative qualities, they "frighten or repel more by their vagueness, which gives free rein to the imagination" ("effraient ou repoussent davantage par leur imprécision qui laisse le champ libre à l'imagination," 24). Ronnet adds: "Thus a grammatical construction can on occasion have an emotional effect" ("Ainsi un tour grammatical peut prendre à l'occasion une valeur affective," 24). And that is certainly the case with τὰ αἴσχιστα.

ὀφλισκάνω here means to "incur a charge of" (LSJ, s.v., II.2) or "to be convicted of" (Smyth §1378). The charge can be either in the genitive or the accusative (Smyth §1378). The use of the perfect in the contrary-to-fact condition indicates a situation that took place in the past but whose effect continues into the present (Smyth §1945). This is exactly the point that D wants to make. The adverb δημοσίᾳ is placed at the end of the sentence to emphasize that the way the Athenians have been acting involves the abandonment of Athenian national traditions and that this will bring shame to the whole city (see Kennedy).

**42.3–4**  The chiasmus in the phrase ἐπιχειρῶν ἀεί τινι καὶ τοῦ πλείονος ὀρεγόμενος makes it striking. Here D is arguing that Philip's hybris leaves the Athenians no choice of whether to act or not. This is exactly the point that he made in section 9. He even uses the same phraseology. The phrase ἔχων ἃ κατέστραπται, for example, appears in both passages. Nine sections from the end of the speech, therefore, he is making exactly the same point that he made nine sections into it.

G.  **Seventh Topic: D draws a contrast between the beginning of the war and how it has ended up and makes a call to action (§§43–44)**

### 43

D continues the critical tone seen at the end of section 42, modulating into the even harsher style of the next two sections. Here anger, frustration, and excitement account for the loose way in which his points are strung together.

**43.5**  θαυμάζω is simply a more polite way of saying "I wonder or am amazed *that*" (cf. LSJ, s.v. θαυμάζω, 6.a); as Davies notes there is "no doubt as to the fulfillment of the dependent clause" (73).

**43.6–9**  The strict parallelism here is striking. The idea expressed in the parallel construction is important, for it really sums up the source of the αἰσχύνη mentioned in the preceding section. Moreover, the neatness and simplicity of the antithesis underscore the totality of the reversal. At the end, the object Φίλιππον is set opposite the agent Φίλιππον. The intended recipient of the action has become its perpetrator. The thesis developed here is reminiscent of the discussion in sections 4–5, where D talks about how the position of Philip and Athens, vis-à-vis each other, has changed.

**43.9–10**  The directness of the phrasing in this sentence, putting the ὅτι clause at the beginning for emphasis, calling attention to it with γε, and the strong contrast in ἀλλὰ μήν all give this sentence an intensity that modulates into the much more excited tone of the rhetorical questions that follow (for the use of the particles ἀλλὰ μήν...γε, see Denniston GP, 119, 341–42). This section shows D's tendency in this speech to move quickly, and frequently, from one tone to another. Here he passes from a fairly calm statement in the first sentence of this section, stated in a long sentence that uses the sort of literary patterns that one associates with a lack of emotion,[18] to impatience in the second and anger in the third and fourth. The length of the first three sentences in this section, which become shorter and shorter, indicates the rising emotion. Blass says: "Swift turns and quick change in thought and tone . . . are generally more typical of Demosthenes than all other orators, and in that respect he imitates a skilled fencer" ("Rasche Drehungen und schneller Wechsel im Gedanken und im Ton . . . sind überhaupt dem Demosthenes vor allen andern Rednern eigen, indem er darin einem geschickten Fechter nachahmt," 186). These quick changes, however, which reveal the excitement of the orator, are particularly characteristic of this speech.

**43.11**   παρὰ τοῦ δεῖνος: D refers below (§45.22) to τὰς ἀπὸ τοῦ βήματος ἐλπίδας. Both phrases probably refer generally to politicians who mislead the people.

## 44

**44.12–14**   The emotional tone at the end of section 43 continues in the first three rhetorical questions of section 44. As Smyth notes, "the future with οὐ interrogative is used in questions in an imperative sense to express urgency, warning, or irony" (§1918). Such ἐρωτήματα are usually used by D in clusters of only three or four (Rowe UL, 196; Ronnet, 121). Here there are five. Longinus cites this passage as a good example of how an orator can use rhetorical questions to give a passage "vigour and tension" (18). Both Demetrius and Longinus note that the piling up of detail such as one finds in these short rhetorical questions is similar to striking an opponent with one blow after another (cf. Wooten A, 501). Demetrius describes such an approach as being "short and sharp, like a close exchange of blows" (274). Longinus says: "Here the orator does just the same as the aggressor, he belabours the minds of the jury with blow after blow" (20). Ronnet points out (116) that there is a greater percentage of rhetorical questions in this speech than in any other of D's public orations.

As he nears the end of the speech, D returns to motifs, here in an emotional context, that he had developed in a more logical fashion earlier: that citizens must fight along with mercenaries (μέρει γέ τινι στρατιωτῶν οἰκείων; cf. §24) and that the Athenians must take the offensive rather than always acting defensively (ἐπὶ τὴν ἐκείνου πλευσόμεθα; cf. §19).

[18] Cf. Hermogenes' discussion of the style that he calls Florescence (269–77) and my discussion of this style in the introduction to my translation (xiv). Demetrius also comments on how parallelism and antithesis can reveal a lack of emotion. He says, in commenting on an elaborate antithesis in the speech *On the Crown* (265): "The elaborate parallelism seems too artificial, and more like word play than honest anger" (250).

**44.12**   μέρει is a dative of military accompaniment, which sometimes uses but does not require a preposition (Smyth §1526).

**44.14–15**   ἤρετό τις: D puts himself in the position of a member of the Assembly and imagines what he must be thinking (cf. Bers, 214). Davies points out (73) that the aorist indicative is more "graphic" than the usual ἔποιτ' ἄν τις would have been. It is more "graphic," or dramatic, because it supposes that someone has actually asked the question. Dilts indicates this by putting it in quotation marks. D uses the indefinite pronoun to imagine what someone in the audience is thinking two other times in this speech: §§4.9 and 29.15. In each of these cases he uses a present indicative (οἴεται). Ronnet calls rhetorical questions "without a doubt the best connector among minds" ("sans doute le meilleur trait d'union entre les esprits," 121). Longinus notes, in reference to this passage: "People who are cross-questioned by others in the heat of the moment reply to the point forcibly and with utter candour; and in much the same way the figure of question and answer actually misleads the audience, by encouraging it to suppose that each carefully premeditated argument has been aroused in the mind and put into words on the spur of the moment" (18). Therefore, Longinus says, the use of this figure "counterfeits spontaneous emotion" and makes the passage "not only loftier but also more convincing."

**44.15–19**   In answering this question, D, somewhat unusually, puts the verb first. The predicate, however, is what Dik would term (cf. discussion at 5.18) the Topic of the sentence, what it is about; τὰ σαθρά ("unsound things," i.e., "weak points") is the Focus, the most important piece of new information that D wants to convey to his audience. The information in the rest of the main clause is predictable. The very positive tone of the main clause is contrasted with the hesitancy seen in the condition that is placed emphatically at the end: ἂν ἐπιχειρῶμεν. To highlight this clause D constructs the next sentence in a chiastic order to the one that precedes (main clause – condition / condition – main clause). This allows him to set the contrastive clause ἂν μέντοι καθώμεθα οἴκοι right next to the ἂν ἐπιχειρῶμεν. The clause ἂν μέντοι καθώμεθα οἴκοι harks back to the end of section 10: μέλλοντας ἡμᾶς καὶ καθημένους περιστοιχίζεται (sc. Φίλιππος). The phrase λοιδορουμένων ἀκούοντες καὶ αἰτιωμένων ἀλλήλους τῶν λεγόντων looks forward to the theme of the detrimental effect of internal bickering that will be developed in sections 46–49.

There is a strong contrast between the two conditional clauses. The same is true of the conclusions. If the Athenians act, the results will be certain. εὑρήσει, a simple future, stating subsequent action conceived of as a fact, is placed emphatically at the beginning of its clause. If they don't act, nothing necessary will happen. The latter thought is expressed as an emphatic future denial; it uses οὐ μή plus the subjunctive and repeats the οὐ in οὐδέποτ' and οὐδέν. Smyth (§2754) notes that this construction is rare in the orators. I am not sure that that is true. He also points out that it "marks strong personal interest on the part of the speaker." That probably is true. The hyperbaton involved in separating the οὐδέν from τῶν δεόντων, again an important motif in this speech (cf. §1.23–24), put at the end of the sentence, emphasizes the last two words.

**H. Eighth Topic: If citizens will participate in the war, the gods will be on Athens' side, but unpaid mercenaries will never be successful (§§45–46)**

## 45

In this section, D picks up ideas developed earlier but combines them in ways not done before, linking citizen participation in the army and the goodwill of the gods, empty measures with a lack of what is necessary, the ridicule by the enemies of Athens and the plundering of her allies. This shows D's ability to emphasize, by repetition, without being monotonous. The manner in which these ideas are combined with one another in ways not seen before in the speech indicates that they are all involved in an intricate nexus of causes and effects that have had a detrimental effect on Athenian foreign policy. It is important that, near the end of this speech, this nexus be brought before the eyes of the audience.

**45.19–21** The interjected οἶμαι creates delay and calls attention to the phrase μέρος τι τῆς πόλεως, and the interjected phrase κἂν μὴ πᾶσα, which is hardly necessary to the thought since that is implied in μέρος τι τῆς πόλεως, allows this important phrase to linger in the minds of the audience before D proceeds. The personification of fortune involved in συναγωνίζεται is striking; D uses this figure only very rarely (Ronnet, 145). The use of the neuter of the article in the singular to form an abstract expression (τὸ τῶν θεῶν εὐμενὲς [sc. ἐστιν] καὶ τὸ τῆς τύχης συναγωνίζεται) is poetic and rare in D. There are only four examples of such a usage in his public speeches, and three of them occur in the *First Philippic*, two of them in this passage. The other is in section 32: τὸ τῶν πνευμάτων ἀσφαλές [sc. ἐστιν]. Ronnet (25) points out that the fourth example, in the speech *On the Crown* (251), is quite different from the three in this speech, since there D uses the article with an adjective announcing an articular infinitive. Therefore, she argues that this should be classified separately and that the usage of the article with a genitive is found only in the *First Philippic*. Ronnet sees this usage as a "youthful figure" ("tournure de jeunesse," 24–25). All of these expressions, however, plus the neuter of the article in the plural in section 12, refer to the operation of the gods or of forces in the universe that are beyond human control. Abstract expression in Greek, much more so than in English, produces what Denniston calls "a degree of elevation" (GPS, 40). It is quite appropriate, therefore, to use such expressions in discussing operations of nature and the divine. Verbs are often omitted in such passages since, as

Hermogenes notes, "substantival words and nouns themselves make diction solemn" (249). Why D essentially abandoned this construction in later political speeches can only be guessed. In this speech he was experimenting with a new style (Pearson AD, 122–23) and was frequently pushing the limits of traditional Greek oratory. Perhaps he decided that it was too poetic for public discourse. This would be borne out by the less artificial style of later speeches (see appendix 2).

**45.19**   ὅποι . . . ἄν: This forms what is in effect the protasis in a present general condition (cf. Smyth §2545c).

**45.21–1**   In the ὅποι clause D reverts to ideas seen earlier in the speech, particularly the need to be realistic and to fund expeditions sufficiently (cf. §§19 and 43). The first clause in the conclusion (οὐδὲν ὑμῖν τῶν δεόντων γίγνεται) reiterates, in a somewhat less emphatic form, but using similar language, the idea at the end of the preceding section (οὐδέποτ' οὐδὲν ἡμῖν μὴ γένηται τῶν δεόντων).

**45.22**   Davies glosses κενόν as meaning "unsupported by any practical measures" and notes that D is intentionally echoing the phraseology in section 43 (τριήρεις κενάς), where the ships are "empty" in that they do not carry soldiers to fight the war because the Athenians have not provided funds for them.

**45.22**   βήματος: Citizens who addressed the Assembly when it met on the Pnyx did so from a raised platform.

**45.1**   ἐκπέμψητε: D switches to the more direct second person when he criticizes the audience.

**45.1–3**   The last two clauses in the sentence are highlighted, since they break the pattern set up earlier by ὅποι clause plus main clause. καταγελῶσιν picks up the idea in section 25 (γέλως) that the Athenians have become objects of ridicule, a clear attempt to shame the audience into action. The clause with which this sentence ends is particularly striking, partially because of the irony seen in the idea that Athenian allies die with fright at the thought of expeditions sent out from Athens to help them. D, however, has developed earlier the idea that Athenian allies suffer at the hands of Athenian mercenaries (cf. §24). What is really striking here is the phrase τῷ δέει τοὺς τοιούτους ἀποστόλους, in which a noun takes a direct object in the accusative; this is very unusual in Greek. The idea that the allies die (τεθνᾶσι) is also striking for its hyperbole. The scholion calls the expression καινοπρεπές and glosses it as μέχρι θανάτου τοῦ φοβοῦντος τοὺς τοιούτους ἀποστόλους ("fearing such expeditions up to death"; Dilts, 101).

46

This section sums up much of what D has already said about Athenian policy. The vagueness of that policy up to this time is conveyed by the indefinite nature of the thought in lines 3–5: the lack of specific referent in ἕνα ἄνδρα, the indefinite adverb ποτε, the imprecise ταῦθ', described by the equally vague πάντα ὅσα βούλεσθε, which is appended almost as an afterthought at the end of the sentence.[19] Its incoherence is reflected in the structure of lines 5–7, consisting of words and short phrases strung together with καί in no apparent sequence or organization, with two instances of hiatus. Its disjointed nature, which has been criticized so many times in this speech (cf. §12: ἀπηρτημένοι καὶ ταῖς παρασκευαῖς καὶ ταῖς γνώμαις), is also reflected in lines 9–10: ὑμεῖς δ' ἐξ ὧν ἂν ἀκούσητε ὅ τι ἂν τύχητε ψηφίζησθε. Of the eleven words in this clause, seven of them are monosyllables, creating a jerky, disjointed effect.

There is a climax in the tricolon in lines 7–10, marked clearly by the δέ that introduces the second and third clause. D moves from one individual to a group in Athens to the entire Athenian population, and the results of the actions of each individual or group become more and more damaging. This intensification of emotion leads naturally to the short indignant rhetorical question at the end.

**46.5**   φῆσαι sometimes means to "say yes" (LSJ, s.v., III), in other words, to agree to be able to do what one could not do.

**46.8**   ὑπὲρ ὧν: see comments at §5.20–21, "concerning (see comments on §1.5) what that one does"; ἄν: see comment at §45.19.

**46.9**   ῥᾳδίως: Best construed with the participle ψευδόμενοι. It is easy for people to lie to the Athenians about what the general does, since there are no Athenians in the army and thus no one in the Assembly who could give an eyewitness account (cf. §33). As usual, D continues to recur to ideas developed earlier.

**46.9–10**   ἐξ ὧν: see on §46.8; ὅ τι: sc. ψηφιζόμενοι; καί strengthens the interrogative (cf. Smyth §2884): "what on earth is one to expect?"

47

I. Ninth Topic: Citizens in the army must monitor the actions of the general (§47)

**47.11–15**   One of D's most fundamental points in this speech has been that the Athenians must be involved in their own affairs. Consequently, to reinforce that point near the end of the speech, the Athenians are emphasized by being referred

---

[19] The phrase ἕνα ἄνδρα may refer to Chares, who was notorious for promising what he could not deliver; cf. Tarbell, 68.

to three times at the beginning of the clause that answers the αἰτιολογία: ὑμεῖς, ὦ ἄνδρες Ἀθηναῖοι, τοὺς αὐτούς. The identification between τοὺς αὐτούς and the words that define them (στρατιώτας, μάρτυρας, δικαστάς), linked together by the homoioteleuton in –ας, reinforces the idea that the Athenians themselves must be participants in working out the salvation of their city. The repetition in ὑμᾶς τὰ ὑμέτερ' αὐτῶν is very emphatic, since αὐτῶν strengthens the reflexive (cf. Smyth §1200.2b). All told, the Athenians are referred to ten times in this sentence, and the participle παρόντας, near the end, sums up D's point.

The result clause develops the contrast between hearing and seeing to emphasize how important it is that the Athenians participate in the war: ὥστε μὴ ἀκούειν μόνον ... ἀλλὰ καὶ παρόντας ὁρᾶν. To emphasize the contrast, these two phrases have the same metrical configuration: ‾ ˘ | ‾ ˘ ‾ | ‾ ˘ ˘ ‾ (Donnet, 416).

**47.12**  ἀποδείκνυμι could mean to "appoint, assign" (LSJ, s.v., I.5) but probably means simply to "make" (LSJ, s.v., II.2).

**47.14**  εὔθυναι were the accounts that had to be given at Athens when a public official went out of office, "the public examination of the conduct of officials" (LSJ, s.v., II). A magistrate, as well as any other citizen who had performed a public function or supervised the spending of public monies, had to submit to an accounting (*euthynai*) at the end of his term of service, when he handed over to a board of ten inspectors (*logistai*) his accounts. The inspectors, who were assisted by ten advocates (*synegoroi*), had to carry out their inspection during the first thirty days of the year or within a month after a public official had completed his duties. The inspectors presided over a court of 501 before which the public officials were summoned. Presumably the advocates appeared as accusers, but any citizen could bring an accusation, even though a man's accounts had been passed by the inspectors. The jury voted only on those officials who had been charged and who had made their defense. The penalty for conviction was usually a fine. This was only the first phase of the *euthynai*. At the second, which took place at least three days after the accounts had been inspected, ten correctors (*euthynoi*), one from each tribe, assisted by twenty assessors (*paredroi*), sat at the Monument to the Eponymous Heroes, each before the image of the hero of his tribe, and received written charges, which could be brought by any citizen or metic, concerning any other offense that might have been committed by the public officials. If the corrector felt that the accusation had any validity, he passed it on to the proper officials who summoned a court to hear the charge. In court the accuser was the person who brought the charge. Any penalty could be assessed by the court. Most public officials must have quickly passed scrutiny; we know of only about fifteen charges that were brought against a named person (Hansen 222–24).

**47.16**  αἰσχύνης is a partitive genitive with τοῦθ': "the situation has come to this point of shame" (cf. ἀσελγείας in §9).

**47.16–17**    As Davies notes (75), we know of historical examples of such cases. D himself mentions Autocles in the speech *Against Aristocrates* (104). Aeschines discusses Callisthenes and Chares in the speech *On the False Embassy* (30, 71), and Diodorus Siculus names Leosthenes (15.95). As is the nature of satire and caricature, D here exaggerates, but he does not invent. The procedure used to impeach generals was called εἰσαγγελία. Any citizen could lodge a complaint in the Assembly, and the Assembly could vote to refer the charge to a court (Hansen, 212–18). From 432 to 355, as Hansen notes (217), we know the names of 143 generals, and thirty-five of them were impeached, in other words, about one-fifth: "Demosthenes' statement about the frequency of trials of generals is not so far from the truth after all" (Hansen, 217).

**47.15–20**    The next sentence, as often in this speech (cf. Rowe SM), contrasts the reasonable ideal, sketched out in lines 11–15, with the ludicrous reality. The result clause uses the figure κατὰ ἄρσιν καὶ θέσιν twice. D first states what the generals do (τῶν στρατηγῶν ἕκαστος δὶς καὶ τρὶς κρίνεται παρ' ὑμῖν περὶ θανάτου) and then describes what they do not do (πρὸς δὲ τοὺς ἐχθροὺς οὐδεὶς οὐδ' ἅπαξ αὐτῶν ἀγωνίσασθαι περὶ θανάτου τολμᾷ). Then, having just stated what they do not do, he restates in a more specific way what they do (ἀλλὰ τὸν τῶν ἀνδραποδιστῶν καὶ λωποδυτῶν θάνατον μᾶλλον αἱροῦνται τοῦ προσήκοντος). In addition to the general contrast between what the generals do and what they do not do, there are several specific antitheses in the result clause, and these contrasts allow D to develop more fully the discrepancy between what one would expect and what actually happens: τῶν στρατηγῶν ἕκαστος/οὐδεὶς ... αὐτῶν (reinforced by the chiastic arrangement of the words), δὶς καὶ τρίς and οὐδ' ἅπαξ, and παρ' ὑμῖν and πρὸς δὲ τοὺς ἐχθρούς, as well as between κρίνεται and ἀγωνίσασθαι. But what really calls attention to the ludicrous nature of the situation is the parallel phrase περὶ θανάτου, used the first time in a technical legal sense ("to be on trial for one's life") and the second time in a military sense ("to fight at the risk of one's life"). κρίνεται is normally followed simply by a genitive of the penalty, although with many verbs of judicial action περί plus the genitive is used (Smyth §1379). Here D uses the preposition to emphasize the contrast between κρίνεσθαι περὶ θανάτου and ἀγωνίσασθαι περὶ θανάτου.

**47.20–21**    D repeats the contrast between what is honorable and what is disreputable in the last two lines of this section. The passage takes the form of an isocolon (thirteen syllables in each clause) with strict antithesis. Moreover, the key words (ἀποθανεῖν, μαχόμενον, πολεμίοις) all have the same metrical configuration: ˘˘‾˘ (Donnet, 416). The structure, therefore, plus the general nature of the thought, turns this sentence into a *sententia* (Greek γνώμη), which is always an effective way to conclude an argument. In the next section of the speech, D will turn from the conduct of the generals to the conduct of politicians and the population in general.

Hansen notes that *kakourgoi* were an official class of criminal that "included kidnappers (of slaves), cutpurses, thieves, muggers, housebreakers, temple-robbers, pirates, adulterers, and certain classes of murderer" (190). D, however, is probably using the term here in a non-technical sense, simply to mean "malefactor," since Hansen also points out that *kakourgoi* could be put to death without a trial and the participle κριθέντ᾿ indicates that that would not be the case here.

κακούργου and στρατηγοῦ are genitives of characteristic, denoting "the person whose *nature, duty, custom*, etc., it is to do that set forth in an infinitive subject of the verb" (Smyth §1304). κριθέντ᾿ and μαχόμενον describe the understood subjects of the infinitive ἀποθανεῖν: "it is characteristic of a criminal that he die having been judged, of a general [that he die] fighting with the enemy."

## J. Tenth Topic: Rumor-mongers deceive the people and only make the situation worse; the Athenians must face facts (§§48–50)

## 48

Here, three sections from the end of the speech, D describes how the Athenians, in spite of all the resources at their disposal (cf. §40.7–8), do nothing but talk. In contrast to this, three sections into the speech, he had described how nobly and decisively their fathers and grandfathers had acted, against overwhelming odds, earlier in the century (§3.17–3).

This section picks up an idea expressed much more sarcastically in section 10: περιιόντες αὐτῶν πυνθάνεσθαι, 'λέγεταί τι καινόν;' Even the language is reminiscent of the earlier section: ἡμῶν δ᾿ οἱ μὲν περιόντες . . . φασὶ . . . λόγους πλάττοντες . . . περιερχόμεθα. The tone, however, is much less harsh, partially because of the straightforward narrative style used here as opposed to the very sarcastic imaginary dialogue used there. Moreover, here D seems to include himself in the criticism (ἡμῶν . . . ἕκαστος περιερχόμεθα); the earlier passage uses the second person plural (πράξετε, βούλεσθε, ὑμῖν). It is important here, near the end of the speech, for D not to alienate his audience with the sort of sarcasm that he had used earlier to evoke from them a strong response, and the best way to do that is to identify himself with them. Hermogenes discusses (256–57) other ways of toning down criticism.

The aimless nature of all this talk is brought out by the way in which D strings together, with no apparent overriding structure or end in sight, the clauses introduced by οἱ δέ. This is the λέξις κατεστραμμένη, the "strung together style," which Aristotle says (*Rhet.* 3.9.2) is unpleasant because it is so open-ended (cf. Denniston GPS, 60). There is a change of construction between οἱ δέ and λόγους in line 3. D does not continue the sequence of indirect statements but breaks off and sums up in λόγους πλάττοντες. Sandys indicates that in his edition by putting a dash after οἱ δέ. The prefix περι-, used twice in this sentence (περιόντες . . . περιερχόμεθα), each time with a verb indicating movement, once at the beginning of the sentence and again at the end, denotes circularity, activity that leads nowhere (cf. LSJ, s.v., F).

**48.22–3**  In other words, Philip was too busy elsewhere to be a threat to Athens. τὰς πολιτείας probably refers to the free states of Arcadia that were being supported by Thebes against their traditional enemy Sparta. The growing power of the Thebans in central Greece, since their defeat of the Spartans at Leuctra in 371, had frightened the Athenians and pushed them closer to Sparta. Thus, any prospect of humiliating Thebes or its allies probably would have been popular with many Athenians (Sealey, 129–30; D's speech *For the Megalopolitans* is an important source). The next clause probably refers to Philip's projected invasion of Persia. The Illyrians, to the north of Macedon, were always a threat to Philip (Sealey, 161–62).

πράττειν ... κατάλυσιν: Here πράττω means to "bring about" (LSJ, s.v., III.1): "to bring about the destruction of the Thebans in conjunction with the Spartans."

### 49

In this section D continues to hark back to earlier ideas. In the two parts of the sentence, each introduced by an oath (νὴ τοὺς θεούς, μὰ Δί'), a rare example of two oaths used in one sentence, there is a contrast that has been developed throughout the speech. Philip is associated with action (πεπραγμένων, πεπραγμένοις, πράττειν, ποιεῖν) and with planning and policy (προαιρεῖσθαι). The Athenians, or at least some of them, are associated with talking (λογοποιοῦντες) and lack of planning or foresight, with foolishness (ἀνοητοτάτους, ἀνοητότατοι). Although D here restricts the group to which he applies these latter attributes, so as not to offend his audience as a whole, he does not want them to forget the basic contrast that he has drawn throughout the speech between people who talk and people who act.

Ronnet points out (12) that μά is always used by D at the head of a negative sentence. She also notes that an oath is usually "tied to an intense effort at persuasion" ("lié à un effort intense de persuasion,"14). Blass remarks (176) that such oaths are rare in other orators but characteristic of D.

D here, as usual in his speeches, draws a sharp distinction between himself and other speakers: "His rhetoric, which is honest and aims solely at the best interests of the *polis*, is beneficial because it is based in reality; the rhetoric of opposing *rhêtores* is harmful because it obscures reality in an effort to please" (Yunis, 264).

**49.5–7**  D reintroduces the idea that Philip is guilty of hybris, seen earlier in section 3 in the first direct reference to Philip (τῇ νῦν ὕβρει τούτου) and explained in greater detail in section 9 (οἳ προελήλυθεν ἀσελγείας ἄνθρωπος... καὶ λόγους ὑπερηφάνους... λέγει, καὶ οὐχ οἷός ἐστιν ἔχων ἃ κατέστραπται μένειν ἐπὶ τούτων). Just as the criticism of the Athenians in the preceding section is milder than that made earlier in the speech, the criticism of Philip here is harsher. μεθύειν and ὀνειροπολεῖν are both strong, vivid verbs, whose metaphorical nature was noted by Athanasius in his prolegomena to Hermogenes' *On Issues* (H. Rabe, ed., *Prolegomenon Sylloge*, p. 178, line 10). The participle ἐπηρμένον, agreeing with ἐκεῖνον, also contains the idea of grasping for too much that is associated with being drunk and dreaming.

Moreover, D pairs with this third reference to Philip's hybris a reminder of what has provoked it (ἐρημίαν τῶν κωλυσόντων). This is an idea that he has been stressing since the outset of the speech (cf. §2, where he first discusses the fact that the Athenians have done nothing to protect their possessions: οὐδέν, ὦ ἄνδρες Ἀθηναῖοι, τῶν δεόντων ποιούντων ὑμῶν). Here, however, unlike earlier, the emphasis is on Philip's aggressions rather than Athenian indifference. In this whole section, there is only one phrase (ἐρημίαν τῶν κωλυσόντων) that is critical of the Athenian population as a whole, and even that is an indirect reference.

**49.6–7** The circumstantial participles are causal: "since he sees the absence of those who are going to prevent him (cf. Smyth §2050a for the use of the participle as a substantive) and has been excited (stirred up) by what he has done." ἐπηρμένον is the perfect passive participle from ἐπαίρω, printed in some editions without a subscript.

**49.9** νοητοτάτους must be a misprint for ἀνοητοτάτους. Otherwise, the sentence does not make any sense.

50

In sections 48 and 49, D discusses λόγοι, rumors that some Athenians spread about Philip's intentions. At the beginning of section 50 he turns to ἔργα, summing up much of what he has been arguing earlier in the speech. The scholion refers to the points made here as τὰ τελικὰ κεφάλαια (Dilts, 105), what Malcolm Heath calls the "standard topics used to evaluate a course of action" (*Hermogenes on Issues* [Oxford, 1995], 254; cf. Lausberg §3), here summing up what is unjust, inexpedient, inappropriate, and intolerable about Philip's actions. The transition is neatly effected by the chiastic contrast between ἀφέντες ταῦτ' and ἐκεῖνο εἰδῶμεν. The first demonstrative refers to what has preceded (cf. Smyth §1261); the second, to what follows (Smyth §1248).

**50.11–12** This part of the indirect statement deals with the present, the basic realities of the situation that faces the Athenians. To make the facts as clear as possible D expresses them in three very simple straightforward clauses: "Parataxis suggests straightforward, plain talk, reflected by lack of complexity in the syntax" (Gotoff, 171).

**50.12**   ἀποστερέω (to "*rob, despoil, defraud* one *of* a thing") can take either an accusative of the person and a genitive of the thing or, as here, a double accusative (LSJ. s.v., I.1).

**50.13–14**   In the next part of the indirect statement D discusses what has kept the Athenians from facing the hard facts that he has just outlined. This part of the indirect statement deals with the past (ἠλπίσαμεν). The style becomes fuller and more complex, reflecting the complicated situation that has existed in Athens in the past because of rumor-mongers and Athenian indifference. This part of the sentence is dominated by aspiration, producing a harsh effect. Of the eleven words in this clause seven either begin with or contain, or both, an aspirated vowel or consonant. Dionysius of Halicarnassus (*On Literary Composition*, 14) uses the adjective δασέα to describe aspirated sounds. The literal meaning of δασύς is "hairy, thick, rough."

**50.14**   εὕρηται: A participle such as πραχθέντα must be understood (cf. Smyth §§2113, 2135): "All things which we ever hoped that anyone would do on our behalf have been found [to have been done] against us."

ἐν αὐτοῖς ἡμῖν ἐστί clearly means "is in our power" or "under our control"; Davies translates the phrase "depends on us" (76).

**50.14–17**   This part of the indirect statement deals with the future (τὰ λοιπά). The style becomes straightforward and simple again (τὰ λοιπὰ ἐν αὐτοῖς ἡμῖν ἐστί). This is also true of the second and third clauses in this part of the indirect statement, although they contain subordination: κἂν μὴ νῦν ἐθέλωμεν ἐκεῖ πολεμεῖν αὐτῷ, ἐνθάδ᾽ ἴσως ἀναγκασθησόμεθα τοῦτο ποιεῖν. The protasis and the apodosis are stated without complication, and the antithesis in ἐκεῖ/ἐνθάδ᾽ and ἐθέλωμεν/ἀναγκασθησόμεθα gives the clauses a pattern that makes them very easy to follow. The past may be complicated, but the present and the future are very clear.

There is a crescendo in the various parts of this indirect statement, which deal with the present (11–12), the past (13–14), and the future (14–16). Ronnet argues (90) that in this apparently loosely constructed sentence, the clauses are arranged in a "gradation tragique." The main clause is forgotten, and the emphasis falls on the last clause in the sequence, ἐνθάδ᾽ ἴσως ἀναγκασθησόμεθα τοῦτο ποιεῖν.

D had begun this sentence with a condition (ἄν . . .) that is long and complex. Therefore, in order to be sure that his audience has not forgotten the basic structure, he repeats the condition.

**50.16–17**   The conclusion to this complex condition is very straightforward. D is making the point that although the situation may be complicated, what must be done to correct it is clear and simple: the Athenians must *do* their duty (τὰ δέοντ᾽) and give up idle *talk* (λόγων ματαίων). In order to make that point, he uses a suspenseful period, piling up subordination at the beginning of the sentence and putting the simple conclusion at the end (cf. discussion of §7).

**50.17–19**   D uses the same language to describe the situation and what must be done about it (φαῦλα, τὰ προσήκοντα ποιεῖν, προσέχειν τὸν νοῦν) that he had used in sections 2 and 3: οὐδ᾽ εἰ πάνυ φαύλως ἔχειν, ἃ προσῆκε πραττόντων, ἐκ τοῦ προσέχειν . . . τὸν νοῦν. Thus, the body of the speech begins and ends with a discussion of similar ideas, expressed in similar language, and these three ideas express three of the most important points made in the speech as a whole: the situation is bad; Athenians must do their duty; they must be attentive. The emphasis here, however, unlike earlier in the speech, is not on the present or the past, but, as in the clauses that make up the condition at the beginning of this section, on the future: ἄττα ποτ᾽ ἔσται.

### 51

### V. Epilogue: D has spoken bluntly in the best interests of the city; he hopes that it will not be to his own detriment (§51)

Kennedy points out that in the *Philippics* D reverted to the fifth-century practice of focusing on a single argument, particularly the argument from expediency, seen most clearly in the speeches in Thucydides. Athenians of the fourth century, however, mindful of the disasters that the amoral policies of the fifth had produced and under the influence of Isocrates and Plato, were more sensitive to morality in politics. Therefore, D identifies expediency with the preservation of Athenian national tradition. This allows him to preserve the vigor and directness of a unified argument, while at the same time avoiding the appearance of an amoral appeal to self-interest. Throughout this speech D has argued on the basis of what is in Athens' best interest, and he underlines that in the epilogue. The verb συμφέρει appears five times here, four times in the future tense. This fits well with the greater emphasis on the future seen at the end of the speech, noted in section 50. In fact, the last word in the speech is συνοίσειν.

**51.20–7**   The first sentence is very fully developed. It uses synonymity, not only in the phraseology within the clauses, but also in the general meaning of each clause. D is using elements of speech, particularly synonymity and balance, that make language impressive, figures, as Hermogenes says, "that call attention to their ornamental nature and show clearly that the style has been embellished" (299). In the second sentence (2–4) there are four examples of antithesis and parallelism, which also create fullness and emphasis.

In the contrastive clauses introduced by ἐπί in lines 4–7 we see the sort of unusual way of speaking that Dionysius (*On Dem.* 9) associates with Thucydides (cf. Smyth §1153b, N. 2): "in the midst of the things going to happen to me from these [acts] being unclear." In the second phrase he uses an articular infinitive (τῷ ... πεπεῖσθαι) on which depends an indirect statement (συνοίσειν ὑμῖν ... ταῦτα): "in the belief that these [proposals] will be beneficial to you if you carry them out."

Dionysius sees the grand style as being far removed from everyday speech (*On Dem.* 1). He gives as examples the style of Gorgias, which uses fullness, particularly balance and antithesis, and the style of Thucydides, which relies upon unusual means of expression (cf. Wooten DH, 576–77). D uses elements of both of these styles in this section, and the grand style that he thus creates calls attention to the solemnity of the occasion and the importance of the topic. It is an appropriate tone on which to end the speech.

**51.20**    πρὸς χάριν expresses purpose (LSJ, s.v. πρός, III.3.a): "with a view to giving pleasure."

**51.21**    πεπεισμένος ὤ: The original statement would have been a present general condition (e.g., "I do not speak if I have not been persuaded, i.e., do not think, that something is beneficial"). When this is thrown back into the past by εἱλόμην, we would expect the subjunctive to become an optative (Smyth §2599). The retention of the original mood is "vivid" (Smyth §2613). What that means here is probably that "it is intended to imply that the speaker's conviction still holds" (Davies, 76). ἃ γιγνώσκω ... πεπαρρησίασμαι recalls τοτ᾽ ἂν αὐτὸς ἐπειρώμην ἃ γιγνώσκω λέγειν from the first section of the speech. Here he claims to have done what he there merely promised to do.

**51.2–4**    D has spoken strongly, even harshly (see the introduction), and he hopes that this will not be detrimental to himself. A secondary tense of the optative with ἄν can be used to denote unreality or an unattainable wish (cf. Smyth §§1786–89). The phrases ἐβουλόμην ἄν and the added ἂν ἥδιον εἶχον, which bracket the expression of hope that the orator's advice will be as beneficial to him as it will be to his audience, would indicate that he is not certain that this will be the case. He uses this idea to evoke sympathy from the audience in the next sentence.

**51.3**    συνοῖσον is the verb in an indirect statement after εἰδέναι; the implied subject is ὑμῖν τὰ βέλτιστα ἀκούειν. What D probably fears here is a γραφὴ παρανόμων, a procedure "whereby the proposer of a decree in Assembly could subsequently be tried in court for having proposed a measure contrary to democratic principles and to Athens' laws" (Ober, 95). The procedure is first clearly attested in 415 but may have been instituted as early as 427. Conviction on the charge meant that the decree was void and the proposer was fined (Hansen, 205–12). Although the procedure was initially instituted to discourage decrees contrary to the laws, Hansen notes that "the notion of illegality was extended in the course of the fourth century from simple breach of some specific provision to breach of the (democratic) principle underlying the laws, and so to the mere accusation of undesirability" (206).

**51.7**  Having contrasted himself strongly with his audience in the preceding two sentences, and indeed in the speech as a whole, where he has cast himself in the role of a teacher, lecturing, in fact, often badgering his audience (cf. Jaeger, 134–35), D associates himself with them in the last sentence (πᾶσι), as he does in section 48, in a hopeful wish for the future: νικῴη δ᾽ ὅ τι πᾶσιν μέλλει συνοίσειν. This speech, which is often pessimistic and critical of his audience, ends on a note that is optimistic and inclusive, with a word of good omen, both for himself and for his audience.

Although much of this speech has been extremely emotional, the epilogue is very calm, as is usually the case in D and indeed in all of Greek oratory. Quintilian, in fact, who seems to think of epilogues primarily as emotional appeals, even says (10.1.107) that D did not use them. Usher notes that "a quiet ending seems to have been characteristic of most Greek oratory, with pathos for the most part to be found elsewhere" (117). I am not sure exactly how to explain this phenomenon. My guess would be that, although the orator may have made many appeals to the audience's emotions, a calm ending allows them to persuade themselves that he has appealed primarily to their reason. We all like to think of ourselves as reasonable people; this was particularly true of Athenians (cf. Ober, 157).

# Appendix 1: *Philippic* II

## HISTORICAL BACKGROUND: D, PHILIP, AND ATHENS FROM 351 TO 344

The *First Philippic* seems to have had no real impact on Athenian foreign policy. The next year, 351/50, D delivered the speech *On the Freedom of the Rhodians*. Like the speech *For the Megalopolitans*, it is an appeal to the people of Athens to broaden their base of power by accepting alliances with states seeking aid against greater powers. In this speech, D supports an appeal by the democratic party on Rhodes to aid them in freeing the island from the influence of Artemisia of Caria, whose husband Mausolus had brought the island under his hegemony after its revolt from the Athenian confederacy in 357 and had established an oligarchy on the island supported by a Carian garrison. D argues that Athenian help for the Rhodian democrats would be a signal for democratic parties in all the islands to rise up against oligarchies and, consequently, could be the beginning of a renewed Athenian confederacy. D also glances (§24) at Philip of Macedon, who, he feared, would come to the aid of states rejected by Athens, as he had done in the case of the Megalopolitans and Amodocus of Thrace, and thereby extend his influence in the Greek world.

In 349, Athens was offered a golden opportunity to resist Philip's extension of his power. Olynthus, the most powerful city in the north, appealed to Athens to make an alliance with it against Philip. In the three *Olynthiacs* D urged the Athenians to accept the alliance. They followed his advice, but (probably because of a lack of funds) sent out only small and ineffectual contingents to aid Olynthus. D realized the necessity for more war funds and in the *Third Olynthiac* broke completely with Eubulus, who had made his reputation as treasurer of the Theoric Fund, normally used only for grants to citizens so that they could attend the theater during major festivals, by proposing that the laws prohibiting the use of this fund for military purposes be repealed. This was not done, and in 348 Olynthus and all the towns of the Olynthian League fell to Philip.

D realized that Athens was too weak to go to war with Philip, and, when efforts to unify all of Greece against Macedonia failed, he supported a proposal by Philocrates that Athens should send ten ambassadors to Philip to negotiate a peace. D was one of the ambassadors, as was Aeschines, who was to become his most implacable political rival. The ambassadors hastened to Pella and pled Athens' case before Philip. D spoke last and, according to Aeschines (2.34–35), after stumbling through his proemium, broke down in the middle of his speech.

In April of 346, the terms were debated in Athens and agreed to. The same ten ambassadors were sent back to Pella to receive Philip's oath to abide by the peace. When they arrived, Philip was in Thrace subduing Cersobleptes, and the ambassadors waited for him at Pella for almost a month. This meant that whatever territory Philip had subdued during this period remained in his control, since the treaty was to be based on the status quo.

Philip stipulated in the peace agreement of 346 that Phocis and Halus, both Athenian allies, were to be excluded from the treaty, and before the ambassadors could reach Athens Philip had marched his army to Thermopylae with the obvious intent of settling the Sacred War that had been going on sporadically in central Greece between Thebes and Phocis since 353. Thebes had applied to Philip for help in 347. Soon after Philip took charge of the war, Phocis surrendered. The towns of Phocis were destroyed, a huge fine was imposed on the Phocians, and Philip was awarded their position on the Amphictyonic Council, which oversaw the sacred site of Delphi. The swiftness with which Philip had moved against Phocis so alarmed the Athenians that they began to make preparations for war in case Philip should invade Attica. He sent assurances, however, that he had no hostile intentions toward Athens, and D himself in the speech *On the Peace* urged the Athenians to recognize Philip's place on the Amphictyonic Council.

The years from 346 to 343 saw nominal peace between Athens and Philip. In 344, however, when Sparta began to threaten some of the smaller states of the Peloponnesus, they applied to Philip for help. Fearing Philip's influence in the Peloponnesus, D went to these same cities to urge them to appeal to Athens, not Philip. This was quite in keeping with his earlier policy, seen in the speech *For the Megalopolitans*, of gaining support of smaller states against larger ones. Philip protested these embassies to the Peloponnesus, and during a debate concerning his protests D delivered the *Second Philippic*.

### GENERAL APPROACH OF THE SPEECH

The *Second Philippic* differs from the first in four ways. First, it is more focused and more clearly organized, dealing with only three main ideas: that Philip is concerned only with improving his own position, that he cannot be trusted, and that those who were responsible for the Peace of Philocrates should be called to account. Each of the three discrete parts of the speech (II, III, and IV in my outline) is devoted to developing a single idea.

Second, the presentation is more measured than that of the earlier speech. *Philippic* I also focuses on a few ideas, but they recur throughout the speech, intertwined with one another, with very abrupt transitions from one idea to the next. There the orator, driven by his emotion, excitement, and anger, passes quickly from one idea to another.[1] In *Philippic* II, on the other hand, he lingers

---

[1] Cicero notes (*Orator* 98–99) that a speech that is overly emotional can convey the image of a speaker who is unstable.

upon each idea, develops it fully, making a much more overt use of ring composition, and then moves on to another thought.

Third, related to this calmer nature of the presentation, the language used in *Philippic* II is smoother and less choppy than that of the earlier speech. There are fewer examples of hyperbaton, fewer direct addresses to the audience, fewer examples, in short, of almost every configuration of language that makes the *First Philippic* seem at times so intense. In this speech, for example, the incidence of hyperbaton is 3.3 examples per page (30 examples in 9 pages of text) as compared with 6 examples per page in *Philippic* I. In this respect *Philippic* II is more like the speeches *For the Megalopolitans* and *On the Freedom of the Rhodians* than *Philippic* I. The same is true of other figures. In *Philippic* II the incidence of direct address to the audience is .77 per page of text (7 examples), as compared with 2.2 in *Philippic* I. There are 10 examples of the figure κατὰ ἄρσιν καὶ θέσιν in *Philippic* II, which gives an incidence of about 1 example per page as compared with about 2 per page in *Philippic* I. The overall average of rhetorical questions is about the same in both speeches (1.9 and 2), but this is mainly because there are so many rhetorical questions in part III of *Philippic* II, which is very emotional (see analysis below).

Fourth, in *Philippic* II D is less critical of his audience than he had been in the earlier speech and devotes a much larger proportion of the speech to attacking Philip. The proemium (§§1–5) and the third part of the body of the speech (§§26.6–32), which together comprise about half of it, are devoted primarily to discussion of the internal situation in Athens. Here D blames the audience for being unwilling to hear the truth, as he does in *Philippic* I, but his criticisms are less frequent and less extended than in the earlier speech and usually take the form of simple assertion rather than scornful caricature. And he does not take the stance of a superior who lectures and badgers his audience, since he assumes some of the blame for the dire situation himself. Moreover, particularly in those sections that deal primarily with Philip, D tries to coax the Athenians into living up to the standards of an earlier day rather than shaming them with reproach and outrage, as he does in *Philippic* I. In fact, in general D is less present in *Philippic* II than he had been in the earlier speech, where he is always telling the audience what they should do, how they should interpret information, what their values should be. He does a fair amount of this, to be sure, in the later speech, but here he is more willing to let the facts speak for themselves, to let the audience reach the right decision on their own, to keep his own emotion out of the presentation, and to focus on the problem more than on his reaction to it. The *First Philippic* focuses too much on the orator and his relationship to the audience. This speech, like the speeches *For the Megalopolitans* and *On the Freedom of the Rhodians*, and also like *Philippic* III, focuses more clearly on the situation under consideration.

The first and second parts of the body of the speech (§§6–28.5), making up about 55 percent of the whole, deal primarily with Philip. The first part (§§6–19) relies mainly on narration and logical argumentation to prove the thesis that

Philip always acts to his own advantage. The much shorter second part (§§20–28.5) is more emotional and attacks Philip in stronger language, foreshadowing the treatment of him in *Philippic* III.

All of the trends that I have outlined above will culminate in *Philippic* III, arguably the greatest deliberative speech from antiquity, but they will be much better integrated into a coherent whole than they are in *Philippic* II, which seems at times to be three separate speeches stitched together. I am not sure how to account for the differences between the later two speeches and the earlier one. D may have come to realize that a very intense, highly wrought speech such as *Philippic* I can be difficult to follow, that it makes too many demands on the audience. He may also have come to realize that criticizing the audience too harshly can be dangerous. But more than anything, I think, the change in approach probably reflects a change in D's political position in Athens. Yunis has noted that "Demosthenes' view of Philip began to gain ground in Athens in the late 340s as the peace eroded and Philip established his power in central Greece, thus closer to Athens" (259). Orators tend to resort to highly emotional speeches when they have a difficult case that is being argued before a hostile audience. That seems not to have been the situation in which D found himself when he delivered *Philippic* II and, even more so, *Philippic* III.[2]

### STRUCTURE OF THE SPEECH

I. Proemium and Partition: Speakers and citizens have not addressed the problems facing Athens, but D will (§§1–6).
II. First Topic: Philip always acts so as to improve his strategic position (§§7–19).
   A. Confirmation (§§7–12).
   B. Refutation (§§13–19).
     1. Philip did not favor the Thebans out of a sense of justice (§13).
     2. Philip was not forced to make concessions to the Thebans (§§14–16).
   C. Confirmation (§§17–19).
III. Second Topic: D quotes from a speech that he gave in the Peloponnesus to warn the Messenians to heed the example of Olynthus and Thessaly and not to trust Philip (§§20–28.5).
III. Third Topic: Those who advocated peace with Philip ought to be called to account (§§28.6–36).

---

[2] In discussing a passage in *Philippic* II (34.13–15) where criticism of the audience is cast in general terms, Sandys notes that this is similar to a passage in the *First Olynthiac* (16.8–11) where the criticism is expressed much more harshly and directly. He explains the change thus: "The same thought is now expressed in a milder form, possibly because the orator has in the meantime brought many of his hearers to a better mind" (Sandys 2, 140).

A. The peace treaty was based on deception and false promises (§§29–31.25).
B. D discusses why he is advising that the authors of the peace be called to account (§§31.25–36).
IV. Epilogue: D prays that what he fears may never come to pass (§37).

### ANALYSIS

We see in the proemium many of the tendencies outlined earlier. In *Philippic* I, D comes across as a hard man, harsh, angry, impatient, shrill at times, scornful of almost everyone else in Athens, particularly his audience and his political opponents, isolated in his firm belief that he is right and everyone else is wrong. He spends too much time discussing internal problems, particularly those Athenians who oppose him, and not enough on the threat posed by Philip. In this speech he is more conciliatory toward his internal opponents and his audience and gives more prominence to the external foe.

The proemium deals primarily with other politicians and the audience, but Philip is mentioned in the first sentence and his name appears in every section. D's only criticism of his political opponents is that the advice they give does not produce results, that they talk but do not make proposals that do anything about Philip's terrible behavior. He does not depict them as being stupid or deceptive, as he did in *Philippic* I (cf. §§48–49) and as he will do even more harshly in *Philippic* III (cf. §2). In fact, he goes on to place much of the blame for their ineffectiveness on the audience (§§3–4) and identifies himself with these other speakers (§3.14–15). He, like them, suffers from the unwillingness of the audience to take action and their tendency to hate speakers who tell them what they do not want to hear (cf. §3.15–16).

But D is also more conciliatory toward his audience. In contrast to the *First Philippic*, where he creates distance between himself and his audience and lectures them about their shortcomings, here he takes some of the responsibility for the situation in which Athens finds itself. He is, after all, one of the group referred to in ἡμεῖς οἱ παριόντες (3.14). D ingratiates himself with the audience in other ways. In lines 17–20, for example, when he makes the distinction between talking and acting, he does not portray the Athenian tendency to discuss rather than take action in a totally negative way, as he usually does in *Philippic* I: at least the audience has more of a sense of right and wrong than Philip and can thus discuss justice and appreciate discussions of it better than he can. In sections 4 and 5, moreover, D does not so much tell his audience what they should do as to lay out the options that they have. At the end of the proemium, rather than emphasizing the difference between speakers and audience, he stresses what they have in common (καὶ τοῖς λέγουσιν ἅπασι καὶ τοῖς ἀκούουσιν ὑμῖν), just as in section 3 he points out that both groups are hesitant to do what must be done.

Moreover, the tone of D's criticisms of the audience and of other speakers, like the substance, is much less harsh, much less emotional than in *Philippic* I. The scholion notes (Dilts, 1b) that sections 3–4 are logically organized, which is normally an indication of a speaker who is calm—unlike the angry, waspish speaker of *Philippic* I. The conclusion (συμπέρασμα) is fully presented in section 2; section 3 gives the confirmation of that conclusion (κατασκευὴ τῆς προτάσεως; Dilts, 4a) with elaboration (ἐπέκτασις; Dilts, 1b). Then, in section 4, D presents the situation that results (συμβαίνει) from the cause that he has described in section 3, that is, the same conclusion that he presents in section 2. In fact, the scholia characterize both section 2 and section 4 as a συμπέρασμα (Dilts, 1b, 8).

The style is also smoother than that of *Philippic* I. In the long sentence in section 3, for example, except for the extended accusative absolute in lines 12–13, which interrupts the development of the thought (and emphasizes the πάντες, which stresses the similarity between speakers and audience), there is none of the interruptive, embedded subordination that appears so frequently in *Philippic* I. Clauses that form complete thought units are tacked on to one another in a logical and seemingly spontaneous manner, which allows the thought to grow incrementally and naturally toward its conclusion.

The structure is also more tightly organized than in the earlier speech. The proemium as a whole, for example, is cast into a ring around the criticism of other speakers and audience in section 3:

A. The nature of public discourse in Athens: speakers (§1).
  B. The λόγοι of the Athenians and the ἔργα of Philip (§2).
    C. Criticism of speakers and audience (§3).
  B. The λόγοι of the Athenians and the ἔργα of Philip (§4).
A. The nature of public discourse in Athens: audience (§5).

Sections 1 and 2 are dominated by discussion of other speakers; sections 4 and 5 by discussion of the audience. Section 3, in the middle of the ring, discusses both, other speakers first and the audience second, and thus acts as a bridge connecting the previous discussion of other speakers with the discussion of the audience that follows.

In *Philippic* I, D begins the argumentation, somewhat abruptly, immediately after the proemium. Here he prepares the audience to receive his arguments. Section 6 functions as a partition in which D (a) indicates what his argument will be (lines 10–13) and (b) asks for the attention of the audience (lines 13–18). The whole section is another example of the control that D exerts over the long sentences in this speech, which are rarely broken up by the speaker's emotion, as so often happens in *Philippic* I. The section is comprised of one long and very complex sentence in which subordinate clauses surround the main verbs (θαυμάζω ... βούλομαι). The first (θαυμάζω) is preceded by the subordinate clauses construed with it, which makes the first half of the sentence look like a suspenseful period. This allows D to achieve surprise with the one-word main clause that follows the two complicated protases. The second half of the sentence, in which the subordinate clauses follow the main verb (βούλομαι), takes the form of an analytical period, whose main function is to create clarity. D thus achieves in this sentence the surprise of a suspenseful period and the clarity of one that is analytical. This sort of sentence is quite appropriate early in a speech. The complexity indicates the gravity of the situation, the surprise evokes interest, and the clarity informs.

The first major part of the speech (§§7–19) is very logically and clearly organized. As in the argumentation of a judicial speech, D first gives arguments that support his own conclusion (ἐχθρὸν ἡγοῦμαι Φίλιππον, §§7–12), then refutes the arguments of his opponents (§§13–16), and then returns to a confirmation of his own position (§§17–19). D introduces this part of the speech calmly, by repeating briefly the point made in the second half of the partition (ἐγὼ τοίνυν, ὦ ἄνδρες Ἀθηναῖοι, λογίζομαι).

Having argued in section 7 that Philip does only what is to his own advantage, in section 8 D very cleverly attributes to their enemy a conception of the Athenian national character that reflects well on Athens. The orator thus ingratiates himself with his audience, without appearing to be a flatterer, and holds out a "beckoning archetype" that he hopes will inspire them to take the course of action that he is recommending. In section 9, D amplifies the praise of the Athenians begun in section 8 by contrasting them with other Greeks, particularly the Thebans, just as earlier he had contrasted them with Philip.[3] Contrast is a common approach in passages of praise and blame (cf. Arist., *Rhet.* 1.9).

In section 10, he compares Philip's evaluation of the Athenians and of other Greeks, which allows him essentially to repeat, for emphasis, what he has said earlier. Much more space (five lines as opposed to one) is allotted to the Athenians, however. Moreover, the praise of the Athenians is stated in a very full and emphatic way, whereas the criticism of the Argives and Thebans is very brief. In fact, the praise of the Athenians, which is continued in section 11, is so extensive and precise and the comments about the Thebans and Argives so abbreviated and vague (ὡς ἑτέρως) that I would see section 10 as part of a frame that rings the negative description of other Greeks in section 9 with praise of the Athenians in sections 8 and 10–11, particularly since some of the language is very similar (cf. τῆς ἰδίας ἕνεκ᾽ ὠφελείας [§8.2–3] and μηδεμιᾶς χάριτος μηδ᾽ ὠφελείας [§10.16]).

In section 12, D concludes the first confirmation (οὖν twice) with the thesis with which he had begun it, that Philip favors Greeks other than the Athenians because it is in his interest to do so. The whole passage, therefore, forms a ring that could be diagrammed as follows:

---

[3] It would seem that at the time of the delivery of this speech D had not yet envisioned an alliance between Athens and Thebes against Philip; contrast his treatment of Thebes in *Philippic III* (§§23–25), which is less harsh.

A. Philip's motivations and intentions (§7).
  B. His evaluation of the Athenians (§8).
    C. His evaluation of other Greeks (§9).
  B. His evaluation of the Athenians (§§10–11).
A. Philip's motivations and intentions (§12).

By putting Philip at the beginning and the end of the frame, D focuses his attention on what is the greatest threat to Athens' well-being, not the Athenians themselves, but the external foe.

In lines 10–14, D continues the orderly and logical argument that is typical of this part of the speech. Having just stated why Philip chose to favor Greeks such as the Thebans, he then rejects, in three sentences introduced by οὐ (οὐδ' ... οὐδ'), other reasons that could explain Philip's action, coupling the affirmative and the negative in an extended κατὰ ἄρσιν καὶ θέσιν. This leads into the next major part of the speech, where the "process of excluding other explanations than that assigned by the orator" continues (Tarbell, 74). One of the ὑποσχέσεις (13) made, not by Philip but by his supporters in Athens, was the disruption of the power of Thebes (Sandys 2, 119), and this reference leads into the next part of the speech, which discusses Philip's treatment of the Thebans.

Section 13 refutes the thesis that Philip favored Thebes out of a sense of justice. In this section there is also an emphasis on logical argument and an attention to clarity of style. The scholion describes the section as an ἀντίθεσις ἐκ τοῦ δικαίου (Dilts, 18). D will deal with the objection expeditiously, since he does not consider it to have any validity; however, the fact that he treats it seriously rather than sarcastically, as he usually does with objections in the *First Philippic* (cf. §§10–11), indicates a heightened respect for the opinions of the audience, here represented by the imaginary τις whose objections the orator answers.

In order to prove that Philip cannot make a plea based on justice, in lines 19–21 D uses an argument from contraries (Lausberg §394), which sets side by side two inconsistent statements. The advantage of this type of argument is that the inconsistency between them is immediately perceptible to the audience.[4] D couples this argument with the one from the more and the less. Davies explains the contradictions involved and the degree of difference between them:

> Philip is now claiming liberty for the Messenians (over whom Sparta has exercised dominion for centuries); his justification can only be the principle that every distinct nationality ought to enjoy independence. But he acted contrary to this principle in the case of O. [Orchomenus] and C. [Coroneia] (though their independence had been maintained until after Leuctra, and they had therefore a much stronger case than the Messenians). (83)

---

[4] Cf. J. J. Bateman, "Some Aspects of Lysias' Argumentation," *Phoenix* 16 (1962): 161, 168.

The inconsistent actions are set forth in the parallel participles (κελεύων, παραδούς), with the example of the Messenians, the specific occasion of this speech, put at the head of the sentence in a prolepsis.

The last sentence in section 13 is another example of a passage that projects the image of a speaker who is very much in control of what he is saying. Hermogenes cites it twice (317, 375) as an example of a concise oratorical period that concentrates many thoughts into one sentence (τὸ κατὰ συστροφὴν σχῆμα). It is not only the fact that several ideas are expressed here that gives this sentence what Hermogenes calls (375) Force (Philip orders the Spartans to free Messene, he handed over Orchomenus and Coronea to the Thebans, he could not claim that these actions are consistent); the ideas are also interwoven in such a way that "the thought is not completed and does not come to a halt in each one, but all are encompassed into one periodic sentence" (Hermogenes, 316). The subject is separated from the verb by πῶς, which would normally come at the beginning of the sentence; the second participial phrase and the articular infinitive separate the interrogative from the verb. These interweavings create an impression of Rapidity, that many thoughts are being developed quickly (Hermogenes, 316).

D has rejected the argument that Philip favored the Thebans out of a sense of justice. In sections 14–16 he will argue that he was not compelled to favor them. Having rejected one of the bases on which public decisions are made (τὸ δίκαιον), he now, in an orderly way, rejects another (τὸ δυνατόν).[5] And he introduces each in the same way (ἀλλὰ νὴ Δία, Ἀλλ' ... νὴ Δία). Moreover, as he had done at the end of section 13, in lines 5–7 of section 15 D calls attention to the inconsistency of his opponents' position by using an argument from contraries, which is given emotional force by being cast in the form of a rhetorical question. Here, however, rather than interweaving the inconsistent actions into a compact period, as he had done in section 13, he sets them side by side in two independent parallel clauses (τοὺς μέν, οὓς δ').

The answer to the rhetorical questions in lines 5–7 is made clear by the short rhetorical question at the end of section 15 (καὶ τίς ἂν ταῦτα πιστεύσειεν;); however, in section 16 he answers it again in a calm and logical analysis of the problem. He first repeats in lines 7–10 his rejection of his opponent's argument in a rhetorical syllogism: "If either *a* [Philip had been compelled by the Thebans] or *b* [he were now abandoning them] were true, *c* [that he is opposing the enemies of the Thebans] would not be true; but *c* is true; therefore, neither *a* nor *b* is true" (Tarbell, 75). If the major premise in a syllogism takes the form of a hypothesis (e.g., "If Philip had been compelled by the Thebans, he would now be helping their enemies") and the minor premise denies the consequence (e.g., "Philip is not helping their enemies"), the conclusion will deny the antecedent (e.g., "Philip was not compelled by the Thebans"). The repetition of οὐ and ἂν underscores the unreality of the argument.

---

[5] For a discussion of the τελικὰ κεφάλαια, see Lausberg §375.

In lines 10–13. D gives the positive, the real explanation, of what he has just expressed negatively, the rejected reason (ἐγὼ μὲν ... ἀλλ'). This leads into the next major part of the speech (II.C), where D will argue that Philip courts states like Thebes as a means of bolstering his power against Athens. He thus returns to ideas discussed at the beginning of this first major part of the speech (II.A) and thereby frames the whole argument about Philip's intentions.

Another indication of the careful construction of the argument in this speech is that in lines 13–16 D picks up the idea that he has just rejected above and argues that Philip's opposition to *Athens*, unlike his support of Thebes, *has* in a sense (τρόπον τιν') been forced on him (ἐξ ἀνάγκης). Athens is the only state standing in the way of his ambition, and the Athenians, therefore, of necessity, must be his enemies. He has thus been compelled to act as he does, but not in the way described by those espousing the excuse that he was compelled (ἐβιάσθη) in section 14 (22).

Maintaining the calm, logical tone of section 16, D will here present the basic facts of the matter in the stark language that is appropriate to logical argument and narration (cf. Quint. 12.10.59). The simple clauses in lines 13–16, consisting of little more than subjects and verbs, convey the impression that these are obvious truths that should be apparent to everyone and that need no shaping or comment by the orator, and the lack of connectives among the sentences indicates that the logical connection among them is so clear that it does not need to be elaborated. The only shaping in these lines is the mild hyperbaton in μόνους ὑπείληφεν ὑμᾶς, which highlights both the adjective and the pronoun, especially the latter, with, I would imagine, a gesture, which may have been preceded by some delay ("namely, you!").

In section 18, D returns to the technique that he had used in section 8, to praise his audience by attributing to Philip thoughts that reflect well on them, in the hope that they will rise to the "beckoning archetype" that he projects. The two sections, in fact, are introduced in a similar way (εἶδε τοῦτ' ὀρθῶς, ἀμφότερα οὖν οἶδεν). D casts the thought in such a way that the consequence of being intelligent must be to hate Philip: "The implication [of the adverb δικαίως] is that any other feeling toward Philip would be a sign of imbecility" (Tarbell, 75). The conclusion of the second main clause is that intelligent people inflict harm on their enemies. The whole sentence could be cast as an enthymeme: intelligent people inflict harm on their enemies; you are intelligent; therefore, you should inflict harm on Philip.

In section 19, D explains the consequences (διὰ ταῦτα) of Philip's realization that the Athenians hate him and are awaiting an opportunity to inflict harm on him if he does not strike first. In discussing why Philip courts allies such as the Thebans, D returns to ideas that he developed in section 12 (cf. ἰδίᾳ τὸ λυσιτελοῦν ἀγαπήσοντας, §12, and διὰ μὲν πλεονεξίαν τὰ παρόντα ἀγαπήσειν, §19) and thereby frames the refutation (II.B) and marks it off from the rest of the speech. The end of the first sentence (διὰ δὲ σκαιότητα τρόπων τῶν μετὰ ταῦτ' οὐδὲν προόψεσθαι) leads into the next major part of the speech (III): Philip thought that his allies were too stupid to understand what he was doing; however (καίτοι), even people with moderate intelligence can understand Philip's intentions, which is why D went on the embassy to the Peloponnesus in 344.

In lines 4–7, D uses an a fortiori argument, an argument based on the common topic of degree that is quite appropriate in this part of the speech, where D is so often drawing a contrast between the Athenians and other Greeks: if even those of moderate intelligence (σωφρονοῦσί γε καὶ μετρίως) can see what Philip is doing, those who are wise (εὖ φρονεῖν ὑμᾶς) ought to be able to understand his intentions easily. Consequently D argues that it is better simply to quote what he said to the Messenians and Argives: if his words could produce the desired effect even among the less intelligent (cf. §26), they should certainly have the same effect on the more intelligent.

Sections 20–25 are an apostrophe in the larger sense of the term, a turning away from the audience at hand to address a second one. Lausberg observes that an apostrophe has "an emotive effect on the normal audience, since it is an expression, on the part of the speaker, of a pathos which cannot be kept within the normal channels between speaker and audience" (§762). In this speech, D has envisioned the Athenians as intelligent people (εὖ φρονεῖν) and has appealed to them mainly by means of calm, logical arguments, which have thus become here the "normal channels between speaker and audience." The next part of the speech, however, in which D quotes from a speech delivered to people to whom he had to make an emotional appeal, since they were not intelligent enough to be susceptible to rational arguments (διὰ . . . σκαιότητα τρόπων), will be more emotional than what has preceded. D, therefore, can appeal to the present audience's emotions but still maintain the view of them— and allow them to maintain a view of themselves—as people who are mainly influenced by reason and who are thus different from other Greeks.

The change in tone is indicated clearly in section 20 by the use of two emotional ἐρωτήματα, coupled with a noun of direct address. D will use seven more such questions in this short reported speech. Earlier, in the part of the speech addressed directly to the Athenians, D has used only two in nineteen sections (§§13 and 15; the questions in §7 are much less emotional αἰτιολογίαι) and has employed a direct address to the audience only five times (§§1, 3, 6, 7, and 9), mainly in the proemium before he begins the argument.

It is not only the rhetorical questions, and the content, which reduces the issue to a conflict between freedom and slavery, that convey emotion in this short reported speech. Section 24 contains a very emotional priamel that focuses on ἕν and culminates in ἀπιστία. W. H. Race defines a priamel as:

a poetic/rhetorical form which consists, basically, of two parts: "foil" and "climax." The function of the foil is to introduce and highlight the climactic term by enumerating or summarizing a number of "other" examples, subjects, times, places, or instances, which then yield (with varying degrees of contrast or analogy) to the particular point of interest or importance.[6]

Race also notes that comparisons can be used to arouse emotion: "What would otherwise be a bare statement of fact or opinion becomes vivid, when measured against specific examples. The element of πάθος—like that of proof—may be present in greater or lesser degree, but when it is present...the effect is striking" (19).

Emotion is certainly present in this passage, as well as at the end of the section. As Quintilian notes (9.3.30) in citing a famous sentence from Cicero's *First Catilinarian* (§1), anaphora at the beginning of successive short clauses (ἐπαναφορὰ κατὰ κῶλον) is particularly insistent and conveys a sense of urgency (*acriter et instanter incipiunt*), and this sense of urgency in lines 10–11 is reinforced by the fact that the two imperatives and the conditional clause, all of which are short, have the same meaning (cf. Hermogenes, *On Invention* 125).

Above (9), D had reduced the attitude that free states should have toward monarchies to a single word, introduced by a simple question. He uses the same approach in line 11 by presenting the basic goal of foreign policy as being a quest for freedom. The γνώμη that ends the argument (13–14) is typical of the sententious tone of much of this reported speech, which, as is appropriate before an unsophisticated audience, tends to reduce complex situations to simple, easily understood eternal verities (cf. §24 and Arist., *Rhet.* 2.21.15). The γνώμη here also forms the major premise of an easily understood syllogism: kings are enemies of freedom; Philip is a king; therefore, he is an enemy of freedom. The final sentence draws the conclusion to be derived from the thesis proven above, again presented as a question. The four questions in this section give it an insistent, urgent tone, which is typical of this reported speech.

Section 28 is transitional: περὶ μὲν δὴ τῶν looks backward; ἃ δέ, forward. The first sentence (3–4) concludes part III: unless the Athenians want to act as foolishly as Messenians and other Peloponnesians, they will have to deliberate about what exactly must be done to oppose Philip (although this cannot be done in the presence of foreign ambassadors, possibly even those from Philip who had come to protest the Athenian embassies to the Peloponnesus). ἂν σωφρονῆτε should be construed closely with βουλεύεσθε and refers to the depiction earlier in the speech (cf. §18) of the Athenians as wise people, thus unlike Peloponnesians.

The second sentence (4–5) introduces a draft of a reply to the ambassadors of Philip and possibly also to those from Messene and Argos, who had come to Athens to protest Athenian support of Sparta. Although some have argued that the draft of this reply would have been read at the end of the speech (cf. Sandys 2, 134; Davies, 89), it seems much more probable that it was read now (see below), and some editors, consequently, have inserted here, although without manuscript authority, ΑΠΟΚΡΙΣΙΣ.

---

[6] *The Classical Priamel from Homer to Boethius* (Leiden, 1982), ix.

μέν οὖν in line 6 of section 28, which, as often at the beginning of an argument, is not correlated with a δέ (Tarbell, 77), looks backward and forward, "Retrospective and transitional οὖν with prospective μέν" (Denniston GP, 470). What the μέν looks forward to is the argument in the next part of the speech (IV). What the οὖν looks back to is less certain. Davies describes this as a "passage not very closely connected with the preceding part of the speech" (89). If, however, the end of the proposed reply to Philip's ambassadors, which D had probably just read, had contained a complaint that Philip had not fulfilled the promises that had been made and that his supporters in Athens, consequently, had deceived the people at the time of the conclusion of the peace, this passage would logically follow. The apostrophe, the first since section 9, and the suspense created by separating the infinitive at the end of the sentence from the impersonal expression at the beginning with which it is construed calls attention to the intervening idea that certain Athenian politicians were the instruments of Philip's deception and that they should be punished as the first step toward revoking the peace, which will be the topic of the next part of the speech.

In this part, D reverts to the more measured, less emotional style that he used in part II, relying for the most part on periodic sentences, which are often quite long, rather than emotional figures of speech such as ἐρωτήματα that he uses so extensively in part III. He does not completely abandon, however, the emotional tone of part III. For example, in line 12 of section 29 D's emotion leads him to create one of the most violent hyperbata in all his speeches. The τούς is separated by twenty–nine words from the participle (λέγοντας) with which it is construed. Even within the interrupting sequence D creates delay and suspense: the subject of the ὅτε clause (ἐγώ) is separated from the verbs with which it is construed by a genitive absolute describing the general situation (γεγονυίας ἤδη τῆς εἰρήνης), a participial phrase indicating time (ἥκων), within which the noun πρεσβείας is separated from the adjective with which it is construed (ὑμετέρας) and described fully (τῆς ἐπὶ τοὺς ὅρκους) before the sentence continues, and another participial phrase that reveals D's motivation (αἰσθόμενος). All of this suspense arouses the attention of the audience, as they look for the participle or noun that completes τούς, and this attention is thus focused on D's actions, which are indicated, in polysyndeton, in a triplet composed of three verbs in the imperfect tense to signify repeated action: προὔλεγον καὶ διεμαρτυρόμην καὶ οὐκ εἴων. The hyperbaton also creates an apt word picture: D tried to forestall the attempts of pro–Macedonian politicians to deceive the people just as these clauses and phrases separate τούς, the men, from λέγοντας, what they did. Even this violent hyperbaton, however, does not disrupt the sentence to the point of creating a lack of clarity, since within the interrupting clause events and descriptions are arranged in a logical, and chronological, order.

Another example of a long period whose structure is influenced by the emotional state of the speaker is found later in the speech. Section 35 is made up of a long periodic sentence that begins with a subordinate clause composed of three short units (15–16), followed by a main clause that is also quite straightforward (16–17), on which depends a very long and somewhat rambling indirect question that grows and swells through five levels of subordination. Ronnet notes (96) that this is the highest level of subordination that one sees in D. She outlines (97) the indirect question thus:

(1) τίς ὁ ... πείσας ... Πύλας προέσθαι

    (2) ὧν καταστὰς ... κύριος ... γέγονεν, καὶ πεποίηχ᾽

        (3) εἶναι τὴν βουλὴν ... ὑπὲρ ... τοῦ πολέμου

            (4) ὃς λυπήσει

                (5) ἐπειδὰν παρῇ.

Ronnet criticizes (96) the second half of the sentence for lacking organization ("son harmonie d'ensemble"). In this passage, D is attacking Aeschines, his most bitter political rival, whose prosecution the next year for malfeasance on the embassy to Philip in 346 he is now preparing, and, as his emotion and anger rise, as he piles one charge on top of another, he begins to lose control of the direction of his sentence. The last part of this sentence, therefore, may very well be lacking "son harmonie d'ensemble," but it is lacking it for a very good reason. Even here, however, the language is more natural than what one often finds in *Philippic* I. There is no interruptive subordination, and each clause logically and smoothly grows out of the one that precedes.

The epilogue (§35), as is usually the case in D, is very simple. It has three functions here: to signal to the audience that the speech is over (νῦν ἱκανῶς εἴρηται), to express a fervent wish that what D has predicted will never happen (μὴ γένοιτο, ὦ πάντες θεοί), and to portray D as a man who cares more about the welfare of the city than getting revenge on its (and his) enemies (οὐδένα γὰρ βουλοίμην). It is indicative of the importance of the third part of the body of the speech (IV) that this conclusion is only to that segment, not to the speech as a whole, the first three parts of which are a prelude to part IV. ταῦτ᾽ clearly refers to what has immediately preceded, and the infinitive used absolutely (ὡς μὲν ὑπομνῆσαι, "for a reminder to you"; Davies, 93) harks back to ἐπαναμνῆσαι in section 35 (17). ἐξετασθείη ("as to any way in which my words might be put to the strongest test," i.e., by Philip's invasion of Attica; Sandys 2, 142) clearly refers to the invasion envisioned in section 36. The assertion that D is not vindictive and is more interested in the welfare of Athens than in getting revenge on enemies, highlighted by the repetition of the negative (οὐδένα ... οὐδ᾽), the doublet (τοῦ πάντων κινδύνου καὶ τῆς ζημίας), and the hiatus and emphatic form of the pronoun in ἔγωγε ἄν, harks back to a similar assertion in section 32 (28–1). δίκην ὑποσχεῖν, coupled with ζημίας, is a forensic phrase (cf. Sandys 2, 143) that foreshadows the prosecution of Aeschines the following year (cf. §28.6–8).

# Appendix 2: *Philippic* III

## HISTORICAL BACKGROUND: D, PHILIP, AND ATHENS FROM 344 TO 341

There was evidently a revival of anti-Macedonian feeling in Athens around 344. Soon after the *Second Philippic* Hyperides, a radical democrat, indicted Philocrates, who had proposed the peace in 346, for corruption and for having deceived the Athenian people. Philocrates fled before the trial and was condemned to death in absentia. Moreover, the Athenians proposed amending the peace they had made to read that Philip and Athens would control "what was their own" rather than "what they possessed" at the time of the treaty. These terms were rejected by Philip.

It was also at this time that D renewed the charges of corruption and treason he had made against Aeschines three years earlier concerning his conduct on the embassy to Philip in 346. It was at Aeschines' trial that D delivered the speech *On the False Embassy*. Aeschines was acquitted, but it is indicative of the growing anti-Macedonian sentiment in Athens at this time that he was acquitted by only 30 votes out of 1501, in spite of the fact that D did not have a very good case. After this trial Philip must have realized that reconciliation with Athens, which he probably truly desired, was impossible, and he began to stir up trouble for Athens throughout the Greek world. This activity played right into D's hands, since he had always viewed the Peace of Philocrates as nothing more than a breathing space in which Athens could prepare for the conflict with Macedonia.

To ensure control of the grain routes, Athens had sent colonists to settle in the Thracian Chersonesus. These settlers had come into conflict with the city of Cardia, which was allied with Philip. The Athenians sent out a military force, led by Diopeithes, to support their colonists, and Philip sent a garrison to Cardia. To maintain his army, Diopeithes attacked shipping in the north Aegean and made raids into parts of Thrace that Philip had incorporated into his kingdom. In 341 Philip sent a strong letter of protest to Athens. It was on this occasion that D delivered the *Third Philippic*. In this speech he depicts Philip as a threat, not only to Athens, but to all of Greece.

## GENERAL APPROACH OF THE SPEECH

The *Second Philippic* is quite different from the one that preceded it and the one that followed. It is shorter, much less complex, and more narrowly focused on a specific historical situation. *Philippic* III, however, is similar to the *First Philippic*. They both deal, in broad, general terms, with the relationship between Athens and Philip and use many of the same arguments and approaches. There are significant differences in the *Third Philippic*, however, as will be noted in the analysis. As in the *Second Philippic*, there is a broader and less abrupt development of the argument, a smoother, less brittle and less excited style,[1] and a more extensive and more overt use of ring composition, all of which contribute to the clarity of the speech. There is in *Philippic* I an undercurrent of emotion that runs throughout, and it frequently erupts into real torrents of strong passion. In *Philippic* II the emotion is relegated to one part of the speech. *Philippic* III, like *Philippic* II, is generally calm, logical, and analytical; however, there are emotional passages, generally directed at Philip, sprinkled throughout. Much of the speech, moreover, is suffused, not with the stronger emotions such as anger and fear, but with weaker emotions such as pride and patriotism, emotions that do not inflame but inspire. The major differences between *Philippics* I and III, however, are D's handling of the audience and his treatment of Philip. In these respects, as in the modulation of emotion, it is also more like *Philippic* II.

The *First Philippic* deals primarily with the Athenians. Much of it is critical, and much of that criticism is quite harsh. In *Philippic* III only about 25 percent of the speech (twenty sections out of seventy-six) is devoted to criticism of the Athenians, and most of this criticism is mild or oblique and even encouraging, written often in a florescent style. About a third of the speech, on the other hand, (twenty-six sections) consists of an attack on Philip, and D's criticisms of Philip are often developed in a harsh style.

In the *First Philippic* D does not mention Philip until the end of section 3. In *Philippic* III he makes it clear in the very first sentence what the topic of this speech will be: ... Φίλιππος ... οὐ μόνον ὑμᾶς, ἀλλὰ καὶ τοὺς ἄλλους ἀδικεῖ. He maintains this critical focus on Philip throughout the speech. Hermogenes cites (260) a passage from this speech (§31) as an example of Vehemence (σφοδρότης), the style to be used for the harshest type of criticism in the Hermogenic system, directed against people for whom the speaker feels contempt and whom the audience is delighted to hear criticized. The reproach, consequently, is made very openly, "almost like slanders" (261), with no attempt to tone down its severity:

> ... ὑπὲρ Φιλίππου ... οὐ μόνον οὐχ Ἕλληνος ὄντος οὐδὲ προσήκοντος
> οὐδὲν τοῖς Ἕλλησιν, ἀλλ᾽ οὐδὲ βαρβάρου ἐντεῦθεν ὅθεν καλὸν εἰπεῖν, ἀλλ᾽

---

[1] I find the following incidences per page of text, as compared with those found in *Philippic* I, given in parentheses: hyperbaton, 4.2 (6.0); rhetorical questions, most of which are clustered in sections dealing with Philip, 1.9 (2.0); apostrophes, .5 (2.2); κατὰ ἄρσιν καὶ θέσιν, 1.3 (1.9).

ὀλέθρου Μακεδόνος, ὅθεν οὐδ' ἀνδράποδον σπουδαῖον οὐδὲν ἦν πρότερον πρίασθαι. (§31)

That D consistently uses this style to describe Philip indicates how successfully he had won the Athenians over to his own point of view.

D opens the argument of the *First Philippic* with the paradox that what is most troubling about Athenian policy from the past is most encouraging with regard to the future: ὃ γάρ ἐστι χείριστον αὐτῶν ἐκ τοῦ παρεληλυθότος χρόνου, τοῦτο πρὸς τὰ μέλλοντα βέλτιστον ὑπάρχει (§2). He then devotes the next two sections of the speech to a discussion of Athenian unwillingness to take necessary action: ... οὐδέν, ὦ ἄνδρες Ἀθηναῖοι, τῶν δεόντων ποιούντων ὑμῶν κακῶς τὰ πράγματα ἔχει (§2). He uses a similar paradox in *Philippic III*; however, it does not come until the beginning of section 5, after a lengthy discussion (§2) in which D places most of the blame for internal problems in Athens on the leaders of the people, not the people themselves: τὸ χείριστον ἐν τοῖς παρεληλυθόσι, τοῦτο πρὸς τὰ μέλλοντα βέλτιστον ὑπάρχει. The answer to the riddle is the same as in the earlier speech: ὅτι ... οὔτε μικρὸν οὔτε μέγα οὐδὲν τῶν δεόντων ποιούντων ὑμῶν κακῶς τὰ πράγματ' ἔχει. Here, however, rather than discussing this problem at length, D expresses it in a brief and pointed sentence that is more encouraging than critical: νῦν δὲ τῆς ῥαθυμίας τῆς ὑμετέρας καὶ τῆς ἀμελίας κεκράτηκε Φίλιππος, τῆς πόλεως δ' οὐ κεκράτηκεν· οὐδ' ἥττησθ' ὑμεῖς, ἀλλ' οὐδὲ κεκίνησθε. Both the brevity of the expression and the parallelism and assonance tend to tone down the criticism. After this mild reproach of his audience, D returns in section 6 to a criticism of those few individuals (ἔνιοι) who tolerate Athenian politicians who blame their political opponents for the war. Unlike the criticism in the *First Philippic*, this is sharply focused on a small group rather than being directed at the audience in general (cf. §2). It is written in a florescent style, with long clauses and much subordination. There are no elements characteristic of Asperity, such as short choppy clauses, rhetorical questions, and exclamations.

The contrast between how D deals with Philip and with his audience can be seen very clearly in sections 26–29. At the beginning of section 26, in discussing Philip's transgressions against Greece and the harm that he has done, D uses a double paraleipsis (ἐῶ ... σιωπῶ), which calls attention to the criticism of Philip, especially since he uses polysyndeton in the first instance to emphasize all the cities that Philip has destroyed so utterly that one could not even say whether they had ever been inhabited (Ὄλυνθον μὲν δὴ καὶ Μεθώνην καὶ Ἀπολλωνίαν καὶ δύο καὶ τριάκοντα πόλεις ἐπὶ Θράκης). The shorter third sentence in this section, more typical of Asperity (cf. Hermogenes, 259), helps to make the transition to the harsher tone that follows: καὶ τὸ Φωκέων ἔθνος τοσοῦτον ἀνηρημένον σιωπῶ. The end of section 26 and the beginning of section 27 are composed of four rhetorical questions, which are also characteristic of Asperity (cf. Hermogenes, 258–59):

ἀλλὰ Θετταλία πῶς ἔχει; οὐχὶ τὰς πολιτείας καὶ τὰς πόλεις αὐτῶν παρήρηται καὶ τετραρχίας κατέστησεν, ἵνα μὴ μόνον κατὰ πόλεις ἀλλὰ καὶ κατ᾽ ἔθνη δουλεύωσιν; αἱ δ᾽ ἐν Εὐβοίᾳ πόλεις οὐκ ἤδη τυραννοῦνται, καὶ ταῦτα ἐν νήσῳ πλησίον Θηβῶν καὶ Ἀθηνῶν; οὐ διαρρήδην εἰς τὰς ἐπιστολὰς γράφει "ἐμοὶ δ᾽ ἐστὶν εἰρήνη πρὸς τοὺς ἀκούειν ἐμοῦ βουλομένους";

This is followed by a very rapid section in which D sketches out some of Philip's other aggressions.

In section 28 the orator turns to the shortcomings of his audience. This criticism is toned down from that in the *First Philippic* in four ways. First, the reproach is made not just of the Athenians but of all the Greeks, including the speaker. The ὑμεῖς that is so typical of critical passages in the *First Philippic* has, as usual in this speech, been replaced by ἡμεῖς: καὶ ταῦθ᾽ ὁρῶντες οἱ Ἕλληνες ἅπαντες καὶ ἀκούοντες οὐ πέμπομεν πρέσβεις. Hermogenes notes (256) that criticisms that are stated in general and do not reproach anyone in particular are gentler than those that are more specific. Second, the criticism is expressed in one long periodic sentence that takes up all of sections 28 and 29, and this sentence contains figures of speech that tend to be pleasing and thus soften and distend the criticism, particularly parallelism (cf. Hermogenes, 299). The synonymity makes the criticism emphatic, but not sharp: ὁρῶντες ... ἀκούοντες οὐ πέμπομεν ... καὶ ἀγανακτοῦμεν ... διακείμεθα καὶ διορωρύγμεθα ... οὔτε τῶν συμφερόντων οὔτε τῶν δεόντων πρᾶξαι δυνάμεθα, οὐδὲ συστῆναι, οὐδὲ κοινωνίαν βοηθείας καὶ φιλίας οὐδεμίαν ποιήσασθαι ... σκοπῶν οὐδὲ πράττων. Third, the expression of hesitation seen in the phrase ὥς γ᾽ ἐμοὶ δοκεῖ (§29. 14–15) also tones down the reproach and gives the passage a gentler tone (cf. Hermogenes, 257). Fourth, D concludes the passage with a simile: ὥσπερ περίοδος ἢ καταβολὴ πυρετοῦ ἢ ἄλλου τινὸς κακοῦ καὶ τῷ πάνυ πόρρω δοκοῦντι νῦν ἀφεστάναι προσέρχεται. Hermogenes says of a similar image in the speech *On the False Embassy* (νόσημα γάρ, ὦ ἄνδρες Ἀθηναῖοι, δεινὸν ἐμπέπτωκεν εἰς τὴν Ἑλλάδα; §259) that "the metaphor, although it is typical of a harsh or vehement passage, has been uplifted in some way, as happens in a brilliant passage and here does not exemplify Asperity as much as it does Brilliance" (270). Hermogenes does not explain this comment, but Syrianus in his commentary indicates (53) that it is the general context of the passage, particularly the long clauses, that makes it more brilliant than harsh.

The same pattern appears in sections 32–35: harsh criticism of Philip, expressed mainly by rhetorical questions coupled with milder criticism of the audience, expressed mainly in periodic sentences. These sections contain eleven rhetorical questions cataloguing Philip's crimes against Greece, beginning with Καίτοι τί τῆς ἐσχάτης ὕβρεως ἀπολείπει; Some of them are quite brief, the sort of impatient questions that Hermogenes sees as being most typical of Asperity: γράφει δὲ Θετταλοῖς ὃν χρὴ τρόπον πολιτεύεσθαι; ... οὐ Κορινθίων ἐπ᾽ Ἀμβρακίαν ἐλήλυθε καὶ Λευκάδα; οὐκ Ἀχαιῶν Ναύπακτον ὀμώμοκεν Αἰτωλοῖς παραδώσειν; This criticism of Philip dominates these four sections of the speech. The reproach of the Greeks is brief and expressed in a period dominated by parallelism, alliteration, assonance, synonymity, and rhyming: ταῦτα τοίνυν πάσχοντες ἅπαντες μέλλομεν καὶ μαλκιζόμεθα καὶ πρὸς τοὺς πλησίον βλέπομεν, ἀπιστοῦντες ἀλλήλοις, οὐ τῷ πάντας ἡμᾶς ἀδικοῦντι. There is, however, some harsh criticism of the Athenians in this speech. In section 39, for example, in discussing the political situation in Athens in the fourth century and how contemporary attitudes differ from those of earlier Athenians, particularly toward bribe-taking, D uses a very choppy style, consisting of phrases as much as clauses: ζῆλος, εἴ τις εἴληφέ τι· γέλως, ἂν ὁμολογῇ· συγγνώμη τοῖς ἐλεγχομένοις·μῖσος, ἂν τούτοις τις ἐπιτιμᾷ. This brief passage of harsh criticism, however, is bracketed, and thus mitigated, by long passages in praise of earlier Athenians (§§36–37 and 41–45), with whom D consistently associates his audience.

### STRUCTURE OF THE SPEECH

I. Proemium: D attacks Philip and his own political opponents and asks his audience to hear him out without penalizing him (§§1–5).
II. First Topic: Is Philip observing the peace? (§§6–20)
  A. Philip's words do not reflect his deeds (§§6–9).
  B. It is foolish to judge reality by words rather than deeds (§§10–14).
  C. Philip's words do not reflect his deeds (§§15–20).
III. Second Topic: Philip poses a danger to all of Greece, but the Greeks are unable to unite against him (§§21–46).
  A. D discusses what motivates the Greeks and contrasts the past and the present (§§21–25).
  B. The present: D discusses (1) the aggressions of Philip and (2) how the Greeks are responding to them (§§26–35).
   1. The aggressions of Philip (§§26–27).
   2. The response of the Greeks (§§28–31).
   3. The aggressions of Philip and the response of the Greeks (§§32–35).
    (a) The aggressions of Philip (§§32–33.21)
    (b) The response of the Greeks (§§33.21–34.1)
    (c) The aggressions of Philip (§§34.2–35.6).
    (d) The response of the Greeks (§35.6–10).
  C. D discusses what motivates the Greeks and contrasts the past and the present (§§36–46).
IV. Third Topic: D advises what Athens must do now (§§47–75).
  A. Practical advice: Warfare has changed, and the Athenians must adopt new tactics (§§47–52).
  B. The cases of Olynthus, Eretria, and Oreus prove the need to resist Philip and his supporters (§§53–66).
   1. Olynthus, Eretria, and Oreus were destroyed because the people let themselves be deceived by pro-Macedonian politicians and did not allow patriots to speak out (§§53–62).

2. The people in Olynthus, Eretria, and Oreus gave more heed to pro-Macedonian politicians because they were unwilling to hear the truth and to face hard facts (§§63–64).

3. Olynthus, Eretria, and Oreus demonstrate that yielding to Philip and his supporters brings nothing but suffering and defeat (§§65–68).

C. Practical advice: The Athenians must organize an alliance of all the Greeks against Philip (§§69–75).

V. Epilogue: What D has proposed will still save Athens; may whatever the citizens decide prove to be beneficial (§76).

### ANALYSIS

The scholia point out that the proemium to the *First Philippic* is taken from the person of the speaker. The proemium to this speech, like that of *Philippic* II, is taken from the nature of the opponent, or opponents, and of the situation (ἐκ τοῦ πράγματος καὶ τοῦ ἐναντίου), and this is typical of the speeches in general (see the second section of appendix 1, on the general approach of *Philippic* II). The proemium is also, as Blass notes, "unusually expanded" ("ungewöhnlich ausgedehnt," 375), being longer and more complex than most of D's proemia. The scholia, in fact, see it as being composed of three separate proemia (Dilts, 7a, 12b). The first attacks Philip and describes the general nature of the situation that has resulted from his aggressions (§1). The second is intended to arouse hostility toward D's political opponents, who have allowed Philip to grow so powerful (§2). The third is a plea for the goodwill of the audience and describes the results of their unwillingness in the past to grant complete freedom of speech to politicians (§§3–4). D concludes the proemium with an encouraging paradox (§5), the second really striking statement in the introduction to the body of the speech, the first being at the end of section 1 (cf. §1.8–11). These two paradoxical statements, plus the elaborate nature of the proemium as a whole, indicate how intent D was to engage the audience's attention before beginning the body of his speech.[2]

We see in the proemium to this speech several tendencies, already noted in the *Second Philippic*, that will characterize the speech as a whole. There is, for example, a more prominent and harsher criticism of Philip than in *Philippic* I,

---

[2] The scholion says (Dilts, 11) that the proemium ends with the appeal to the goodwill of the audience in section 3. The description, however, in section 4 of the negative consequences of not allowing freedom of speech to all orators is closely connected with the plea for indulgence in section 3, and the paradox in section 5 is intended to arouse the audience's attention, one of the primary functions of the proemium. It makes much more sense, therefore, to conclude the proemium after section 5 (cf. Blass, 375–76).

where he is not even mentioned by name until section 4. Here, however, as in *Philippic* II, he is introduced in the very first sentence. In addition, D ends the proemium to the *Third Philippic* as he begins it, with a reference to Philip, thus keeping at the forefront what will be the major topic of the speech. In *Philippic* II he ends the proemium with a discussion of internal politics in Athens. In fact, the proemium to this speech, like the proemium to *Philippic* II, forms a perfect ring, but what is emphasized, in the frame, is not the internal problem, but the external threat:

A. The external problem: Philip (§1.1–6)
   B. Attempt to arouse interest: striking statement (§1.6–11)
      C. Internal problem: other politicians (§2)
         D. Appeal for goodwill (§3)
      C. Internal problem: the audience (§4)
   B. Attempt to arouse interest: paradox (§5.21–27)
A. The external problem: Philip (§5.27–29)

The center of the ring is an appeal to the goodwill of the audience. This is similar to the προδιόρθωσις in *Philippic* I. It is also different in several significant ways, all of which, like the long and involved proemium itself, show a heightened sensitivity to the reaction of the audience. First, the plea for a fair hearing in the *First Philippic* (§§14–15) is used as an introduction to the specific proposals only, which come about a third of the way into the speech. The one here prefaces the entire speech. Second, this προδιόρθωσις is more insistent than the one in the earlier speech. There D had made a request based only on need (δεηθείς, §13.11). Here he makes a demand of his audience based on what he deserves (ἀξιῶ, 5). Third, in keeping with the idea that he deserves to be heard fairly, the explanation of why this is the case is cast in a more striking way in this speech. In the *First Philippic* D had claimed that the audience should listen to him simply because he had better advice to give than his opponents (§§14–15). Here he uses a very elaborate a fortiori argument to prove (σκοπεῖτε γὰρ ὡδί) that he deserves to be heard: if freedom of speech exists in Athens where one would not expect it to exist, that is, among foreigners and slaves, it should certainly exist where one would expect it to exist, that is, among citizens who are politicians. The a fortiori argument that D uses is triple in nature and complex. He compares, first, foreigners and slaves in Athens with Athenian citizens (9–10); second, servants in Athens with citizens in other Greek states (10–12); and, third, Athenian politicians with everyone else in Athens (12–13). The conclusion of each comparison is the same: complete freedom of speech should be granted to politicians as it is to everyone else in the city. κοινήν (8), separated by five words from the noun with which it is construed (παρρησίαν), is very emphatic, as is the phrase πᾶσι τοῖς ἐν τῇ πόλει (9) placed at the end of the clause. Fourth, the negative reaction that D is trying to forestall in *Philippic* I is simply an unwillingness to hear him out (μὴ πρότερον προλαμβάνετε, §14.12–13). Here he envisions a much stronger reaction, ὀργήν. The separation, again by five words, of the adjective μηδεμίαν (6) from the noun ὀργήν (7) creates a fairly violent hyperbaton that calls attention to the noun. D envisions here an audience that is sensitive and easily provoked, one that must be approached and handled with the greatest care: he fears that simply saying something that is true (τι τῶν ἀληθῶν μετὰ παρρησίας λέγω, 5–6) might provoke them.

D is here more hostile to Philip than in *Philippic* II. He is also more hostile to other speakers than in the earlier speech and, related to that, his criticism of the audience is less harsh. Early in both *Philippic* II (§2) and in this speech, for example, D uses a similar phrase to introduce a result clause: εἰς τοῦτο ἤδη προηγμένα τυγχάνει πάντα τὰ πράγματα, εἰς τοῦθ' ὑπηγμένα πάντα τὰ πράγματα (9.1.6–7). In *Philippic* II, however, the result clause expresses an idea that reflects badly on the audience: the more Philip is proven to be violating the peace and plotting against the Greeks, the more unwilling the audience is to hear what must be done. Here, however, what follows reflects badly both on the audience and on other speakers, but the implication, seen in sections 2 and 4, is that other speakers are more responsible for the terrible situation in which Athens finds itself since they have misled the audience. In fact, in this speech D consistently ingratiates himself with his audience by blaming other politicians for the mistakes that the Athenians have made.

There is some criticism of the audience in section 4. In keeping with the more cautious handling of them in this speech, however, the criticism is somewhat muted. First of all, as Hermogenes notes (257), the indirect means of expression, saying ὑμῖν συμβέβηκεν τρυφᾶν rather than τρυφᾶτε, tones down the criticism. Second, the Athenians are depicted as giving themselves airs (τρυφᾶν), to be sure, but they do so mainly because they are flattered (κολακεύεσθαι) by politicians who refuse to tell them the truth. This picks up the idea in section 2 that politicians who gratify the people are the real cause of Athens' problems (τοὺς χαρίζεσθαι μᾶλλον ἢ τὰ βέλτιστα λέγειν προαιρουμένους, 14–15). Here the audience is flattered; in the *First Philippic* the Athenians are depicted as flattering themselves (φενακίζειν ἑαυτούς, §38.22). There they practice self-deception; here they are deceived by their leaders. They are victims of politicians who use them to advance their own career and who, in the process, put the population into the greatest danger (περὶ τῶν ἐσχάτων ἤδη κινδυνεύειν). That is why the deception of the Athenians is here limited to public meetings (ἐν ταῖς ἐκκλησίαις), where the people are being influenced by their leaders, whereas in the *First Philippic* it is much more widespread (περιόντες αὐτῶν πυνθάνεσθαι, §10.11; ἡμῶν δ' οἱ μὲν περιόντες, §48.22). Moreover, the Athenians as a whole here listen to what is pleasant, but they are not depicted as generating harmful rumors themselves, as is the case in the *First Philippic* (cf. §§10–11, 48). They listen, but they do not speak. Moreover, in keeping with the gentler treatment of the audience, at least in this part of the proemium, when D refers to what the Athenians have lost (19), he uses a passive verb (προεῖται) with no agent.

In lines 16–18, by means of parallel and antithetical division, D offers his audience a clear-cut choice, as he does at the end of the proemium to *Philippic*

II: εἰ μὲν ..., οὐκ ἔχω τί λέγω, εἰ δ' ..., ἕτοιμος λέγειν. What D considers to be the inappropriate response is described in a vague, almost euphemistic way (οὕτω διάκεισθε), so as not to offend the audience. What he considers to be the right reaction is described in a much more graphic way, using positive language (ἃ συμφέρει χωρὶς κολακείας), so as to create a "beckoning archetype" (Black, 119) for his audience.[3]

The paradox in lines 21–23 is very similar to the one used in *Philippic* I (§2.12–13). In fact, the second half is exactly the same (τοῦτο πρὸς τὰ μέλλοντα βέλτιστον ὑπάρχει). Here, however, unlike in the *First Philippic*, D introduces the paradox and thus calls attention to and apologizes for it (καὶ παράδοξον μὲν ἴσως ἐστὶν ὃ μέλλω λέγειν, ἀληθὲς δέ). The striking statement in section 1 is introduced in a similar way and with the same effect (βλάσφημον μὲν εἰπεῖν, ἀληθὲς δ' ᾖ).

In *Philippic* I, after stating that there is hope for the future because the Athenians have done nothing in the past to protect their interests, D devotes ten sections (3–12) to proving the latter point by contrasting the Athenians of his own day with their ancestors and with Philip. Here he makes his point in three lines (27–29). Not only is the criticism much briefer than in the *First Philippic*, it is also milder. D's purpose is to be encouraging rather than critical. The key phrase here is οὐδ' ἥττησθ' ὑμεῖς, and it is stated directly to show the confidence that the orator has in what he says. Moreover, D casts his idea in a positive way. He makes a distinction between the apathy of its citizens and the city itself. Philip, who appears at the end and the beginning of the proemium, each time in an emphatic position in the clause, has defeated one but not the other.

We see in section 2 a good example of another tendency that distinguishes this speech from *Philippic* I: the extreme control that D exerts over his very long sentences. The entire section, like the previous one,[4] is composed of a single, unusually elaborate and complex sentence that involves a triple division, the only such sentence that I know of in D.[5] In this remarkable sentence, which uses three pairs of μέν/δέ clauses, each δέ clause is itself divided into μέν/δέ clauses, which creates what looks like an unusually complex sentence. There is, however, a very clear informing principle that makes the sentence easier to follow and allows D to emphasize what he wants to highlight: the δέ clause in each pair is the more important of the two and contains information to which D wants to call attention. Moreover, in each μέν clause there are delaying devices that create suspense, whose primary purpose seems to be to emphasize the more important δέ clause, which in each case is more specific than the μέν clause with which it is paired. There is thus a steady progression from shorter to longer, from the general to the specific, and from the less to the more important. This creates a spiraling effect by which, as the thought becomes more precise and more

---

[3] Cf. the discussion of Black's conception of a "beckoning archetype" in section 13 of *Philippic* I.
[4] Dionysius analyzes the first half of section 1 (*On Dem.* 9).
[5] A detailed analysis of this sentence can be found in my article, "A Triple Division in Demosthenes," *Classical Philology* 94 (1999): 450–54.

significant, the clauses become more expansive. The resulting pattern, planted clearly in the mind of the hearer, might be compared to an unbalanced metronome in which one beat is louder and longer than the other, and this architectural pattern guides the reader or hearer through this complicated passage.

In the final pair the μέν clause (1–2) once again uses a delaying device that can be seen elsewhere in the sentence: the second half really says the same thing as the first (ἡ μὲν πόλις παρ' αὐτῆς δίκην λήψεται καὶ περὶ τοῦτ' ἔσται). D is once again simply delaying the δέ clause that contains the ultimate problem that this speech addresses: Philip can do and say whatever he pleases. D manages to emphasize this clause, the climax of the sentence, in several ways. First, he delays it. Second, he here breaks the pattern that he has set up in the rest of the sentence, because this final δέ clause is shorter than the μέν clause with which it is paired (twenty syllables as opposed to seventeen) and, unlike the other δέ clauses, is not itself divided. This foils the hearer's expectations and thus forces his attention onto the clause, which seems abrupt. Third, in the rest of the sentence the speed varies. The expression holds back or lunges forward. Here, however, the flow is steady and sure. Fourth, the very simplicity of the clause calls attention to it. Every other clause in this sentence contains within itself synonymity, subordination, or hyperbaton (e.g., ἐν οἷς εὐδοκιμοῦσιν αὐτοὶ καὶ δύνανται in lines 15–16, which describes the ταῦτα that follows). This clause, however, is plain and stark. As D presents the situation, causes may be complex and complicated, but the result that they produce is plain for all to see.

D has moved steadily from general causes (πολλὰ μέν) to particular causes (μάλιστα δ') and finally to results (ὅπως). He has built up a pattern that emphasizes particular causes rather than general, traitors rather than complacent politicians, and Philip's freedom of action rather than the bickering among the Athenians. καὶ λέγειν καὶ πράττειν ὅ τι βούλεται is the most important phrase in this sentence because, as D says later in the speech, this type of free rein is ὑπὲρ οὗ τὸν ἄλλον ἅπαντα χρόνον πάντες οἱ πόλεμοι γεγόνασιν οἱ Ἑλληνικοί (§22). This speech is a call to war. There is no better way to arouse the Athenians than to show that Philip now holds a power that the Greeks have never allowed to anyone before.

As in *Philippic* II, after the proemium D does not launch immediately into the argumentation as he does in *Philippic* I but leads the audience gently from the proemium to the body of the speech. Sections 6–7 are a transitional passage that gives a résumé of the proemium, which D might have considered to be necessary for the sake of clarity because of the length and complication of the introductory material. This leads to the specific charge that D's opponents accuse him of fomenting the war, which raises the question of whether it is still possible to debate about war and peace.[6]

---

[6] For a discussion of the longer and shorter versions of *Philippic* III, see appendix 3. I am assuming that the longer version was the one that was delivered. There is a mistake in Dilts's text in section 6 (line 2): ἀλλ' should be ἄλλ'.

In section 8, D discusses the two options mentioned at the end of section 7, setting them out in a fairly equal division (μέν . . . δέ) of about three and a half lines each. The first option (14–17) is stated in a very calm and general way: Εἰ μὲν οὖν ἔξεστιν εἰρήνην ἄγειν τῇ πόλει . . . φήμ᾽ ἔγωγε ἄγειν ἡμᾶς δεῖν. The second (17–20), however, is much more specific and emotional: εἰ δ᾽ ἕτερος τὰ ὅπλα ἐν ταῖς χερσὶν ἔχων. . . . ἕτερος personalizes the conflict by seeing the opponent as an individual; τὰ ὅπλα ἐν ταῖς χερσὶν ἔχων is a concrete image of hostility. This part of the division concludes with an emotional ἐρώτημα(τί λοιπὸν ἄλλο πλὴν ἀμύνεσθαι;). Moreover, the first possibility, keeping the peace, which D does not see as a real option, is dropped immediately as a topic of discussion. The second, that Philip is already at war with Athens, is developed in the next twelve sections, until, in section 20, he makes a transition to a new topic. This underdeveloped division is similar to an unfinished or incomplete one and makes it clear that D does not consider the first option worthy of discussion, that he is so focused on the second that he completely forgets about the first. Unfinished or incomplete divisions also convey a sense of spontaneity (Hermogenes, 362).

In the *First Philippic* D frequently discusses the discrepancy between what the Athenians say and what they do, and the theme is used to reveal his audience's apathy. Here in lines 17–20, in keeping with the greater emphasis on Philip, the theme is applied to him and underlines his treachery and deceit. In the *First Philippic* (§§5–7) D holds up Philip as an example that the Athenians can imitate. Here he invites them to do the same. The emphasis, however, is not on his energy and activity but on his willingness to deceive, in fact, to use any means at his disposal, in order to achieve his goals. This is in keeping with the more negative and sinister portrayal of Philip in this speech and also with the more desperate nature of the conflict, which is here seen as a struggle between Hellenism and barbarism (cf. §20).

The highly patterned language at the end of section 9 (1–2) is an appropriate way to conclude the πρόθεσις of the first major part of the argument, that Philip is already at war with Athens. It makes the same point that D states briefly at the beginning of section 6 (Φίλιππον τῇ πόλει πολεμεῖν καὶ τὴν εἰρήνην παραβαίνειν) and thus creates a ring that marks off the four sections (6–9), in which the first point in D's argument, that although Philip uses the words of peace he engages in the acts of war, is developed.

D states his next thesis, that Philip never reveals his true intentions until the last moment, in section 10 and then proves it with four historical examples, a very orderly and logical presentation. τεκμαίρεσθαι (6), meaning "to judge from signs and tokens" (LSJ, s.v., II.1), is an apt way to introduce the induction. Aristotle uses τεκμήριον in the *Rhetoric* (1.2.17), which is roughly contemporary with this speech, to refer to irrefutable evidence. The examples are arranged in chronological order, beginning with Philip's attack on Olynthus in 349 and ending with his intrigues in Oreus in 342, the year before the delivery of this speech. As Sandys notes, there is also an intensification in that "each example gives a still stronger proof of his treachery" (Sandys 2, 199), since in each instance there is a greater discrepancy between what Philip says and what he does. In the case of Olynthus, he did reveal his true intentions, but only when he was forty stades from the city. He marched against the Phocians as an ally (ὡς πρὸς συμμάχους). When he captured Pherae, he claimed to be both a friend and an ally (ὡς φίλος καὶ σύμμαχος). In his intrigues against Oreus, he concealed his true intentions with the language of concern. His troops, he argued, were like a doctor coming to visit a patient who was sick (ἐπισκεψομένους, νοσοῦσιν), whose only concern was the sick man's welfare (κατ᾽ εὔνοιαν). Sandys notes: "All these gradations of tone must have been effectively distinguished by the orator's delivery" (Sandys 2, 199).

In sections 13 and 14, D presents the conclusion that can be drawn (εἶτ᾽) from the historical examples recounted in sections 11 and 12 as an a fortiori argument: if something existed where you would not expect it to exist, that is, if Philip used deceit and treachery against cities and peoples who could have done him no real harm, it will certainly exist where you would expect it to exist, that is, Philip will use treachery and deceit against Athens, which can, in fact, do him harm.

Dionysius cites (*Dem.* 9) the sentence in section 13 as an example of the grand style, language far removed from everyday speech, which he associates with Gorgias and Thucydides. The long relative clause (οἳ ἐποίησαν . . . ἴσως), which precedes the pronoun that it describes (τούτους) and separates the subject αὐτόν from the verb with which it is construed (αἱρεῖσθαι), creates a violent hyperbaton, the sort of contorted arrangement of words that Dionysius associates (9) with Thucydides and which is unusual in this speech. D's sentence, however, in addition to the Thucydidean elements already noted, also contains antithesis (τούτους μὲν/ὑμῖν δ᾽), especially the sort of quick antithesis of similar length that Dionysius associates (1) with Gorgias: ἐποίησαν μὲν οὐδὲν ἂν κακόν, μὴ παθεῖν δ᾽ ἐφυλάξαντ᾽ ἂν ἴσως. This sentence contains the point to which sections 10–12 have been building, and D uses this unusual means of expression, containing both Thucydidean and Gorgianic elements, to give the sentence the sort of striking configuration that would impress it upon the audience.

The question in section 13 looks like an ἐρώτημα. It is emotional in tone, and the answer to it is obvious. D, however, treats it as if it were an αἰτολογία and answers it, not once (οὐκ ἔστι ταῦτα) but, in effect, twice (καὶ γὰρ ἂν ἀβελτερώτατος εἴη πάντων ἀνθρώπων). This dwelling upon an idea, seen in *Philippic* I to some extent but much more frequently and clearly here, is typical of what Blass calls the "the broader character of the presentation" ("breitere Charakter der Darlegung," 381) in this speech as compared with earlier deliberative speeches such as the *First Philippic*: "Generally the orator lingers for a long time on a thought or on a sequence of thoughts, whereas in speeches such as the *First Philippic* he is every moment with swift transitions on a new thought" ("Ueberhaupt weilt der Redner lange bei einem Gedanken oder bei einer Folge von Gedanken, während er in Reden wie der ersten Philippika mit raschen Uebergängen jeden Augenblick bei einem neuen Gedanken ist," 381–82). There are other examples of this tendency, on a larger scale, later in the speech. There is ring composition in this part of the speech (II.B in my outline). D begins section 10 with the idea that the Athenians are the most foolish of all (πάντων ἐσμὲν εὐηθέστατοι) if they expect Philip to agree that he is at war with the city (ἕως ἂν ἡμῖν ὁμολογήσῃ πολεμεῖν). He ends section 14 by saying that Philip would be the most foolish of all (ἂν ἀβελτερώτατος εἴη πάντων ἀνθρώπων) if he should allow his agents to make such an admission (λέγοντες ὡς ἐκεῖνός γε οὐ πολεμεῖ τῇ πόλει). Ring composition, used more frequently and more explicitly in this speech than it is in the *First Philippic*, is related to the "breitere Charakter der Darlegung" mentioned above. The presentation is fuller, less excited, and more orderly than in the earlier speech. The less emotional tone probably explains the absence of nouns of direct address in large parts of the speech. ὦ ἄνδρες Ἀθηναῖοι has not been used since section 3.

In the third part (II.C) of the first major block of argument (II), D returns to the same idea that he had discussed in the first (II.A), particularly in sections 8 and 9, that Philip's words do not correspond to his deeds (τοὔνομα μὲν τὸ τῆς εἰρήνης ὑμῖν προβάλλει, τοῖς δ' ἔργοις αὐτὸς τοῖς τοῦ πολέμου χρῆται, §8.18–20; ἐκ τῶν ὀνομάτων μᾶλλον ἢ τῶν πραγμάτων τὸν ἄγοντ' εἰρήνην ἢ πολεμοῦνθ' ἑαυτῷ, §15.4–6). He thus encloses in a larger ring part II.B, which itself is organized by ring composition. D's discussion of the discrepancy between Philip's words and his deeds in II.C, however, differs from the one in II.A in two significant ways. It is more emotional, and it is more specific and detailed. Since sections 6 and 7 are transitional in nature, D really devotes only sections 8 and 9 to this idea. In II.C, however, he devotes five sections to it. In I.A the discussion is general and calm; in II.C he backs up his thesis with many specific examples. The tone is heated in places.

To convey the more emotional tone, there is something rapid about this part of the speech (Hermogenes, 312–20). D presents much information and passes quickly from one point to another. Since, however, every point he makes supports one general thesis, that Philip is breaking the peace, Hermogenes would probably describe this as "apparent Rapidity." His description of a sentence from the speech *On the Crown* (71), which he sees as being typical of such a style, could apply to this passage:

> In this sentence Demosthenes seems to be saying a lot and to pass quickly from one topic to another, which produces an element of Rapidity and an impression of conciseness. But in fact he does not really say very much and does not really pass quickly from one topic to another. He lingers upon the same topic, which is typical of Abundance, and that is the opposite of Rapidity and concision. Here general classes are mentioned with particular examples, and wholes with the

parts that make them up, and undefined concepts with defined ones, and other devices are used that create Abundance. (318)

This part of the speech (II.C) is a good example of what Blass calls the "breitere Charakter der Darlegung," since D lingers upon the same idea by presenting it in different ways. He has given specific instances of Philip's violation of the peace in sections 15–17, coupled with general descriptions of their significance. Then he sums them all up with a concrete image of what Philip is doing (§17.25–27). Finally, to cap it all off, D uses what looks like a proverb, an *epiphonema*, placed at the end of a series of arguments to sum them up (Lausberg §879). D has thus moved from specific facts, to an image that sums up what they have in common,[7] to an abstract principle based on them.

The sentence in lines 1–3 of section 17 is very tightly constructed, like a proverb (cf. *Rhet. to Her.* 4.24). In fact, Hermogenes cites it twice (294, 376) as an example of the figure τὸ κατὰ συστροφὴν σχῆμα. The hyperbaton involved in placing each of the descriptive clauses or phrases before the word that it describes, like the brevity, gives the sentence the sort of artificial structure often found in proverbs. It also features the sort of responsion between the two halves of the sentence that the author of the treatise *On Invention* sees (180) as being typical of "gnomic" periods. The long phrase ὁ γὰρ . . . κατασκευαζόμενος describes οὗτος; the relative clause οἷς ἂν ἐγὼ ληφθείην describes ταῦτα. The metrical configuration of the condition at the end also makes this sentence extraordinary: it is composed almost exclusively of heavy syllables, which gives it great weight. The clausula is composed of a cretic and a spondee (μηδὲ τοξεύῃ, ‾ ˘ ‾ | ‾ ‾). Dionysius of Halicarnassus notes that the phrase μηδὲ τοξεύῃ is not necessary to the sense: "Here the reference to 'arrows' is added not out of necessity, but in order that the last clause, 'though he is not yet firing missiles at me', being shorter than it ought to be and not pleasing to the ear, may be made more elegant by this addition" (*On Comp.* 9). Dionysius doubtlessly found μήπω βάλλῃ "not pleasing to the ear" because it involves two spondees, each of which corresponds to a single word, which seems artificial.[8] Hermogenes also notes (253) that it creates a more solemn effect to end a clausula with a word of at least three syllables, a word long enough to anchor the end of the sentence. Two short words would seem choppy. The single light syllable in μηδὲ τοξεύῃ relieves the heaviness of the line and makes it seem more natural, as does the fact that the cretic is spread over two words.[9]

In section 18, D continues to linger upon ideas already developed by repeating the image of the siege-engine. There are differences, however. In section 17 the image is developed in a very general way through the use of the

---

[7] Hermogenes discusses (342) this image as an example of a style that he calls Subtlety.

[8] Cf. the note in Usher's edition in the Loeb Classical Library, 64–65.

[9] As is clear from the many references given in the testimonia in Dilts's text, this is one of the passages in the Demosthenic corpus most frequently discussed by ancient rhetoricians.

plural (τοὺς τὰ μηχανήματα ἐφιστάντας) and the absence of any particular enemy against whom the actions are directed. Here he is much more specific. There is only one man (τὸν ... ἱστάντα); the action is directed against a specific enemy (ἐπὶ τὴν πόλιν); and the siege-engine is pointed at with a demonstrative (τοῦτο τὸ μηχάνημα). D also connects this sentence with the proverb at the end of section 17 in that he uses the same pattern here that he had used there, a long descriptive phrase that precedes the demonstrative that it describes: τὸν ... ἱστάντα, τοῦτον (cf. ὁ γὰρ ... κατασκευαζόμενος, οὗτος).

D also compares his own reaction to this situation to the reaction of his audience. In section 17 he presents specific violations of the treaty, followed by the image of the siege-engine, followed by the reaction of his audience (οὐ φήσετε). Here he uses the same pattern: the results of specific violations of the treaty, the image of the siege-engine, and his own reaction (φῶ). D thus reacts to this situation as his audience had reacted and thereby creates the sort of identification with them that is so lacking in the *First Philippic*. The repeated pattern also creates clarity and makes the argument easier to follow.

With ὁρίζομαι (19.9) D begins to close the ring that encircles the first major part of the argumentation (II, §§6–20). In the second section of this part of the speech (§7.11–14), D had said that his main task was to determine (διορίζομαι) whether it was still possible to deliberate about war or peace. In lines 10–13 D continues to close the circle. At the beginning of section 6 he had said that the only object of deliberation should be how the Athenians might defend themselves against Philip (ὅπως ἀσφαλέστατα καὶ ῥᾷστα αὐτὸν ἀμυνούμεθα). Here he returns to that idea (ὑμᾶς δέ, ἐὰν ἀμύνησθε ἤδη, σωφρονήσειν φημί). D has been discussing Philip primarily since section 6. ὑμᾶς, placed emphatically at the beginning of the sentence and separated by the condition from the infinitive with which it is construed, indicates that he is now turning to the actions that the audience must take. The δέ, without a preceding μέν, is abrupt. In the second half of section 6, D had mentioned his disagreement with other politicians. He returns to that idea here also: τοσοῦτόν γε ἀφέστηκα τῶν ἄλλων, ὦ ἄνδρες Ἀθηναῖοι, τῶν συμβουλευόντων.

The apostrophe at 19.12 is the first one used since section 3 and indicates that an important idea will follow. The last apostrophe had been used in the proemium to the entire speech; this one appears in what is in effect an introduction to the second, and most important, segment of argumentation, where D will argue that it is not only Athens, but all the Greeks that are being threatened by Philip.

D has announced what the topic of the next major part of the speech will be. Now, as in a partition, in lines 16–1 of section 20 he describes how he will deal with it. D here puts his reputation on the line and envisions negative consequences for himself if what he says is not true, which, according to pseudo-Aristides (1.95), lends credibility to the argument. Pseudo-Aristides cites as examples of this technique this passage and a similar one, also at an important point in the speech, just after the specific proposals, in the *First Philippic* (§29).

In the third major part of the speech (III), D will develop the thesis that Philip poses a threat to all of Greece and that the Greeks are unable to unite against him, but first he will discuss (§§21–25) what motivates the Greeks and will contrast the past and the present. The first sentence in section 21 exemplifies what Hermogenes calls (267–68) an ἀπόστασις, an indication of a fresh start, here involving a broad review of the relations between Philip and Greece and the situation within Greece itself. D claims to pass over what will be the two major topics dealt with in this part of the speech: that Philip has grown so powerful as to threaten all of Greece and that he has grown great mainly because the Greeks will not unite against him. D uses a παράλειψις in order not to appear to be dwelling on facts that are painful to the audience (cf. Lausberg §888.b), quite in keeping with the greater sensitivity shown to the audience in this speech in general. The suspenseful period, however, actually calls attention to the information put early in the sentence.

In this central part of the speech (III), D, like any good courtroom advocate, generalizes his case as much as possible. He has already argued that this is not simply a conflict between Athens and Philip over the issue of Athenian troops in the Thracian Chersonesus, but a struggle between Philip and all of Greece, between barbarism and civilization. In section 22 he continues his attempt to broaden his case by arguing that what is at stake is a fundamental principle over which Greeks have always gone to war, and that is not to allow any one state to dominate completely the others. Earlier he had said that some politicians in Athens had created a situation in which Philip could πράττειν ὅ τι βούλεται. Here he argues that all men (ἅπαντας ἀνθρώπους), not just those Athenian politicians τοὺς ἐπὶ τοῖς πράγμασιν ὄντας αἰτιώμενοι καὶ διαβάλλοντες, have granted him the right τὸ ποιεῖν ὅ τι βούλεται. D no longer thinks in terms of "the old formulae of Greek internal politics" (Jaeger, 172), but in much broader, more general categories. Five times in sections 21–23 D uses an expression referring to all the Greeks, each time emphatically placed at or near the end of the clause in which it appears and separated by a mild hyperbaton from the word or words with which it is construed: οἱ Ἕλληνες (§21.6), οἱ Ἑλληνικοί (§22.12), τῶν Ἑλλήνων (§22.14), τῶν Ἑλλήνων (§23.16), and ὑπὸ τῶν Ἑλλήνων (§23.21). D also thinks in large terms chronologically: in this speech he will contrast the way Greeks are now, in the fourth century, with the way they used to be, in the fifth. Thus, geographically, morally, and chronologically D expands the scope of his argument as much as possible in order to give it more weight.

καίτοι at the beginning of section 23 introduces an objection, raised by the speaker himself, which makes what he has just said appear surprising (Denniston GP, 556). D is here using an a fortiori argument: if the right to do as they pleased was never extended to the Athenians and the Spartans, it should certainly not be extended to Philip, particularly since they, at least, were true sons of Greece (cf. §31) who held the hegemony for long periods of time. To emphasize this last point, as Sandys notes (Sandys 2, 208), in indicating how long the Athenians were the leaders of Greece, D puts the larger number first (ἑβδομήκοντα . . . καὶ τρία), whereas later in section 25, when he wants to emphasize how short Philip's hegemony has been, he reverses the order (τρισὶ καὶ δέκα).[10]

In section 24, D follows the pattern outlined at the beginning of section 23, another indication of the full and orderly presentation that is characteristic of this speech. He will discuss first the Athenians and then the Spartans. μᾶλλον δέ in line 22 introduces an ἐπιδιόρθωσις, "the correction of the speaker's own utterance" (Lausberg §784). In keeping with the sensitivity to the reaction of the audience noted elsewhere in this speech, and also with the "point on which the whole speech focuses and under which all arguments are subsumed,"[11] D consistently associates his audience with the glories of their ancestors but is careful not to alienate his contemporaries by imputing to them the faults of earlier Athenians: "The correction is suggested by the thought that it seems unwise to associate the present audience with the discredit of their predecessors: elsewhere, in speaking of the past glories of Athens, Demosthenes makes his contemporaries partakers in the actions of their ancestors" (Davies, 104).

The sentence in section 24 is a good example of the interrupted development that Dionysius and Longinus see as being typical of D. The interruptions in this speech, however, tend to be much less disruptive than those in *Philippic* I in that they insert qualifying information into natural pauses between units that make up the sentence. They thus interrupt the flow of the sentence as a whole but not of the smaller units that make it up. The hyperbata thus created, in this case at least, call attention to the interrupting phrases, particularly μᾶλλον δὲ τοῖς τότ' οὖσιν Ἀθηναίοις, for reasons noted above, and καὶ οἱ μηδὲν ἐγκαλεῖν ἔχοντες αὐτοῖς. The latter phrase involves an a fortiori argument: if those Greeks who had no complaint against states that were acting aggressively rose up against them, surely the Athenians, who have many grounds of complaint against Philip, should resist him. The embedded causal clause also involves the argument from the more and the less. The Athenians had only *seemed* to *some* to behave aggressively. The understatement in the litotes οὐ μετρίως also attenuates the reproach. Philip, on the other hand, as D has made clear from the beginning of the speech (cf. §1), is wronging *all* the Greeks. The antithesis brings out nicely the difference between fourth-century Greeks and those of the fifth that is so crucial to the argument in this speech and that also reflects the argument from the more and the less that is so frequently developed in it. Earlier all (πάντες) had gone to war although only some (τισιν) felt

---

[10] Seventy-three years must cover, counting inclusively, the period from 476, the year that the Delian League became fully operational, to 404, the battle of Aegospotami. The twenty-nine years during which the Spartans had the hegemony must run from 404 until the battle of Naxos in 376. The Thebans were in the ascendancy for about nine years, from the battle of Leuctra in 371 to the death of Epaminondas in 362.

[11] George Kennedy, *The Art of Persuasion in Greece* (Princeton, 1963), 225.

wronged; now, although all are being wronged (οὐ μόνον ὑμᾶς, ἀλλὰ καὶ τοὺς ἄλλους ἀδικεῖ; §1.3–4), no one fights back.

Section 25 is transitional, a hinge passage that begins by marking the conclusion of the first topic discussed in this part of the speech (III.A) by restating the thesis developed in section 24, but in particular rather than general terms, which is appropriate to the fullness with which the argument is developed in this speech. There D had discussed how all the Greeks (πάντες) reacted to Greek states that were aggressive; here he cites the Athenians and the Spartans as particular examples of states that went to war against an ambitious aggressor even though they themselves had no complaints. The language, therefore, is very similar to that used in section 24.

Lines 3–6 look backward; the rest of the section foreshadows, again using the common topic of the more and the less, the next idea to be discussed in this part of the speech (III.B), which will be, not the way in which the Greeks have treated one another, but the way in which Philip has treated all of them and how they have reacted to his aggressions.[12] D calls attention to the importance of this idea by using the apostrophe ὦ ἄνδρες Ἀθηναῖοι, employed only ten times in this speech. This more moderate use of approaches that create emphasis is one of the reasons why *Philippic* III is a more effective speech than *Philippic* I, in which every point is introduced by an apostrophe: when every argument is emphasized the emphasis loses its effect. The mention of Philip's wrongs against Greece leads naturally into a discussion of his transgressions in sections 26 and 27.

The discussion of the relationships among the Greeks in sections 22–25 is calm, detached and philosophical in tone, developing the thought by means of well constructed periodic sentences. The tone becomes more emotional as D begins to discuss Philip. Dionysius muses on how this passage would have been delivered:

> Here the words themselves show what kind of delivery is needed for them. Having specified the numbers of cities in Thrace destroyed by Philip he says he will not give them. Surely this requires an ironic tone of delivery, with an undertone of indignation and with heightened intensity of utterance. Then, although he says he cannot recite the list because of their terrible, or worse than terrible fate, he nevertheless goes on to give a pathetic list of the cities and describes their complete destruction, implying that not a vestige was left of their former habitation. Surely this demands an overwhelmingly angry and tragic manner of delivery? What, then, are the tones and accents of voice, the facial expressions and manual gestures that portray anger

---

[12] D rounds off the number of years during which the Athenians and the Spartans held the hegemony, which he had given in section 23 as seventy-three and twenty-nine, respectively. The thirteen years during which Philip has been prominent must date from 353, when he took Methone, defeated the Phocians, and threatened Thermopylae.

and grief? Those which men actually experiencing these emotions employ; for it would be silly to reject real life, and look for another school to teach us delivery. (*On Dem.* 54)

There are also stylistic features that reveal D's emotion. The polysyndeton in lines 12–13 allows him to highlight, by dwelling on, each of these cities or groups of cities,[13] although D gives the appearance of being hesitant to mention them. One sees here, as in much of D's oratory, a combination of speed and retardation.

Hermogenes, also citing this passage, argues that a παράλειψις reveals a modest character:

> To choose to omit some point that you could say against your opponent or on your own behalf seems to be indicative of a modest character. Such omissions add much credibility because of the impression of Modesty that they produce.... Of these two kinds of omissions, the one that narrates the fact, such as I just cited, creates trustworthiness and reveals Character. (351)

Demetrius explains how such a passage creates trustworthiness: "In these words Demosthenes has actually stated everything he wanted, yet he claims to pass over them, to imply that he has other more forceful points to make" (263). Ronnet notes (134) that such an approach also shows a sensitivity to the audience in that a discussion of facts that are well known could seem tedious. The cities that are mentioned in the two παραλείψεις had been destroyed before 348 and had been discussed by D in earlier speeches. As D moves closer to the contemporary moment (Philip had invaded and reorganized Thessaly in 344), he becomes more emotional, switching to a series of four rhetorical questions.

In this part of the speech D is heaping up charges against Philip. In lines 18–2 of section 27, he twice makes a statement and then adds an even more damning circumstance—what Hermogenes calls "the overrunning figure" (τὸ ἐπιτρέχον λεγόμενον σχῆμα, 314). This creates an intensification of emotion throughout the passage. He begins with παραλείψεις, switches to more emotional rhetorical questions, and then to rhetorical questions with aggravating circumstances piled onto them. These aggravating circumstances are like ἐπικρίσεις, which Hermogenes sees (361) as being characteristic of animated passages. In the first instance, D calls attention to the fact that Philip's activity is near Attica and threatens both Athens and Thebes, setting off the important phrase, and city, by means of hiatus (καὶ ταῦτα ἐν νήσῳ πλησίον Θηβῶν καὶ Ἀθηνῶν). He thus prepares the way for the alliance that he will propose between these two states. In the second (καὶ οὐ γράφει μὲν ταῦτα, τοῖς δ' ἔργοις οὐ ποιεῖ), he proves his thesis with a rapid succession of short statements (2–4), what the scholion calls τὸ σχῆμα ἐπιτροχασμός (Dilts, 33). In this entire

---

[13] The thirty-two cities on the borders of Thrace refer to the cities of the Olynthian League, destroyed by Philip in 348.

passage, D relates much information and frequently changes construction. The scholion notes: ὅρα τὴν σχημάτων ποικιλίαν (Dilts, 32). This constant variation in the presentation of Philip's aggressions reflects how energetic and unexpected his activity is. D caps off this passage with a summarizing statement, similar to an *epiphonema*, that indicates that this part of the speech is at an end: οὔθ᾽ ἡ Ἑλλὰς οὔθ᾽ ἡ βάρβαρος τὴν πλεονεξίαν χωρεῖ τἀνθρώπου.

When D turns to a discussion of the Greeks, he switches abruptly from a series of rhetorical questions and short statements put together without connectives to a long, complicated analytical period dominated by polysyndeton and synonymity. As he does so often in the *First Philippic* (cf. comments on §§34–35), D uses a rapid style to describe Philip and an abundant one to discuss the Greeks.

The main clause of the period is composed of four verbs joined by polysyndeton, all of which refer to the same idea, the inability of the Greeks to unite and their isolation from one another (οὐ πέμπομεν ... καὶ ἀγανακτοῦμεν ... οὕτως δὲ κακῶς διακείμεθα καὶ διορωρύγμεθα). The parataxis and polysyndeton reflect the divisions among the Greeks, as does the hiatus (καὶ ἀκούοντες, καὶ ἀγανακτοῦμεν; cf. Pearson VP, 227–28). The first result of the divisions described in the main clause is an inability to act. This is conveyed by the heaping up of negatives (οὐδὲν οὔτε ... οὔτε ..., οὐδὲ ..., οὐδὲ ... οὐδεμίαν), the use of full and emphatic phrases (ἄχρι τῆς τήμερον ἡμέρας), and synonymity (συστῆναι, κοινωνίαν ... ποιήσασθαι).

The second result, seen in section 29, is a complicated situation, reflected in the complicated structure of the second half of the sentence, in which individual Greeks look out for themselves and show no concern for the welfare of Greece as a whole. To emphasize this idea, D switches from the plural (περιορῶμεν) to the singular (ἕκαστος). The frequent interruption in the development of the thought (ὥς γ᾽ ἐμοὶ δοκεῖ, οὐχ ὅπως ..., ἐπεί, ὅτι ...), unusual in this speech, reflects the inability of individual Greek states to form a unified plan of action against Philip, and the discrete nature of the clauses and phrases thus produced reflects the isolation of the individual states. The succession of three mild hyperbata in lines 12–17, created in each instance by putting an object before the verb with which it is construed (τὸν χρόνον κερδᾶναι, ὅπως, ὅτι), produces a disjointed effect and, by creating suspense, slows down the presentation. D caps off the long period with an image.[14]

To conclude this part of the speech dealing with the Greeks, D uses in sections 30–31 a very elaborate a fortiori argument similar to the one developed at the end of section 25, but this time emphasizing, not the extent of the injuries inflicted by the opponent, but the nature of the opponent himself. In section 25 the a fortiori argument had acted as a transition from attitudes of the Greeks to the aggressions of Philip; it has the same function here, creating a bridge between the discussion of the Greeks in sections 28–29 and a reversion to the

---

[14] See the section "General Approach of the Speech" for further discussion of this image.

aggressions of Philip in sections 32–33. Juxtaposition of the present and the past and of Philip and the Greeks is the most basic principle that organizes this part of the speech (III). Sections 30 and 31 are highly patterned and filled with the sort of repetitions that make the style full and abundant. They have the kind of weight that is appropriate to a passage that concludes a major segment of the speech.

In sections 26–27 (III.b.1), D had dealt with the aggressions of Philip against the Greeks, and in sections 28–31 (III.b.2) with how the Greeks had responded to those aggressions. In this, the third segment of this part of the speech (III.b.3, §§32–35), D twice repeats the contrast between Philip and the Greeks. In lines 11–21 (a), he catalogues Philip's aggressions, and in lines 21–1 (b), he discusses how the Greeks have reacted. Then he repeats that contrast. In lines 1–6 (c), he describes Philip's aggressions and in lines 6–10 (d), the reactions of the Greeks. Here, as earlier, the actions of Philip are related in emotional rhetorical questions (ἐρωτήματα), an unusually long series of six; the response of the Greeks is described in more complicated periodic sentences. This part of the speech, therefore, which summarizes and restates what has been discussed in parts III.B.1 and III.B.2, is a good way to bring this segment of the speech (III.B) to a conclusion (III.B.3 = III.B.1 + III.B.2) and is once again typical of the broad development of the argument in this speech.

D calls attention to the next segment of the speech (§§36–46) by using it to close the ring that organizes the middle part (III), returning to the theme that he had discussed in the first major segment of this part of the oration (III.A). This is a very important passage, falling in the center of the speech, dealing with the national character of the Greeks, the most pervasive argument in the oration.

D goes to great lengths to highlight the importance of section 36. First, he opens it with an αἰτιολογία, which he answers with an enigma (ἦν τι), thus creating more suspense (cf. Ronnet, 135). This means that he has to use another αἰτιολογία at the beginning of section 37 in order to explain the enigma (τί οὖν ἦν τοῦτο;). Second, there is something very solemn about this passage. Hermogenes argues (246) that Solemnity is created when the orator deals with great and glorious human deeds. The thoughts should be presented by means of direct statements made without hesitation (246), using short direct clauses (251), which contain more nouns than verbs (249–50). This is an apt description of the style of this passage. Third, there is something poetic about the passage, which also lifts it onto a "higher level than that of ordinary prose" (Sandys 2, 217). Davies comments, for example, on the use of ἦγε in line 16: "more usually διῆγε. The use of the uncompounded verb is a touch of poetical colouring, helping to give elevation to the passage, as does the personification of the τι, and the turn of phrases ἐκράτησε πλούτου and μάχης . . . ἡττᾶτο" (109). The word πλούτου is striking and leads nicely into the following section on bribery: *they* defeated Persia's *wealth*; we let Philip's wealth defeat us. Here it is not an individual or a state that is never defeated; it is a feeling, an attitude (Ronnet, 160). This personification is striking since the figure is rare in D (Ronnet, 145). Finally, D calls attention to this passage by the use of the apostrophe ὦ ἄνδρες Ἀθηναῖοι, only the seventh example so far in this speech and the first one since section 25. He also creates emphasis, and suspense, by means of the epanadiplosis, what Sandys calls "the pathetic repetition" (Sandys 2, 216), in ἦν τι τότ', ἦν, which is coupled with the apostrophe, which also creates suspense by separating the subject of ἦν from the prepositional phrase with which it is construed.

οὐδ' ὅλως τοιοῦτον οὐδέν, at the end of section 38, referring to the past, followed by νῦν δ' at the beginning of the next section is the exact center of the speech and reflects its organization. The first half has dealt mainly with the past. The last major part of the body of the speech (IV) will deal with the present. The loss of opportunities offered by fate, because of neglect and apathy, described in section 38, is not an idea that has appeared very frequently in this speech, but it is one that is prominent in *Philippic I* as part of the description of affairs in Athens. By denying that a situation that he had earlier described as existing in the present existed in the past, D begins the transition to a discussion of the present state of politics in Athens, which will begin in the next section (νῦν δ').

Sections 39 and 40, dealing with the present, are framed by a ring. D begins the passage by describing how Athens' advantages are sold by traitors (ἐκπέπραται ταῦτα); he ends the passage with the same idea. He thus emphasizes this important thought by putting it at the beginning and end of the passage.

The first sentence in section 41 indicates to D's audience that one stage of the argument, the presentation of the thesis (οὕτω ταῦτ' ἔχει), is over and that another, the proof of the thesis, is to begin. ταῦτα is divided into τὰ μέν, referring to the present, and τὰ δ', referring to the past. D shows confidence in his audience by stating twice that they are informed about the present situation (ὁρᾶτε ... οὐδὲν ἐμοῦ προσδεῖσθε μάρτυρος). As often in this speech, he identifies the audience with himself: they perceive the present situation as clearly as he does. They may not, however, be so well informed about the past, and he will thus inform them about that. By citing an inscription set up by fifth-century Athenians as proof of his thesis, D not only gives his argument more objectivity but also avoids putting himself in a superior position. He is not the one instructing his audience; their ancestors instruct them all. The orator merely calls attention to their precepts.

D then restates the decree in his own words, adding explanation and commentary, typical of the broad nature of the development in this speech, in order to insure that its content is firmly planted in the minds of the audience before he describes what was the intention of those who passed it. ἀτίμους dangles at the end of the sentence in section 43; this is what D will explain in the next section. It is also typical of the broad development in this speech that D explains to his audience what ἄτιμος means, although this explanation is not really necessary to the point that he wants to make (cf. Blass, 381). This discussion does have a stylistic function, however: as in the second half of the preceding section, D is holding back, for effect, the explanation promised at the beginning of section 43 about why the Athenians passed this decree.

This explanation, which involves a discussion of the differences between fifth- and fourth-century Greeks, is in a very important position in the speech. It is the conclusion not only to the third part of the central segment of the discourse (III.C) but also to the central segment itself (III). As usual, however, D devotes more space to those heroic attitudes that motivated past Athenians than to the shortcomings of his own contemporaries. In this section, seven lines (17–23) are devoted to former Athenians; only two (23–24) to those of his own day. Moreover, the description of his contemporaries is vague and general (οὐ ... οὕτως ἔχετε) so as not to alienate the audience. οὔτε πρὸς τὰ τοιαῦτα οὔτε πρὸς τἆλλα might have conjured up all sorts of self-reproaches in the minds of his audience, but it is not D who makes them. His goal here, unlike in the *First Philippic*, is not primarily to criticize his audience, but to inspire them. The αἰτιολογία (ἀλλὰ πῶς;) introduces the next major part of the speech (§§47–75) in which D will advise his audience about what they must do now.

So far, D has analyzed the situation, but he has not made any proposals as to what to do about it, as he did in the central part of *Philippic* I. D may have remembered a negative reaction to the demands made on his audience in that speech (cf. his foreboding in §51.2–4). Therefore, he tries to forestall such a response by pretending that he is speaking only at the urging of his audience and asking them not to be angry (εἴ πω κελεύετε;). In the *First Philippic* D had made very concrete proposals. Here, he will limit himself to general advice (keep Philip as far away as possible from Attica, beware of traitors, face facts, realize what is at stake, become the leader of a general alliance against Philip). In a sense, this part of the speech corresponds to part II. There D had outlined the problems that Philip had caused for Athens; here he will suggest how to solve those problems. Parts II and IV, therefore, which focus on Athens, frame part III, which deals more generally with all of Greece.

D begins section 47 with an idea that appears toward the beginning of part II, that the Athenians delude themselves into believing that Philip does not really pose a threat to Athens. There he had referred to them as being εὐηθέστατοι (§10.4); here he uses the phrase εὐήθης λόγος to describe what many of them believe. The τοίνυν indicates a return to ideas discussed earlier (Denniston GP, 574). D also picks up the theme of the false advisors who tell the people, not the truth, but what they want to hear (cf. §4). ὡς ἄρα "is often used in quoting an opinion with which one does not agree" (Tarbell, 91).

D uses direct speech to represent what this objector to his position might say, and he represents the imaginary interlocutor as speaking forcefully, which is an indication of D's confidence in his own position. In the *First Philippic*, D quotes his opponents, but always with ridicule and scorn (cf. §§10–11). Here he takes them seriously, which is another indication of respect for his audience, many of whom probably believed this εὐήθης λόγος.

The presentation in this part of the speech (IV.A) is very orderly. D states a thesis at the end of section 47. In sections 48–50 he will prove that thesis. In sections 51 and 52 he will make a recommendation based on it. As usual in this speech, D gives much specific information to support his contention. ἀκούω (14), "a modest way of referring to the facts of history" (Sandys 2, 226), is another attempt not to put too much distance between himself and his audience. In section 49 he will say that hearsay is also his audience's primary source of knowledge (ἀκούετε, 22). Tarbell argues: "The Athenians are sarcastically represented as knowing nothing about Philip's methods of warfare except by hearsay" (91). The use of ἀκούω, however, in reference to both orator and audience, is an attempt to effect identification between them.

D ends (3–4) this part of the speech that demonstrates the difference between the past and the present with a reference to closed and open seasons for warfare, exactly as he had begun it at the beginning of section 48. He thus closes the ring and indicates that a new idea will follow, here the conclusion.

D has consistently tried to make his audience a participant in his reasoning. At the beginning of section 51, therefore, he prefaces his conclusion to this part of the speech (IV.B) with a reference to what they know (εἰδότας καὶ λογιζομένους [sc. ὑμᾶς]). D here presents his ideas, not so much as advice given by the orator to the audience, but as a conclusion that the audience reaches on its own based on the information that it has acquired. This is very different from the presentation of advice in the *First Philippic*, where the orator clearly instructs his audience as to what they should do (cf. the use of κελεύω in §§24.26 and 25.10).

D first states his thought very simply (οὐ δεῖ προσέσθαι τὸν πόλεμον εἰς τὴν χώραν) and then restates it several times in more complicated ways. The first restatement of it uses the figure κατὰ ἄρσιν καὶ θέσιν (οὐδ'... ἐκτραχηλισθῆναι, ἀλλ'... φυλάττεσθαι). The meaning of ἐκτραχηλισθῆναι has been disputed. Since it seems to be the opposite of keeping Philip as far away as possible, it probably means fighting at close quarters. It could be an image from wrestling, meaning to be taken by the throat or have the neck bent back (Sandys 2, 229). Taken with βλέποντας, it would thus mean to be distracted during a wrestling match and then caught off guard. This interpretation would not only fit the figure in which the word is used; it would also jibe with the use of συμπλακέντας in line 10, which is clearly an image taken from wrestling ("coming to close grips"; Davies, 114), and with the phrase εἰς δὲ ἀγῶνα... ἤσκηται at the end of section 52, which is also an athletic term and probably there refers to wrestling (Tarbell, 92). D calls attention to the basic point that he has made in the conclusion by using two examples of hiatus near the end of section 52 (δὲ ἀγῶνα ἄμεινον).

Section 53 is transitional. In lines 15–16 D recapitulates the point that he had made in IV.A. In lines 16–20 he states the thesis that he will develop in IV.B. In IV.A he had presented information before stating the recommendation or conclusion based on it. Here he presents his thesis before the information that supports it. This is partially for the sake of variety. The tone of this part of the speech, however, will be much more emotional than that of the preceding one. Indeed, the emotional high point of a Greek speech often comes about two-thirds of the way into the speech. Kennedy, for example, notes that the speech *On the Crown* "ebbs and flows like the tide of a great sea, reaching full flood two thirds of the way through, and gradually withdraws into a more philosophical tone in picturing the tragic confrontation between Demosthenes' personal fortune and that of Aeschines."[15] It is important, therefore, that the structure be such that the tone of the presentation can rise from calm to emotional, which is more likely to happen in the presentation of specific examples than in the elaboration of a thesis. Of the seven oaths used in this speech five appear in the last third of it (§§54, 65, 68, 70, and 76).

The first piece of advice concerns the nature of the warfare that the Athenians should use against Philip. The second concerns the internal situation in Athens. Section 54 is one of the most emotional passages thus far in the speech and one of the few where the orator is very critical of his audience. The Athenians' willingness to tolerate speakers who lead them astray and who serve their enemies, however, as D will demonstrate with the historical examples that follow, is an extremely dangerous tendency. D thus plants in the minds of his audience the conclusion to be derived from the facts he will narrate in order to influence how they listen to the narration. He is intentionally provocative in sections 54 and 55 in order to arouse their attention.

In proving his thesis, D will draw on information that the audience already knows (ἃ πάντες εἴσεσθε), again making them collaborators in his argument (cf. §41.17–18). To a great extent, however, the audience knows the facts that D will narrate because he has already used them in previous arguments: D "shows extraordinary skill in using the same familiar facts to prove Philip's duplicity (§11), and the danger thus accruing to Athens (§18), his injustice towards Greece and his restless aggressiveness (§26), his contempt for the Greeks in general, and his remorseless conduct towards individual states (§33), the frightful consequences of a policy friendly towards Macedonia (§56), and the slavery which befell his victims when it was too late for them to repent" (Sandys 2, 231).

In sections 56–62 the same historical pattern is repeated three times, and it is reinforced by similar patterns in language. In each city there was a pro-Macedonian faction and a pro-Athenian party (τινὲς μέν, τινὲς δέ; οἱ μέν, οἱ δ'; Φιλιστίδης μέν, Εὔφραῖος δέ). One represents slavery, the other freedom. The pro-Macedonian politicians were servants of Philip (πάνθ' ὑπηρετοῦντες ἐκείνῳ, χορηγὸν ἔχοντες Φίλιππον καὶ πρυτανευόμενοι); those who favored the Athenians were trying to keep their city free (ὅπως μὴ δουλεύσουσιν, ὅπως ἐλεύθεροι καὶ μηδενὸς δοῦλοι ἔσονται). The people were persuaded to drive out the pro-Athenian

---

[15] George Kennedy, "Oratory," in *The Cambridge History of Classical Literature*, vol. 1, pt. 3, ed. P. E. Easterling and B. M. W. Knox (Cambridge, 1989), 111.

patriots (ἐκβαλεῖν ... ἐπείσθη, ἐπείσθησαν ... ἐκβαλεῖν), which resulted in disaster ("Ολυνθος ἀπώλετο, οἱ ταλαίπωροι καὶ δυστυχεῖς Ἐρετριεῖς, τῆς πόλεως δ᾽ οὕτως ἀλούσης αἰσχρῶς καὶ κακῶς).

D ends section 56 with a specific example of someone who suffered from Philip's intrigues, put emphatically at the beginning of the result clause and set off by hiatus (τόν γε Ἀπολλωνίδην),[16] just as he will end the discussion of Philip's intrigues in Oreus, and this whole passage on traitors, with the vivid example of Euphraeus's cutting his throat rather than yield to Philip (§62.25–2):

> To create emotion it is essential to be specific. General notions and abstract schemes have hardly any effect on the imagination. Whateley relates how an audience that had remained unmoved by a general description of the carnage that occurred at the battle of Fontenoy was moved to tears by a little detail concerning the death of two young men.[17]

D ends the passage with a thought that relates to his own *ethos* in the speech, that people who oppose Philip do it out of a sense of justice (δικαίως), from motives that are pure and disinterested (καθαρῶς), and out of a concern for their fellow citizens (ὑπὲρ τῶν πολιτῶν). As Sandys notes, "the participial clause is at least as important in sense as the principal verb" (Sandys 2, 236).

In sections 63 and 64 D sums up what he has established in sections 56–62. By making the people of Olynthus, Eretria, and Oreus the subjects of the same verb in the articular infinitive (ἔχειν), he extracts from the preceding narrations the most basic mistake that they all made: they listened to advice that was pleasant to hear rather than what they needed to know. And those politicians who said only what was pleasant to hear were in Philip's pay. Thus, the people of these three cities made the same mistake that D had earlier accused the Athenians of making (ὅπερ καὶ παρ᾽ ὑμῖν) in the introduction to the narrative (§§53–54). And it is only to be expected, consequently, that they will suffer the same fate (65.17–19). Therefore, in order to frighten his audience, D returns to the examples of Olynthus, Eretria, and Oreus to demonstrate how much they have suffered from entrusting themselves to the supporters of Philip. He deals with them, however, in the reverse order to the one that he had used earlier. This creates a chiasmus that frames the important discussion of the differences between traitors and patriots in sections 63–65 and signals, by closing the ring, that this part of the speech (IV.B) is coming to an end. In fact, the entire fourth part of the speech is arranged around a triple ring that frames the discussion of the differences between pro-Macedonian and patriotic politicians in sections 63–64 (IV.B.2):

---

[16] Apollonides was later awarded Athenian citizenship. D does not mention that it was eventually revoked because he seemed unworthy; cf. Sandys 2, 232.

[17] C. Perelman and L. Olbrechts-Tyteca, *The New Rhetoric: A Treatise on Argumentation*, trans. John Wilkinson and Purcell Weaver (Notre Dame, 1969), 147.

A. External affairs: advice about the war (§§47–52).
B. The dangers of traitors (§§53–55).
C. The examples of Olynthus, Eretria, and Oreus (§§56–62).
D. Internal affairs: beware of politicians who mislead (§§63–65.21).
C. The examples of Oreus, Eretria, and Olynthus (§§65.21–66).
B. The dangers of traitors (§§67–68).
A. External affairs: advice about the war (§§69–75).

Not only is the order of presentation different, the tone is also. In sections 56–62 D had dealt with these examples in a narrative mode. He has a point to make, to be sure, and this is a *narratio instructa*. But the tone is basically that of narration. In sections 65–66 it is very ironic. Quintilian notes:

Under the type in which meaning and the words are *contrary* comes Irony, or, as people call it, *illusio*. This is revealed either by delivery, by the character of the speaker, or by the nature of the subject. If any of these is incompatible with the words, it is clear that the speech intends something totally different. (8.6.54)

Here all three elements would probably have revealed that καλός is used in a way that is different from normal speech.

In sections 67–68 D returns to the idea of how dangerous it is to trust traitors. He here presents the idea differently from above, however, again demonstrating his tendency in this speech to linger on basic ideas and to present them from different points of view or in a different key. First he makes a gnomic statement that expresses a general principle to be derived from the preceding narration (§67), and then he dramatizes how people deceived by Philip's agents would have reacted after the fact. The summary sentence at the end of section 68 indicates that this whole argument about traitors and politicians who deceive the people is coming to a close.

In section 69 D turns to the advice that he would give based on the lessons to be learned from the preceding narrations, and he explains this with an image from navigation. It is indicative of his emotional state that he introduces the image with no formal introduction, giving the impression that his excited mind is leaping from one topic to another without pause (Hermogenes, 357).

The allegory makes it clear that Philip is a power that can be resisted and that the audience must take some responsibility for the welfare of the "ship of state," which is only appropriate in a passage that introduces a discussion of what they should do to combat Philip. Philip is like the sea, D is like the pilot, and the Athenian people are like the sailors on the ship. The sea can be dangerous, to be sure, but it is an element of nature against which the pilot and the sailors can take precautions.[18] In order to impress upon the audience

---

[18] See my article, "La funzione delle metafore e delle similitudini nelle orazioni di Demostene," *Quaderni Urbinati* 29 (1978): 123.

how important it is to take these precautions before the ultimate crisis arrives, D develops the first sentence in the comparison very fully, using an abundant style. Once the sea is high, however, nothing can be done, and the second sentence in the comparison, therefore, is developed very quickly, only one line as compared to four to describe what must be done before the storm breaks out. In fact, to increase the speed, in the last clause D omits the verb and uses the two-termination form of the adjective (μάταιος) rather than the feminine (μάταια) to avoid hiatus, although he does use hiatus at the beginning of the sentence (δὲ ἡ) in order to call attention to thought that it introduces.

In keeping with the tendency to linger upon ideas, at the beginning of section 70 καί introduces the "personal application" (Sandys 2, 239) of the comparison to the particular situation in Athens, and τοίνυν indicates that D will now present the conclusion to be drawn from what precedes. Much of this speech has dealt with Philip and other Greeks. Now D must bring it home, make his audience realize that the fate of Greece now depends on them. The apostrophe, only the tenth used so far in this speech, coupled with the pronoun (ἡμεῖς), lays great stress on the audience, and the pronoun, at the head of the sentence and far separated from the verb with which it is construed (ποιῶμεν), is very emphatic. ἕως ἐσμὲν σῷοι, similar to ἕως ἂν σᾐζηται in the comparison, links up the particular application of the comparison, indicated by the indicative, to the general principle, conveyed by the subjunctive. The objects of the participle ἔχοντες sum up much of what D has argued so far. The final term, ἀξίωμα κάλλιστον, summing up the argument in the important central part of the speech (III), is particularly insistent. τί ποιῶμεν; indicates the topic that will take up the rest of the speech. Given its placement in the sentence, after all the advantages that Athens possesses, particularly its prior reputation for saving Greece against overwhelming odds, the answer is self-evident. Before he proceeds, however, D calls attention to the bond between himself and his audience by indicating that his question is the same as theirs and by assuring them that he will address (ἐγὼ νὴ Δί' ἐρῶ) the issue that they have been expecting for some time (πάλαι). Sandys notes that ἀγωνιστέον at the end of section 70 is "more expressive than πολεμητέον," and implies that "all the Greeks will be witnesses to the contest" (Sandys 2, 240). This struggle will not simply be a war; it will be a contest between two ways of life. δουλεύειν and ἐλευθερίας sum up, in stark terms, what is at stake.

After the lively and emotional presentation in sections 65–70, which is intended to engage the audience's attention, the tone becomes calm, as it often does at the end of a Greek speech. D makes several recommendations: the Athenians must send aid to the mercenaries commanded by Diopeithes, prepare themselves for war, and rouse the other Greeks. He concludes with a very patterned sequence of four infinitives, which "are to be read in two pairs, and συνάγειν, which adds nothing to the sense, is inserted simply to give this effect of balance" (Davies, 121). He concludes the section with the idea of Athens' reputation (ἀξίωμα), which is so prominent at the beginning of this part of the speech (cf. §70.1), thus surrounding his advice with the word that sums up those attitudes that should make the Athenians want to take it. The expression of this idea is fuller, however, than it was earlier, since ἀξίωμα is described by a clause (ἠλίκον ὑμῖν ὑπάρχει) rather than by a simple adjective (κάλλιστον). D thus calls attention to an idea that he will develop more fully in the next section.

In expanding on the idea stated at the end of section 73, D, as often in this speech,[19] looks at it first from a negative (3–6) and then from a positive (6–8) point of view. He picks up here the contrast between Athenians and other Greeks that he had developed at the beginning of this part of the speech (cf. §70.5–6) and thus tightens the ring that encloses it. The argument here is developed very fully, as in a rhetorical *epicheireme*, in which a reason is given for each premise: the other Greeks will not save Greece (major premise), because they will be content if they themselves are saved (reason); you have the reputation for saving Greece in times of crisis (minor premise), because your ancestors left it to you (reason); you, therefore, must save Greece (conclusion).

The conclusion is stated very abruptly at the beginning of the second half of the division (ὑμῖν τοῦτο πρακτέον). ὑμῖν is repeated three times in this passage, which gives it special emphasis (cf. §§73.3 and 74.6 and 7), each time in an emphatic position at or near the beginning or end of the clause in which it appears. The anaphora of this word in rapid succession at the head of the last two clauses in the section is particularly emphatic. γέρας is a word that is associated with noble actions and noble men (cf. LSJ, s.v.,1), and, in keeping with the heroic connotations of the word, the end of the section takes the metrical configuration of a series of dactyls and spondees, characteristic of epic poetry: -πον μετὰ πολλῶν καὶ μεγάλων κινδύνων (˘ ˘ | ˉ ˉ | ˘ ˘ | ˉ ˉ | ˉ ). καὶ κατέλιπον, which D wants to stress, creates a hyperbaton in that it separates ἐκτήσαντο from the prepositional phrase μετὰ πολλῶν καὶ μεγάλων κινδύνων, which is logically construed with the first rather than the second verb. Presumably he wants to put κατέλιπον nearer to the emphatic ὑμῖν at the head of the sentence, and metrical factors may have been a consideration as well.

In this speech D has been gentle with his audience. He has praised them, tried to inspire them, coaxed rather than threatened them into making the right decision. At the very end of the body of the speech, however, in section 75 he warns them harshly, very much as he did at the end of *Philippic I* (cf. §50). He must not let the audience forget that the situation has reached a crisis and that it is imperative to act quickly. D had begun the speech with an expression of fear (cf. §1.7–8); he ends the body of it in the same way. He thus surrounds the speech, which in many ways is very positive, with expressions of foreboding and apprehension.

---

[19] Cf. §§41 (two examples), 44 (two examples), 48, 51, 54, 64, 73, and 75.

As is usually the case in D's speeches, the epilogue is very calm. He backs away from the threatening, hostile tone of section 75 and becomes encouraging and conciliatory toward his audience. This speech is really a preface to specific proposals that D will make later. Thus, as in the preface to the specific proposals in *Philippic* I (cf. §15.21–22), he invites his audience to participate in the formulation of policy. He ends the speech on a solemn note (ὦ πάντες θεοί), which is appropriate to the grave crisis that threatens the state (Sandys 2, 243). The last word (συνενέγκοι), however, as in the *First Philippic* (συνοίσειν), is one of good omen.

# Appendix 3: The Longer and Shorter Versions of *Philippic* III

Quite a few passages of *Philippic* III do not appear in manuscript S, the oldest medieval manuscript of D, dating from the end of the ninth or the beginning of the tenth century and the principal one used in all editions since Bekker's 1823 Oxford text.[1] These passages were added by a later hand in the margins and appear in other manuscripts, not derived from S. This produces what have been called the "longer" and "shorter" versions of the speech, and it is usually assumed that these derive from the delivered version, circulated soon after delivery, and an edited version published months or even years later, although there is disagreement over which is which.

Raphael Sealey, drawing on earlier arguments of M. P. Treves, argued that the longer version was the delivered version of the speech, published soon after its delivery. The shorter version, he felt, was published about two years later as a pamphlet, mainly for dissemination throughout Greece. The basis for this argument is that many of the passages in the longer version that are omitted in the shorter version would have appealed exclusively to an Athenian audience.[2]

This is an attractive argument. The *Third Philippic* is addressed to the Athenians, but it is also directed at a larger pan-Hellenic audience (see appendix 2), which would not have been able to hear the speech when it was delivered and could have had access to it only if it had been circulated after its delivery in Athens.[3] Moreover, as one would expect, if Sealey's argument is right, and I think that it is, the passages that are omitted in the shorter version often exhibit

---

[1] Cf. the preface to Dilts's edition, xvi. These passages are found in sections 2, 6–7, 26, 32, 39, 41–42, 44, 46, 58, and 71. Dilts, as Butcher had done, indicates the passages that are in the longer version but not in the shorter one by printing them in smaller type. He considers sections 6 and 7, however, the longest passage in question, to have been accidentally omitted from S and thus does not print them in smaller type, unlike Butcher's earlier edition and most other modern editions of the text.

[2] "Dionysius of Halicarnassus and Some Demosthenic Dates," *Revue des Études Grecques* 68 (1955): 101–4.

[3] This is, as far as I know, the only instance of a Demosthenic speech for which two copies were circulated. The *Third Philippic*, however, because of its double audience, is unique in the corpus of D. That D's speeches were circulated is indicated by the story in Plutarch (*Dem.* 11.4) that D's contemporary Aesion said that he had read them and also by the story in pseudo-Plutarch (*Lives of the Ten Orators* 845C) that when Philip read copies of the *Philippics* he said that if he had heard them delivered he would have voted for war against himself.

characteristics that are typical of delivered speeches, and that is what I want to discuss now.

Let us look first at the longest passage in question, which comprises sections 6 and 7. Pearson, using Croiset's Budé text (1955), which, like most modern editions, prints sections 6 and 7 in smaller type, argues (AD, 151) that if 6 and 7 are omitted the argument of 8 follows naturally the conclusion to 5. Having pointed out that Philip has not really defeated Athens (§5), D would then begin: "If, therefore, it is possible for the city to keep the peace and this is in our power, in order that I might begin from here, I say that we should" (§18.14–16). This is certainly possible, although it is rather abrupt. D does make abrupt transitions in *Philippic* I (cf. §12.18), and the transition from the proemium in section 1 to the beginning of the argument in section 2 of that speech could be described as sudden. The elaborate proemium to *Philippic* III (see appendix 2), however, would indicate that D was more sensitive to keeping the audience's attention, to avoiding abrupt transitions, to guiding them carefully through the speech, and that desire may explain sections 6 and 7.

Pearson argues that "6 and 7 offer an alternative to 8, that Demosthenes's own text contained both versions and he did not decide until the last moment which was the better" (151). One of the arguments that he adduces is that at the end of 7 "the text breaks off in the middle of a sentence" (εἰ ἐφ᾽ ἡμῖν ἐστι τὸ βουλεύεσθαι περὶ τοῦ πότερον εἰρήνην ἄγειν ἢ πολεμεῖν δεῖ) and that it "is difficult to see how the sentence can be completed so as to link up with the beginning of 8" (151). It seems to me, however, that the clause that Pearson cites as being only a partial sentence could be construed as an indirect question dependent on διορίζομαι (Smyth §2671) and putting a comma, or no mark of punctuation at all, rather than a semicolon before it would solve the problem. Davies, who keeps the semicolon, remarks, nevertheless, that εἰ here means "namely, whether" and describes the clause as being "explanatory of τοῦτο" (98). Sandys argues (Sandys 2, 196) that this is not possible since διορίζεσθαι is always followed by an accusative and infinitive, or by ὅτι, or by ὅπως. In D's speech *Against Timocrates*, however, it is followed by ἃ χρὴ ποιεῖν (92), which I would interpret as being an indirect question (see Smyth §2668). In Aristotle, moreover, it is followed by an indirect question introduced by τίς (*Pol.* 1323a15) and in Andocides by the same construction introduced by ὁπότερον (4.8).

If we read the end of section 7 as I have done, the beginning of 8, then, quite logically takes up the first alternative stated at the end of 7 (πότερον εἰρήνην ἄγειν): Εἰ μὲν οὖν ἔξεστιν εἰρήνην ἄγειν τῇ πόλει καὶ ἐφ᾽ ἡμῖν ἐστι τοῦτο. The second alternative (ἢ πολεμεῖν) is examined beginning in line 17 (εἰ δ᾽ ἕτερος . . .). This is similar to the way in which D offers his audience two alternatives at the end of the transitional passage (§6) in the *Second Philippic*. I am less convinced that section 9 could logically follow 7, as it would have to do if section 8 were an alternative to 6–7. To say "But if someone supposes this to be peace, from which that one, having taken all the other things, will come against you" right after "if it is in our power to deliberate concerning whether it is necessary to keep the peace or fight" seems very abrupt to me. The only way to make the transition clear, as Pearson himself admits by his paraphrase (151), would be to add text to the manuscript. Changing a mark of punctuation seems a much easier solution.

I would argue, therefore, that sections 6 and 7 are not an alternative to 8 but a preparation for it, that D had these sections in his text, to be used if he felt that he needed to explain himself more fully in order to keep the audience's attention between the end of the proemium and the beginning of the argument. These sections involve a very full development of the thought. There is first a résumé of the proemium, which D might have considered to be necessary for the sake of clarity because of the length and complication of the introductory material. This leads to the specific charge that D's opponents accuse him of fomenting the war, which raises the question of whether it is still possible to debate about war and peace. Sections 6–7 could thus be seen as a transitional passage, leading the audience carefully from the proemium to the argument of the speech, as D does in *Philippic* II (§6). D may have felt, as he was preparing the speech, that such a transitional passage might be necessary to keep the audience's attention and to make very clear to them how he gets from the proemium to his first argument.

D's copy of the speech may have circulated soon after its delivery. Later, in a more formally published version, directed at all the Greeks, he may have deleted sections 6 and 7 on the grounds that they were somewhat repetitious and unnecessary for a reading audience, which can reread passages, check earlier parts of the text, and pause for reflection, tightening up the presentation, just as people do nowadays when they turn delivered papers into published articles. The inflammatory and provocative clause οὐκοῦν οὐδ᾽ ὑμᾶς οἴονται δεῖν ἔχειν in section 2 (17–18), which does not appear in the shorter version of the speech either, might also be an example of a passage that seemed appropriate in a delivered speech before a live audience but would have been cut from the published version. Or, if I have correctly analyzed the stylistic function of this clause,[4] D may have felt that the effect that it produces was less necessary in a version of the speech that would be read than in the one that was delivered.

I certainly do not mean to imply by the preceding comments, however, that D spoke with a written text in his hand; Athenian orators did not use notes. It is clear, however, that D prepared very carefully when he knew that he was going to speak in the Assembly. In fact, Plutarch tells us (*Dem.* 8) that D once said that it was insulting to the people for an orator not to prepare his speech and practice it beforehand if possible. It is equally clear that this careful preparation involved working with a written text.[5] Jeremy Trevett, in fact, argues that the speeches that we have are the versions that D produced as he was preparing to speak in the Assembly, which he never intended for any other purpose and

---

[4] Cf. Wooten TD, 452.

[5] Plutarch, *Dem.* 8; Quintilian 12.9.16, 12.10.51–54.

which were circulated, that is, "published," only after D's death, probably by his nephew Demochares.[6]

I cannot agree with Sandys, who argues (Sandys 2, lxv) that the shorter version, without sections 6 and 7, probably corresponded to the speech as it was actually delivered and that this version was circulated informally soon after its delivery for purposes of propaganda. Sections 6 and 7 would have then been added to a subsequent version, written with a view to formal publication, according to Sandys, who, like Pearson, argues that they were an alternative to 8 rather than a transition to it. According to this argument, D had come to realize, possibly during the delivery itself, that 8 was too abrupt a transition from 5 to 9 and thus substituted 6 and 7 as a more fully developed transitional passage. But D had obviously learned in the *Second Philippic* the value of a transitional passage between a long proemium and the body of the speech (see appendix 1) and surely would have foreseen the need for a substantial transition in this speech, which is considerably longer and more complex than *Philippic* II. Sandys argues that 6 and 7 must have been an alternative to 8 rather than a preparation for it, since if they were an addition "then we must not only strike out εἰ ἐφ' ἡμῖν - πολεμεῖν δεῖ, but also the previous sentence ἐγὼ δὴ τοῦτο πρῶτον ἁπάντων - διορίζομαι, the sense of both these sentences having already been expressed in the shorter draft" (lxv). Hermogenes notes (289–90), however, that D uses Abundance, which involves repetition and elaborate patterning, more often than any other style, and that is particularly true of this speech, where much of the presentation is very broad and full (see appendix 2). Hermogenes says, in fact, about D's style that there is "really no passage in his speeches that does not exemplify Abundance" (289). And there are sections of other speeches that seem to me just as repetitious and patterned as the one here (cf. 18.4–6). Sandys also argues that "when Demosthenes revised his speech, possibly at a time when war had already broken out, he may have felt it desirable to meet the criticisms of his opponents in more definite terms, and to emphasise the fact that he had not provoked the war" (lxv). But it is just as likely that he would have defended himself against such a charge at the discussion concerning whether Athens should declare war or not. It also seems to me fairly unlikely that he would have published this speech, which is a call to war, after war had already broken out.

An examination of other passages that appear in the longer but not in the shorter version of the speech also suggests that the longer version was the one that was delivered:

---

[6] "Did Demosthenes Publish his Deliberative Speeches?," *Hermes* 124 (1996): 425–41. I find this argument unconvincing. If the texts had been intended only as scripts with which to practice for speeches in the Assembly, which were all that mattered, why would D have kept copies of them, sometimes for over thirty years? Also, if the stories in Plutarch and pseudo-Plutarch (see note 5) have any validity, how did Aesion and Philip get copies of these speeches?

**26.11–12:**   A comment like this might well be made in the delivered version of a speech, where it would be necessary to make it very clear to the audience where the argument is proceeding (cf. Hermogenes, 235–36), but could be deleted from a published version intended to be read, where the connection of what follows to what precedes could be inferred without being explicitly stated.

**32.14–18:**   Piling up example after example is an approach that could be justified in a delivered version of a speech, when the orator's emotion drives him to heap outrage upon outrage (cf. Demetrius, 274, and Longinus, 20), but which might seem tedious in a published version going to be read by someone who is not driven by the same emotion.

**39.9–10:**   συγγνώμη τοῖς ἐλεγχομένοις is not in the shorter version of the speech and is deleted by some editors on the grounds that it "mars the symmetry of the three clauses in the context, and, as compared with them, is weak in point of sense" (Sandys 2, 218). It also destroys the crescendo and temporal sequence in the tricolon: someone takes a bribe, admits it, and is reproached for it (cf. Quintilian 9.4.23). Since ἐλεγχομένοις and ἐπιτιμᾷ have a similar meaning, the synonymity would weaken the crescendo effect in the tricolon. It is typical, however, of people who feel strong emotion to break patterns (cf. Longinus, 22). Here again the emotion of the orator may have made the break in the sequence seem natural in the delivered version of the speech, although D may have decided that in the published version, unaided by the delivery of the orator, it was better to delete it. There is a similar sequence presented in section 37: to take bribes, to be convicted, and to be punished (λαμβάνοντας, ἐλεγχθῆναι, ἐκόλαζον). In some manuscripts a fourth item is added, καὶ παραίτησις οὐδεμία ἦν οὐδὲ συγγνώμη, which has been deleted by most editors, including Dilts, on the grounds that it breaks the pattern of the tricolon, usually preferred by D, and παραίτησις does not appear elsewhere in the orator (Sandys 2, 217). This makes sense. The presentation in that passage is much less emotional than it is in section 39, which is one of the most emotional parts of the speech, and it could not be argued that it is his emotion there that drives D to break a pattern that he generally prefers.

**41–42.21–24:**   These lines are typical of the sort of expansion that could be suitable in a delivered speech but that might seem tedious in one that was being read. D uses here the figure κατὰ ἄρσιν καὶ θέσιν, stating the same idea negatively and then positively (οὐχ ἵνα ... ἀλλ' ἵνα), which he uses frequently in the *Philippics* in order to emphasize a thought (cf. Hermogenes, 293–94). Moreover, here, since the negative is put first and then drawn out by the parenthesis, the orator creates suspense, quite appropriate in the delivered version of a speech, in that having told his audience what something is not he arouses a desire in them to know what it is. The αἰτιολογία at the beginning of section 42, which D immediately answers, is also typical of speeches that are actually delivered.

**44.13 and 15:**   The two phrases in question here also create examples of κατὰ ἄρσιν καὶ θέσιν. In the first instance, οὐ τοῦτο λέγει (13) is the negative of γέγραπται; in the second, εὐαγές ᾖ τὸ ἀποκτεῖναι (15) is the positive of μὴ διδῷ. In each case, the figure allows the orator to delay, and thus to emphasize, the positive by prefacing it with the negative (see above).

**46.1–4:**   Most of section 46 is not in the shorter version of the speech. It must have been in the delivered version, however, because, if lines 1–4 (ἴστ' to τίνος;) are omitted the passage simply does not make sense. If εἴπω κελεύετε; comes right after πῶς;, we would expect examples to follow that demonstrate how the Athenians of D's own day do not live up to the example of their ancestors, but that is not the case. What is in the longer version of the speech, however, is a perfect fit and quite in keeping with tendencies seen elsewhere in this speech (see appendix 2). First, D calls on his audience to collaborate with him, as he does at the beginning of section 41 (ὁρᾶτε); he trusts them to understand a situation without being instructed by him (ἴστ' αὐτοί). In fact, at the beginning and end of this discussion of Arthmius of Zelea, D shows confidence in his audience to understand the present and to contrast it with the past. Secondly, he refrains from criticizing the audience openly, as has been the case elsewhere in this speech (τί γὰρ δεῖ περὶ πάντων ὑμῶν κατηγορεῖν;) and attenuates whatever criticism is inherent in his comments by generalizing it (παραπλησίως δὲ καὶ οὐδὲν βέλτιον ὑμῶν ἅπαντες οἱ λοιποὶ Ἕλληνες). Since, however, the Athenians have not risen to the challenges offered by Philip, they need advice (βουλῆς ἀγαθῆς), and that is exactly what D will give in the next major segment of the speech (§§47–75). The sentence beginning with διόπερ thus makes an appropriate transition to the next part of the speech; "the connexion is perfect" (Sandys 2, 225).[7]

**58.27–28:**   In a delivered version, the neat antithesis τότε μέν/πάλιν δέ would make a suitable coda to the sentence, and to this part of the speech dealing with Eretria (cf. Arist., *Rhet.* 3.9.5–8 and Demetrius, 22). The metrical configuration of Παρμενίωνος, which takes the form of a dactyl and a spondee, has the same effect (cf. Hermogenes, 251). This sort of closure may not have been consid-

---

[7] I do not know how to explain the illogical sequence in the shorter version of the speech. If the longer version was abbreviated for publication, I can understand how lines 1–2 may have been cut out on the grounds that they would be useful in a speech before a large audience whose goodwill the orator was trying to obtain before he suggested how the situation could be remedied but were not really necessary in a speech intended to be read. The sequence πῶς; ἴστ' αὐτοί· διόπερ φήμ' ἔγωγε…would make perfect sense. In the redaction, however, more of the passage may have been inadvertently omitted. Sandys also argues (Sandys 2, 225) that there must have been a lacuna of some sort in the shorter version.

ered necessary in a version intended to be read. Moreover, a large audience of uneducated people may not have been expected to know about Philip's subsequent interventions in Eretria in the summer of 342; a better-educated reading audience may have been assumed to know this information.[8]

**71.9–11:**   The embassies envisioned here were sent out soon after the speech was delivered (Sandys 2, 241). In a redacted version published quite some time after its delivery, therefore, reference to these particular missions would quite naturally have been omitted.

---

[8] Michael Gagarin also describes as being typical of delivered speeches, as opposed to written versions, some of the stylistic features noted above, particularly approaches that create Distinctness, which he calls "signposts," short antitheses, and emotional appeals; "The Orality of Greek Oratory," in *Signs of Orality*, ed. Anne Mackay (Leiden, 1999), 168, 170, 179.

# Historical Index

# Rhetorical Index

CPSIA information can be obtained at www.ICGtesting.com
Printed in the USA
BVOW08s0037200716

456159BV00001B/28/P